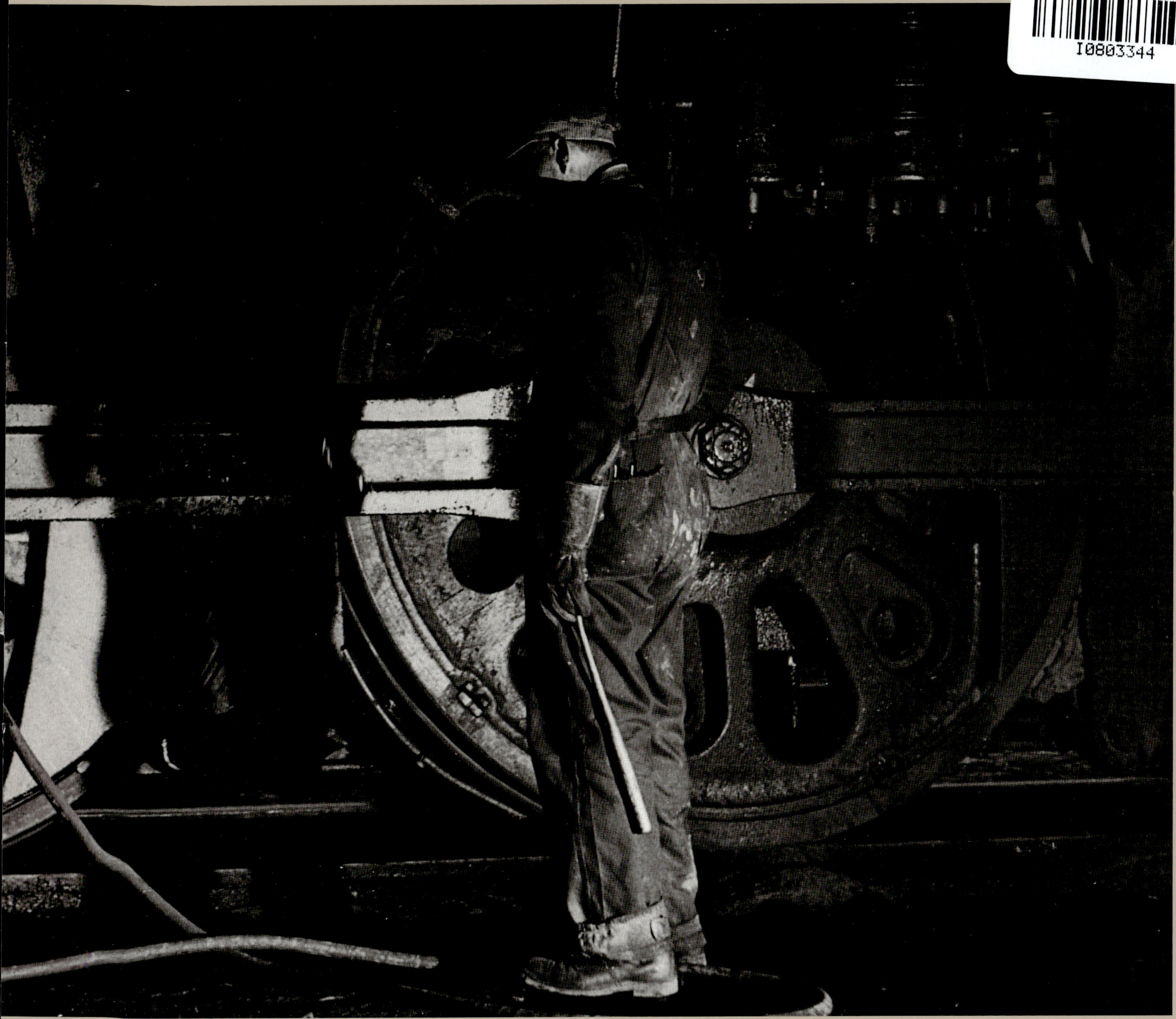

STARLIGHT ON THE RAILS

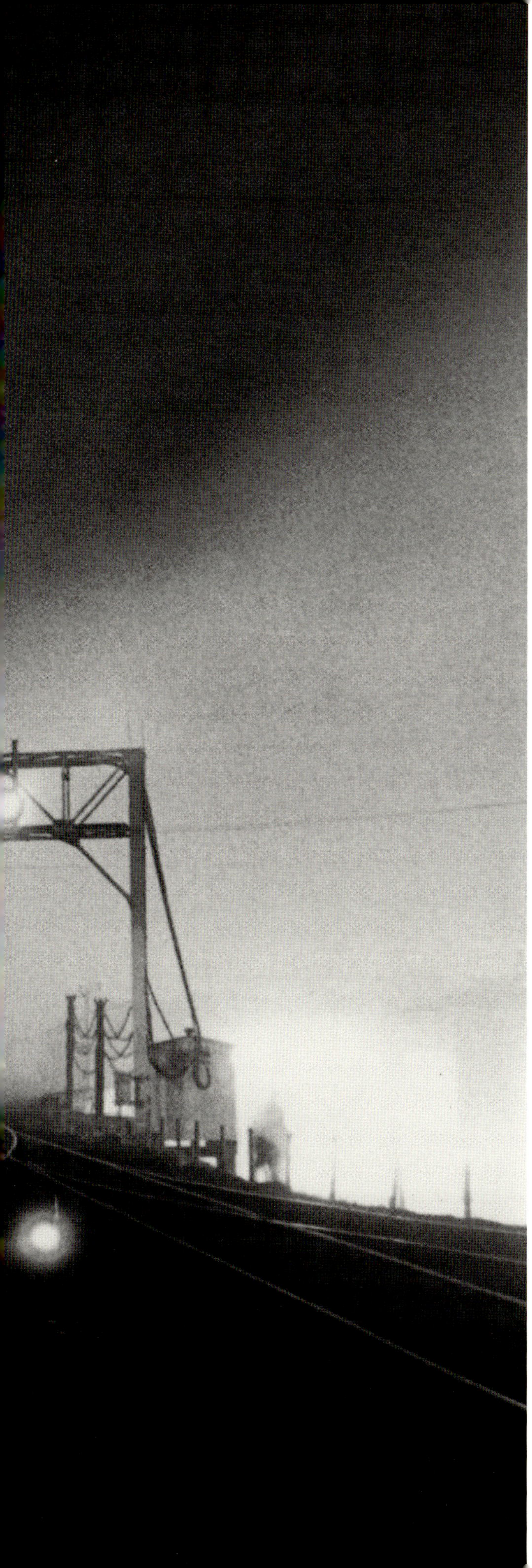

STARLIGHT ON THE RAILS

photographs selected by Jeff Brouws and Ed Delvers
text by Jeff Brouws
with an introduction by Richard Steinheimer

HARRY N. ABRAMS, INC., PUBLISHERS

This book is dedicated to Richard Steinheimer and Philip Hastings, and my parents: Richard and Annette Brouws and my mother, Yvonne LeMay Gerlitz—JB

This book is dedicated to Mr. Nishio Katsusaburo, and Mr. Hirota Naotaka, and my parents Frank and Alicia Delvers—ED

The authors would like to acknowledge the California State Railroad Museum for graciously allowing us to publish images from the Philip Hastings, M.D., Collection, CSRM © 2000

Grateful acknowledgment is also made to the following for permission to reprint previously published material:

Excerpt from *Lonesome Traveler* by Jack Kerouac, reprinted by permission of Sterling Lord Literistic, Inc. Copyright 1988 by the Estate of Jan Kerouac

Excerpt from *The Sportswriter* by Richard Ford, reprinted by permission of Vintage Books, a division of Random House, Inc.

Excerpt from *Of Time and the River*, copyright © 1935 by Thomas Wolfe, published by Charles Scribner's Sons, reprinted by permission of MacIntosh and Otis, Inc.

cover, top:
AMTRAK'S CALIFORNIA ZEPHYR crosses the Utah desert, October 1995.
Mel Patrick

cover, bottom:
THE RIO GRANDE ZEPHYR glides past Prospect Junction at Denver, Colorado, in 1972.
Mel Patrick

endpapers:
TWO RAILROAD WORKERS service the running gear of their GS4 locomotive at San Luis Obispo, California, in the mid-1950s. Train #75, The Lark, is right "on the advertised" for its run north.
Richard Steinheimer

frontispiece:
CB&Q 4-8-4 Northern #5632 leads an Illini Railroad Club excursion, Aurora, Illinois, April 1964.
John Gruber

following page:
WESTERN PACIFIC'S Golden Gate Merchandise slides by the west switch at Clifside, Nevada, behind a rebuilt GP35 in August 1982.
Ted Benson

Editor:
Eric Himmel

Designer:
Jeff Brouws / For a Small Fee, Inc.

Library of Congress
Cataloging-in-Publication Data

Brouws, Jeffrey T.
Starlight on the rails: photographs selected by Jeff Brouws and Ed Delvers; text by Jeff Brouws with an introduction by Richard Steinheimer.
p. cm.
ISBN 0-8109-4167-8
1. Railroads—pictorial works.
2. Night photography.
I. Delvers, Ed. II. Title.

TF149 .B76 2000
385'.022'2—dc21 00-31319

Published in 2000 by Harry N. Abrams, Incorporated, New York

Printed and bound in Japan

Harry N. Abrams, Inc.
100 Fifth Avenue
New York, N.Y. 10011
www.abramsbooks.com

Exhibition schedule for Starlight on the Rails:

Robert Mann Gallery
October 26–December 7, 2000
210 Eleventh Avenue, 10th floor
New York, New York
212.989.7600
www.robertmann.com

I will go up and down the country,
and back and forth across the country
on the great trains that thunder over America.
I will go out West where States are square;
Oh, I will go to Boise, and Helena,
and Albuquerque. I will go to Montana
and the two Dakotas and the unknown places.
The rails go westward in the dark.
Brother, have you seen starlight on the rails?

from Thomas Wolfe
Of Time and the River

CONTENTS

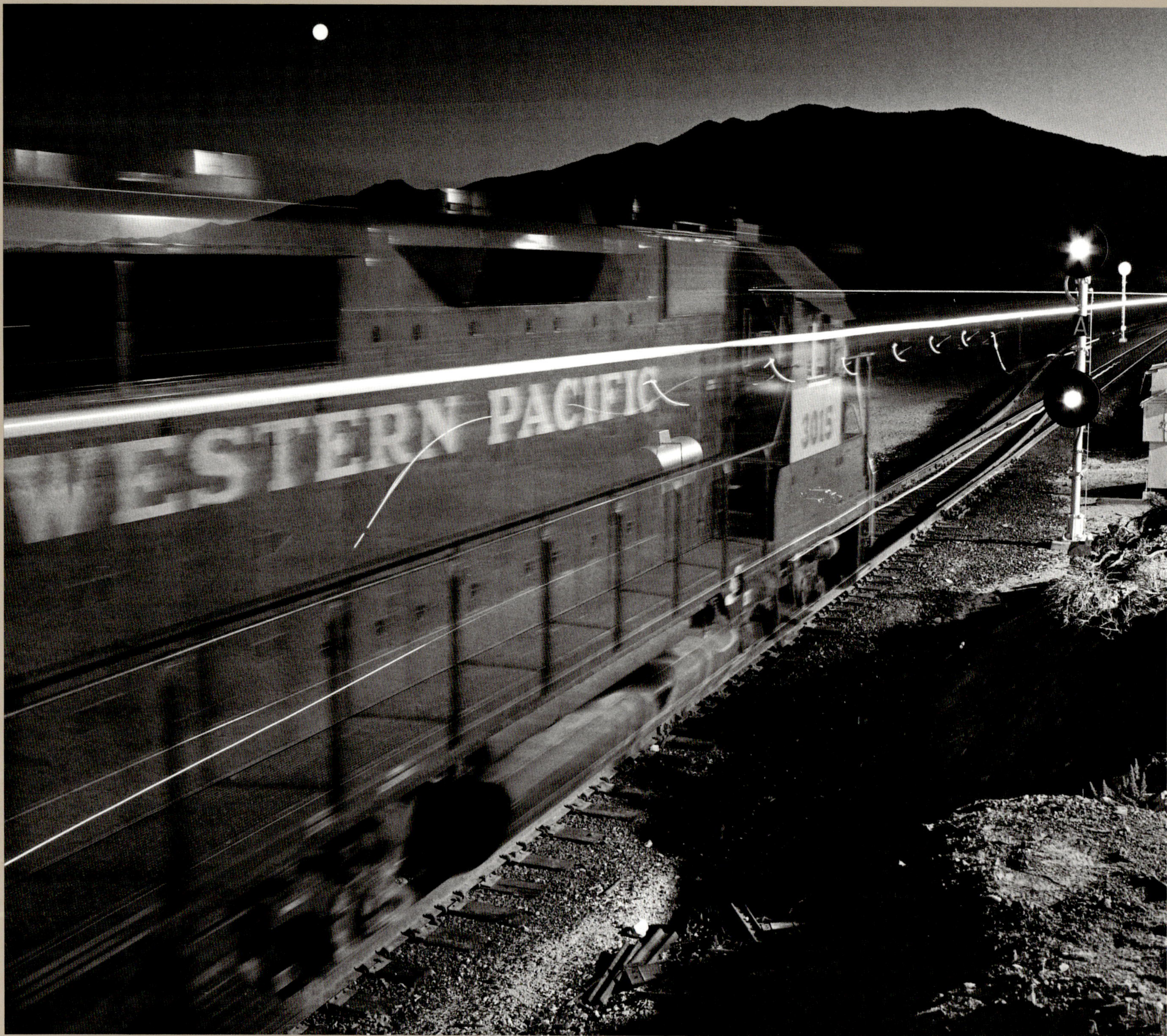
WESTERN PACIFIC
3015

INTRODUCTION

INTRODUCTION *Richard Steinheimer*

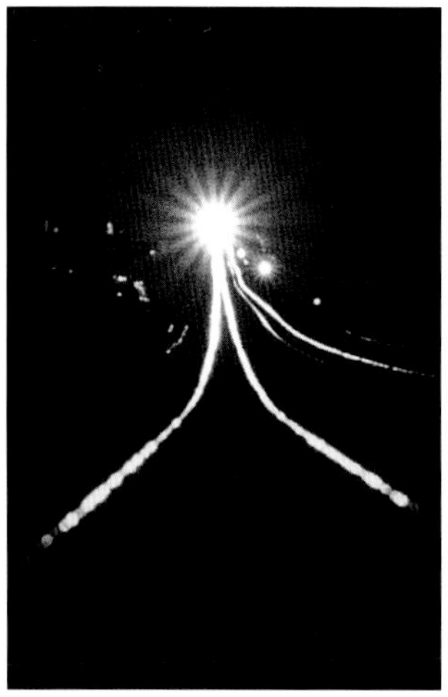

THE HEADLIGHT OF a Santa Fe freight train six miles from the camera forms a "Christmas tree" near Amboy, California, in the 1970s.
Richard Steinheimer

right:
THE LIGHTS OF BROADWAY beckon LA cosmopolites to shop, spend, and take in a double bill, as Los Angeles Railway streetcar #1416 pauses at a busy 6th Avenue intersection. This type H "yellow car," of 1923 vintage, had been in operation for thirty years in this 1953 view.
Richard Steinheimer

LOOKING WESTWARD DOWN the Sunset Route mainline into the rural darkness outside the perimeter of suburbanized Los Angeles, I see a tiny speck of light rising from the dark edge of the horizon. Sixty seconds later, the speck of light has expanded, growing larger and brighter as it rises higher above the rim of the earth. With rapidly increasing intensity, the light's brilliance spreads to the shiny rails ahead. In a rush of activity, I place my camera on a tripod and extend the legs as the beam grows more vivid. Poised now at the apex of several miles of brightly shining rails, I see a "Christmas tree" of light take shape in front of the train.

By the time the far-off exhausts of the oncoming locomotive are audible, I also sense its slow pace of deceleration, both by the sounds of the stack talk and the now unhurried approach of the headlight's glare. Finally, the giant Southern Pacific 4-8-4 towers overhead as it brings train #44 to a stop. The air pumps pant like an animal regaining its breath after a fast pursuit.

Several passengers walk quickly to an open vestibule and climb aboard the Californian. A black attendant assists them onto the train with their luggage. A highball is quickly passed to the head end, as Ontario, California, is only a short flagstop on the cusp of civilization. The hoghead responds with two quick blasts of the whistle. The bright Mars headlight resumes its characteristic figure-eight dance back and forth across the rails. The locomotive begins to move, imperceptibly at first. As the engineer releases the air and slowly notches out the throttle, the cars behind the locomotive grudgingly respond. The slow building cacophony of exhaust grows more insistent as the train's speed increases. The head-end cars keep accelerating as they pass, shaking the ground with the deep concussive beats of flanged wheels against steel rail.

The wheels click faster now over the joints as the train picks up speed, fleeing this insignificant country station with a hasty finality. The last sleeping car flies past into the night. Looking ahead into the darkness I see the locomotive's black smoke rising, its oscillating headlight still delivering an all-important "get-off-the-tracks" message.

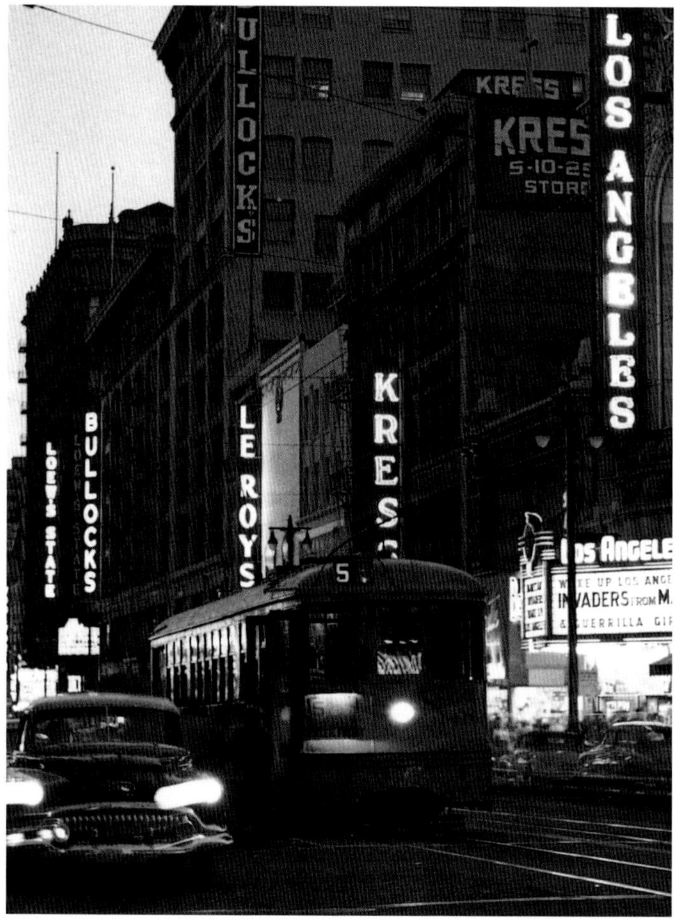

The rear-end marker lights retreat into the gloam, growing smaller as they withdraw from my field of vision. The diminishing sounds of the engine's exhaust are a fading roar. In a minute the train is lost completely from sight.

MY INITIAL EXPERIENCES around the nighttime railroad environment are probably very similar to those of other photographers whose work appears in this book. Something from our youth fashioned deeply powerful impressions and feelings within us concerning trains. As Americans we have a collective psyche that compels us to be on the move. Call it our myth of mobility. We believe that going somewhere else, down a distant track, away from present situations, can only mean broader fulfillment: a remedy for what ails us. It's our restlessness that best understands and appreciates the symbolism trains and railroads play in our lives.

This characteristic mood is heightened by a night train. It must be so. Inventorying great American literature—from Thomas Wolfe and F. Scott Fitzgerald to more contemporary works by Jack Kerouac and Richard Ford—we begin to understand that these writers have been our witnesses. They have recorded in words the feelings we've had, much like the photographers in this volume have captured on film visions we've seen. The pictures are equivalents in moody black and white or dynamic color for our emotions.

Throughout the pages of Richard Ford's novel *The Sportswriter*, his lonely, going-through-a-divorce protagonist, Frank Bascombe, takes solace and comfort in trains at night and the surrounding railroad environment. While watching husbands stepping off trains to meet their wives at suburban depots in waning twilight and trainmen busying themselves during a station stop, he reflects:

> I enjoy this closeness to trains and the great moment they exude, their implacable hissing noise and purpose. I read somewhere it is psychologically beneficial to stand near things greater and more powerful than you yourself, so as to dwarf yourself (and your piddlyass bothers) by comparison. To do so, the writer said, released the spirit from its everyday moorings.

Kerouac was also a writer pivotal to our understanding of the railroad landscape—but from the inside. In the early 1950s he worked as a brakeman out of the Southern Pacific's Bayshore Yards near San Francisco, making nighttime runs on the Zipper and Overnight freights to all points on the Coast Division.

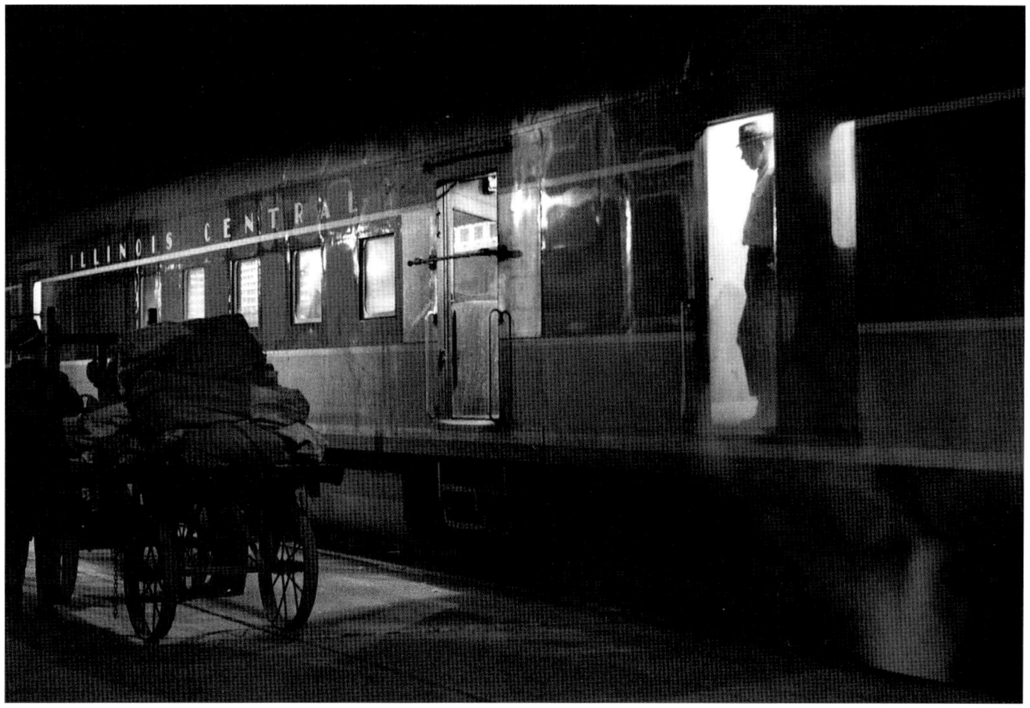

A RAILWAY POST OFFICE clerk pauses from sorting duties as a conductor manages the night's mail pouches during a brief station stop. It's the late 1950s on the Illinois Central and the nation's railroads have yet to lose lucrative mail contracts—the fuel that helped bolster, until 1965, sagging revenues on America's passenger trains. This "hidden" government subsidy amounted to hundreds of millions of dollars a year.
Philip Hastings / CSRM

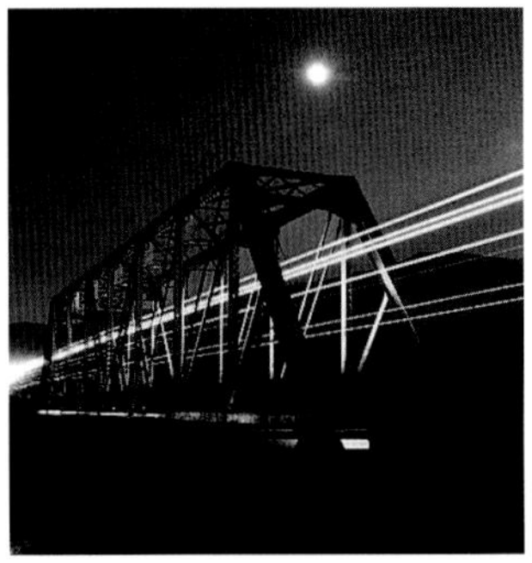

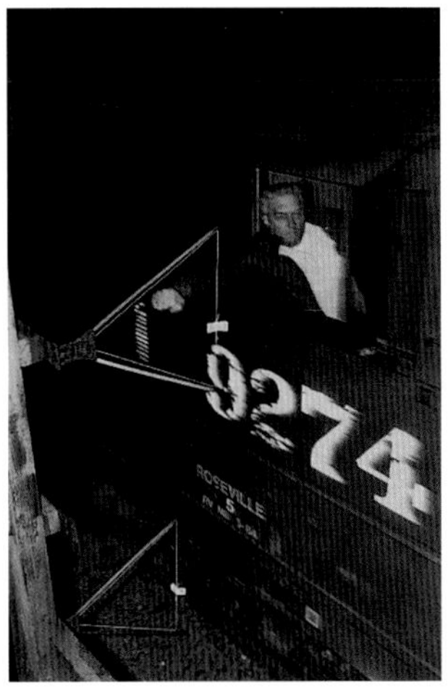

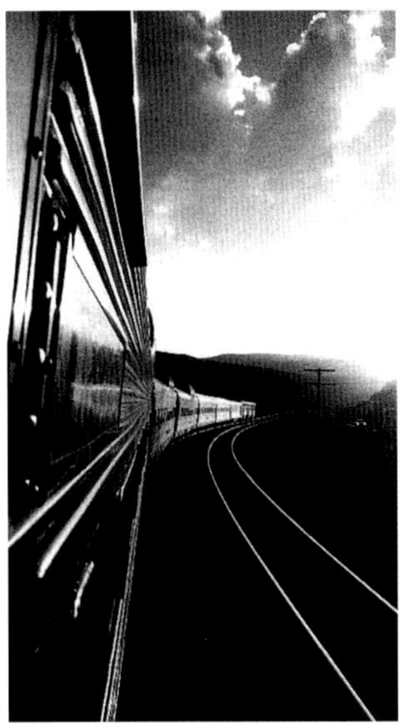

Some of his prose, such as this description of "picking up orders on the fly," provides us with a written artifact of this fast-paced, stream-of-consciousness activity, captured vividly by several photographs in this book (pages 10, 74–75):

> The train goes around the curve there and gently I lean out of the grabiron darks and look and there's our little clearance and train order sitting in a piece of string which is stretched between the two train order bamrods, as the train passes the trainman simply (usually the fireman) reaches out with whole arm so to make sure not to miss and hooks the string in passing (the string being taut) and off it comes the string and the two bows which are rigid sorta ping a little and in yr arm is looped the train orders on yellow onionskin tied by string, the engineer upon receipt of this freight takes the string and slowly according again to habit unfolds the paper to read and sometimes they even put glasses on like great professors of ivy universities to read as that big engine goes chug chugging across and down the green land of California.

The "Railroad Earth" chapter in *Lonesome Traveler* may be the finest piece of contemporary literature to describe mid-century life as a railroader, and it gives us a glimpse into what might have inspired the photographers herein. Jeff Brouws' work, in particular, has been very influenced by these two books. After he read *The Sportswriter,* the station platform in his hometown took on a renewed meaning that he attempted to record visually.

MOST OF THE PICTURES for *Starlight on the Rails* have been gathered by Brouws and Ed Delvers, who jointly conceived of a trains-at-night photo book compiled from the archives of many contemporary image makers. Most record scenes in the United States, but Ed's own photos from Japan, where he spent the first eighteen years of his life, also grace these pages, as do the works of two other Japanese photographers, Naotaka Hirota and Katsusaburo Nishio. Nishio has one of the earliest images in this book, taken in 1949 (page 112).

As a youth, Ed ventured far afield, shooting Shay locomotives on Taiwan as well as the steam engines lumbering by his own Yokohama backyard. Later, as a student at MIT working on a photography degree (under the tutelage of Harold "Doc" Edgerton—father of the electronic strobe), Ed often took the rocket-scientist approach to film and processing, concocting his own developers to use on film that he routinely pushed to ASA 64,000. This extremely fast film allowed him to record scenes that otherwise would have been unobtainable at 1/125 of a second in almost total blackness (pages 11, 79). These images from Japan prove the international allure of railroads at night and remind us that all human beings, across the sometimes dividing obstacles of country and culture, share a commonality in their love of trains and railroading.

When Brouws and Delvers set out on their quest eighteen years ago, they received over a thousand photographs from contributors. In order to edit them down to manageable numbers, it was necessary to formulate a plan that would bring cohesion to the project. The solution: to group the photos according to locations on the railroad, as well as in sunset and sunrise sections, typically two times during the day when photographers favor the low angle of light. The authors weren't concerned with creating a treatise on motive power or railroad history, nor were they concerned with depicting just one era, steam or diesel, foreign or domestic. Their mission, instead, was solely photographic. They wanted to arrange the pictures according to how the images played off one another, within the themed structure, showing the "art" of railroad photography.

With this in mind, *Starlight* begins at sunset ("Toward Nightfall"), goes to the depot ("Sentimental Journey"), visits the mainline ("Chasin' the Train"), and then takes us through the mysterious environs of the freight yard ("Night Moves") and roundhouse ("'Round Midnight"). Ending at sunrise ("Softly as a Mornin' Sunrise"), the book completes a twelve-hour tour of the work-a-night world of railroading. The chapter openers are first-person accounts of Brouws' own involvement within the railroad milieu. "Toward Nightfall" and "Night Moves" recount two freight train riding experiences. The first was made on a hot July day during his sixteenth year, as he and a buddy hopped a Western Pacific drag bound for Bieber through the "Inside Gateway"—a secondary mainline used jointly by the Western Pacific and Great Northern between California and southern Oregon. As you can see, it was an interesting bordering-on-the-magical sunset ride, with some danger attached. Not enough, however, to keep him from making further expeditions, like the late-night run discussed in "Night Moves," between San Luis Obispo and Watsonville, California, on the Southern Pacific's fabled Coast Line.

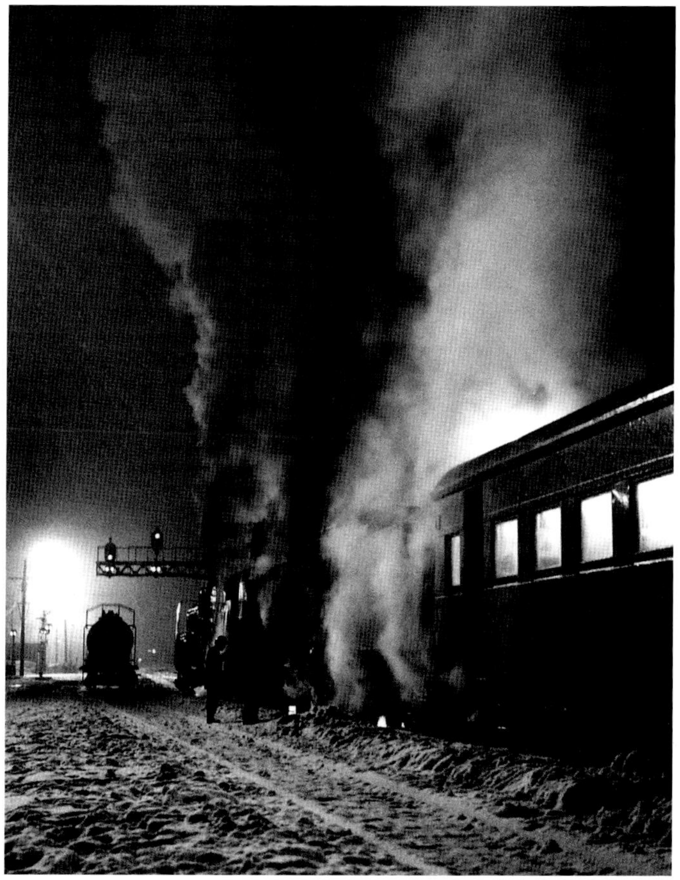

Other chapter introductions—"Sentimental Journey" and "'Round Midnight"—blend actual experience with historical research, since Brouws wasn't yet born when the described scenes took place. He did, however, have firsthand experiences with the places he writes about—Los Angeles' Union Station being a favorite haunt in the 1980s and Bayshore Yards and Roundhouse near San Francisco the focal point of his first night photos, taken in 1972.

"'Chasin the Train" and "Softly as a Mornin' Sunrise" complete the narrative. The mainline introduction chronicles a rainy ride across Nebraska in an aging Volkswagen beetle ("the wipers had long since stopped working"), circa 1974, pacing a Union Pacific freight train. In the sunrise text, we find Brouws and Delvers emerging from their frost-covered sleeping bags, California's Mount Whitney towering above them, to indulge in their favorite pastime—some early morning picture-taking while the local freight made up its train.

far left, top:
THE MOON ASCENDS as Burlington Northern train #138 races neon-like across the bridge at Home Valley, Washington.
Wayne Depperman

far left, middle:
AN ENGINEER ON Southern Pacific's Coast Line picks up train orders at Surf, California.
John Roskoski

far left, bottom:
A CLASSIC VIEW FROM the dutch door vestibule finds the Rio Grande Zephyr traversing the curves at Soldier Summit, Utah, during its westbound run to Salt Lake City in 1975.
Jeff Brouws

left, this page:
AN EXPRESS TRAIN stops at Kutchan, on the Hakodate mainline of Japanese National Railways in 1971. Located on the island of Hokkaido, this small rural village saw the passage of twenty daily passenger trains.
Ed Delvers

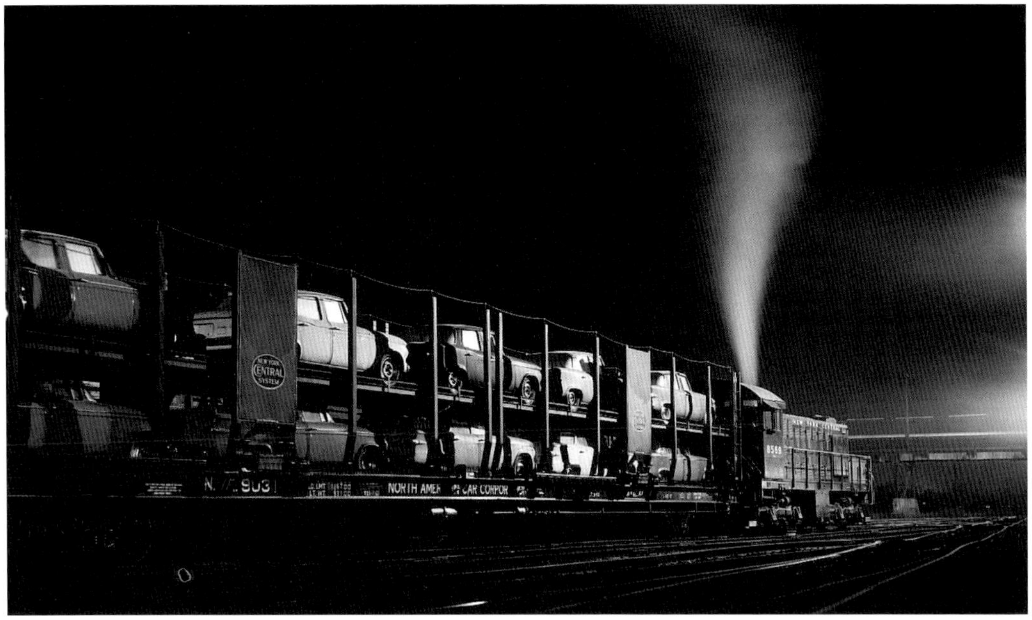

A STRING OF AUTORACKS filled with late-model Studebakers glides past the camera in the New York Central yards at Albany, New York. It's November 1959, and a venerable Alco S2 makes light work of the switching action.
Jim Shaughnessy

It's precisely the everyday ordinariness of these descriptions that helps us appreciate the lyricism that is railroading—past, present, and future—and the oftentimes mundane beauty of the environment it inhabits. The authors want you to feel the romance inherent in the nocturnal passage of a long freight wending its way over Cajon, the brief poignancy of the St. Claire pausing near the architecturally resplendent Niles, Michigan, depot (pages 54–55). To feel the thrill of travel for the railfan/photographer, whose best images are often made in out-of-the-way places. In short, to have you there, behind the camera, at the moment of exposure.

In *Starlight* we see the outstanding pictures of such Eastern seaboard photographers as Jim Shaughnessy, Howard Pincus, Robert Hart Jr., Victor Hand, and Jim Boyd; western talents Ted Benson, Wayne Depperman, Dick Dorn, Ed Delvers, Jeff Brouws, David Styffe, John Roskoski, Thomas L. Taylor, Stan Kistler, Joel Jensen, Paul Lukens, and myself; and midwesterners Philip Hastings, William D. Middleton, and such "second-generation" geniuses as Mel Patrick and John Gruber. A good crew to have on board.

THE LATE DR. PHILIP HASTINGS, trained as a psychiatrist, was a superb railroad photographer beginning in the early 1940s. In his quiet, thoughtful way, he seemed to equate people's search for meaning with their interest in trains. His educated and considered approach created beautiful visual explorations of the stately and the humble, of the inanimate and the vital. Concentrating on the human side of the photographic equation, these studies (pages 9, 13, 50–51, 76, 100) are some of the most genuine and unobtrusive glimpses into the world of railroading that have come down to us. Hastings' equipment was simple: a twin lens reflex, light tripod, and one or two flash guns. Relying mostly on available light from station platforms or quickly vanishing daylight (he was a superb master of low-light, mixed source photography), his techniques were straightforward—the direct antithesis of the more elaborate setups of Patrick, Pincus, and Benson.

Hastings' photography took him many places. He was involved in his craft twenty-four hours a day, and any excuse was good enough to get him out into the world on a moment's notice. Whether fighting blizzard conditions on Cumbres Pass, enduring the frigid winter environments of New Brunswick, or just hanging out for the 10 P.M. departure of the Ak Sar Ben (Nebraska spelled backwards) Zephyr from Omaha on a humid summer night, he was there. At one point early in his medical career, while living in Albany, New York, he and Jim Shaughnessy roamed the Northern territories together in search of subject matter and made similar photographs simultaneously (page 51 for Hastings's contribution; see the cover of *Night Train* {Golden West Publications, 1961} for Shaughnessy's image).

Phil and I shared the belief that to suffer a bit for your art was a good thing—inclement weather, hunger, or a staying-up-all-night tiredness made for better pictures. The adrenaline rush of being in a new location shooting a new railroad could make you forget the human essentials. In fact, every artist showcased here has experienced this—it seems to be *de rigueur* for the rail photographer.

Hastings' legendary night cab-ride story, "Into the Freezing Darkness" (*Trains,* April 1956), was made while riding a Denver & Rio Grande Western narrow-gauge freight train into the Rockies west of Alamosa, Colorado. The trip led him to ponder the battles between men and nature (page 71) as the little train fought its way through the darkness and snowdrifts to surmount one of the most forbidding mountain passes in all of Colorado.

Two thousand miles to the east, a commercial photographer named O. Winston Link was conducting a successful photography business in New York City when he became aware that the Norfolk & Western Railway was the last major American railroad to operate exclusively with steam power. A lucky assignment to a small town in Virginia gave him the chance to watch its locomotives at work, and he acted on a decades-old dream: to photograph a steam railroad at night so as to control the light and focus the drama of the scene. He created splendid nighttime action photographs of the N&W in many locations and later documented the N&W's Abingdon Branch in a series of exemplary daylight photographs as well. With the full cooperation of the railroad, Link planned his photos in advance, before he and his assistants deployed their kits of heavy flash equipment. The quality of their teamwork shows in their carefully orchestrated images: they combined imagination with plenty of flashbulbs. Link contacted trackside residents while scouting locations and made them, with their permission, the supporting actors in his photographic swan song to big-time mainline steam railroading. This all before the final curtain fell on a small-town American culture that would be forever altered by the diesel locomotive, automobile, and "mallification" of the urban landscape. Link's masterwork of twentieth-century photography has been documented in two previous books: *Steam, Steel & Stars* (Harry N. Abrams, Inc., 1987) and *The Last Steam Railroad in America* (Harry N. Abrams, Inc., 1995).

Link's prodigious efforts in the late 1950s had a profound impact on a younger generation of railfans. Every photographer featured in this book saw the work in early issues of *Trains* magazine and fell under its influence. Patrick, Pincus, Benson, Hart, and I would be inspired to try our own "light-up-the-night" scenarios: I, while working during the time Link was doing his best N&W work; Patrick in the late 1960s and early 1970s; and Benson, Pincus, and Hart in the 1970s, 1980s, and beyond.

ACTUALLY, THERE HAVE BEEN many means employed in the past century for the night photography of trains and locomotives. The earliest night train photograph may have been made by H. L. Arey using existing light from his own locomotive's headlamp near Tillamook, Oregon, circa 1914 (see Lucius Beebe's *Great Railroad Photographs* {Howell-North, 1964}). Before the advent of flashbulbs or electronic strobes, magnesium—in wire, ribbon, or powdered form (flash powder)—was

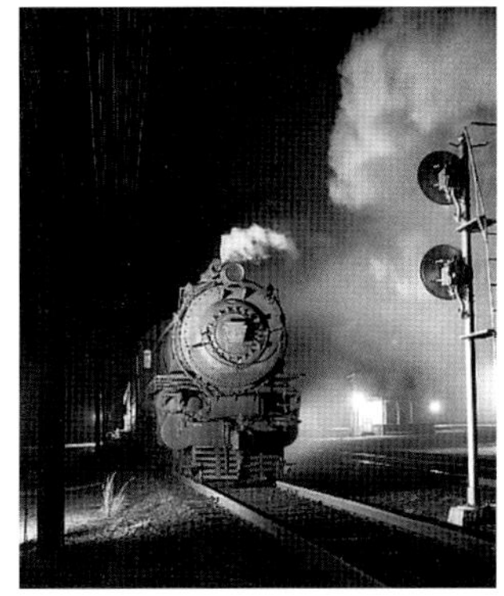

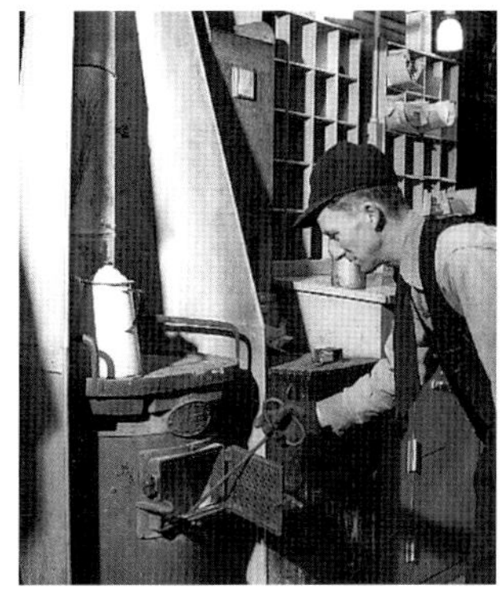

PENNSYLVANIA RAILROAD
4-4-2 #645 waits on the Ocean City Branch for a mainline connection to Camden, New Jersey, 1956.
Philip Hastings / CSRM

A CANADIAN NATIONAL
Railway baggageman adjusts the stove fire in the baggage car of train #52, traveling from Quebec to Moncton, New Brunswick, in March 1955.
Philip Hastings / CSRM

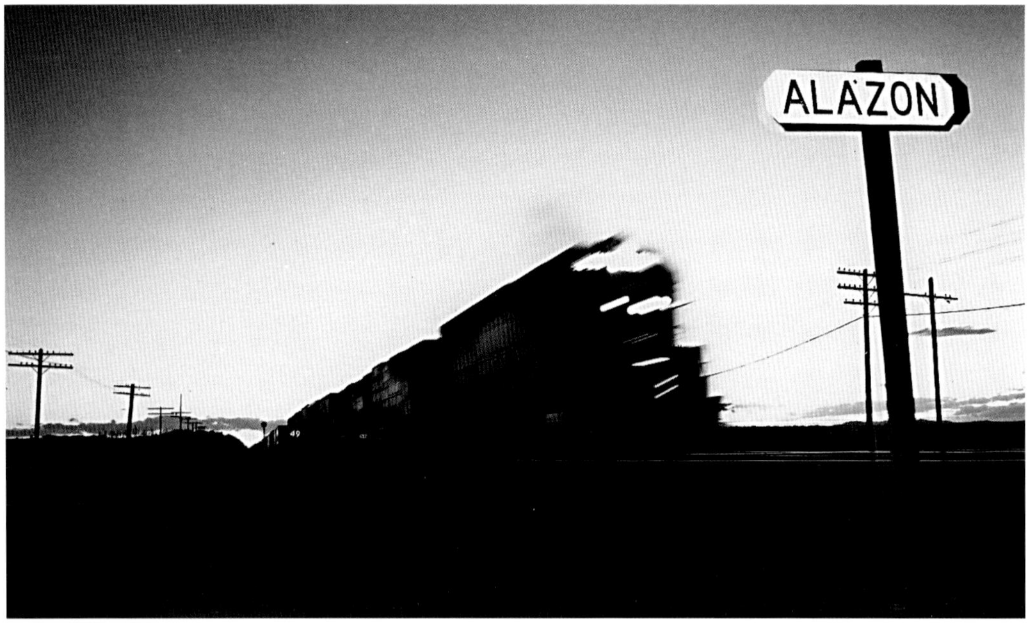

OPERATING ON PAIRED Western Pacific/Southern Pacific trackage, an Espee freight highballs past Alazon, four miles west of Wells, Nevada, in 1979. In 1853, Congress appropriated $150,000 to scout four possible rail routes to the West Coast, to aid in the settlement and development of a fledgling nation. The two tracks depicted above, crossing the Humboldt Sink, follow original alignments explored by U.S. Army engineers during the Pacific Railway Survey made the following year. *Dick Dorn*

used by commercial and news photographers. It was a very powerful light source. Flash powder was used for both indoor and outdoor photographs of many subjects, including exteriors of complete passenger trains. They were often lit by a photographer moving along the length of a train at night, illuminating several sections by repeated firings. One photograph in *Starlight*, taken in 1949 by Nishio (page 112), was made using magnesium. Because of magnesium's inherently volatile nature, most photographers soon switched to flashbulbs, invented in Germany by Paul Vierkotter in 1925, perfected by J. Ostermeier in 1929, and introduced into the American market as the Photoflash lamp in 1930. High-speed electronic flash was used as early as 1852 in experiments conducted by Henry Fox Talbot. It was also used in laboratory settings by Ernst Mach in Czechoslovakia in 1887 and Harold Edgerton starting in 1940. Kodak soon made larger units—called strobes—for studio use in the 1940s. A small portable flash was invented in 1939 by newspaperman Edward Farber.

Flashbulbs and electronic flash each have advantages and disadvantages. Flashbulbs provide fuller illumination (up to 1000 times more intensity than electronic strobes) with a softer edge, capable of filling in deep shadows. Slower shutter speeds have to be used, however, because of the duration of the actual flash (1/50 of a second). Electronic flash, on the other hand, is shorter in duration (1/10,000 of a second) and produces a colder, sharper light, incapable of much fill-in. Its advantage is that one does not have to remove, or otherwise deal with, still hot, burnt flashbulbs, when walking around a scene "painting with light" (open flash). Cost is also a factor: flashbulbs can be used once (and in recent years have become scarce and expensive, solely manufactured by Electrodyne of Ireland), whereas the electronic flash can be fired repeatedly (if running off batteries or a pack).

Whether a photograph is being made by professionals or amateurs, the work of setting up lights for night-train photography still requires good planning, muscle and nerve, safety consciousness, and a lighting configuration that will enhance what might otherwise be a dark, mundane scene. The more ambitious "light-painters" represented in this book—Mel Patrick, Ted Benson, and Rails After Dark (Howard Pincus, Bob Hart Jr., and Al Papp)—worked assiduously with railroad authorities to insure that all safety precautions were taken and that unsuspecting train crews might be alerted to "the gang with all the lights" as they passed by a photo location. Long hours and late nights were often required to string wire and insure proper conductivity to all flash units. Anywhere from three to thirty individual bulbs of varying wattage were employed in any given photograph. Pincus mostly favored clear #2 and #22 bulbs—the bigger ones for large areas that needed broad illumination and the smaller ones for lanterns and platform lights. Most were operated by a portable battery-capacitor unit. Patrick employed upward of thirty flashbulbs either wired in series or triggered by "slave" units. Patrick did many setups around his home base of Chicago in the late 1960s and early 1970s (pages 15, 48, 49, 53, 54–55, 66-67, and 80–81), as well as making images in the Denver area when he was transferred to the Rock Island traffic department in 1972 (page 70). Rails After Dark worked from 1983 to 1987, creating more than sixty-five different setups, concentrating on motive power and railroads that would soon be vanishing from the scene (pages 56–57 and 68). Benson, while employing simpler methods, nonetheless explored the full creative possibilities of artificial lighting (pages 6, 16, and 85), making many photographs along the Western Pacific and Sierra Railroad mainlines that are contemporary classics.

Most of the photographs in the book were made with available light or in combination with one of the two types of flash described above. In some cases, the photographers counted on the veiled presence of light to create the desired mood in their images. Gruber's Madison, Wisconsin, photograph (page 45) is a striking example: the headlamp of the oncoming train scatters and creates sharp contrasts between the shadowed

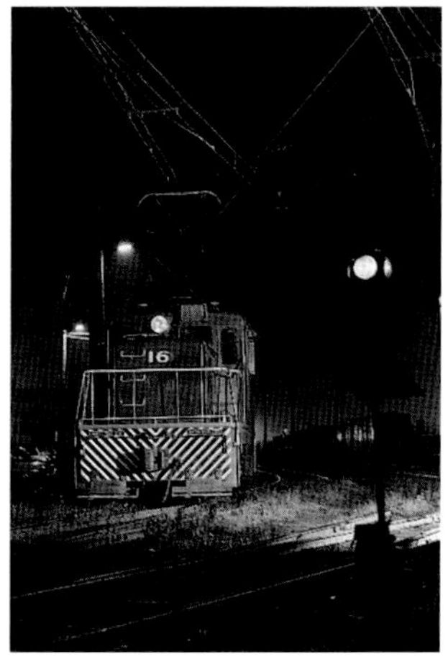

A NIAGARA JUNCTION Railway juice jack switches the yard at Niagara Falls, New York, in 1959. A kerosene lantern atop a target switchstand lights the way. Number 16, a GE unit built in 1952, lasted on the property until the catenary came down in 1979—the year Conrail diesels took over.
Jim Shaughnessy

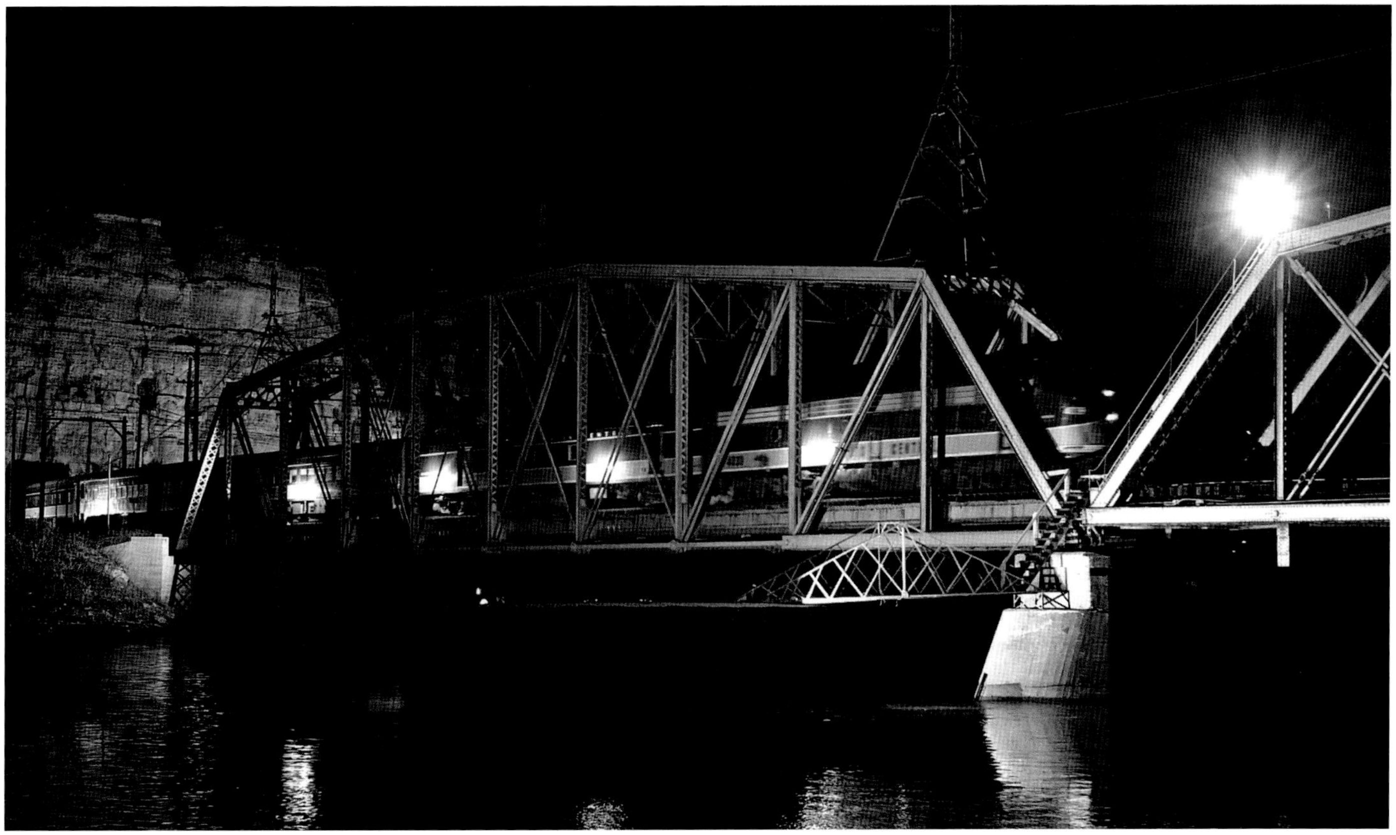

left:
WITH THE AID of nineteen flashbulbs, Illinois Central's crack passenger train, the Hawkeye, is caught midspan crossing the Mississippi River at East Dubuque, Illinois, in 1971.
Mel Patrick

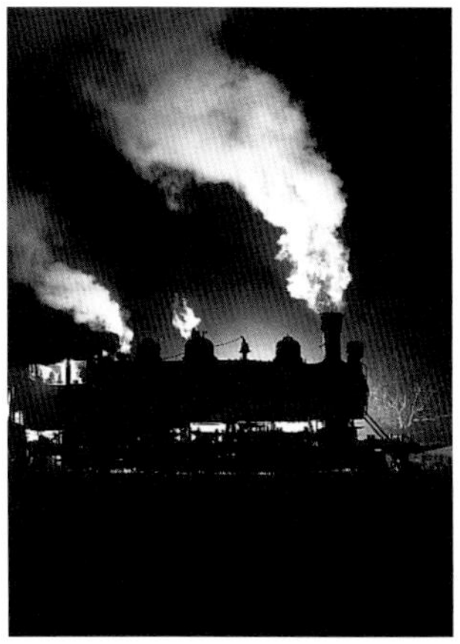

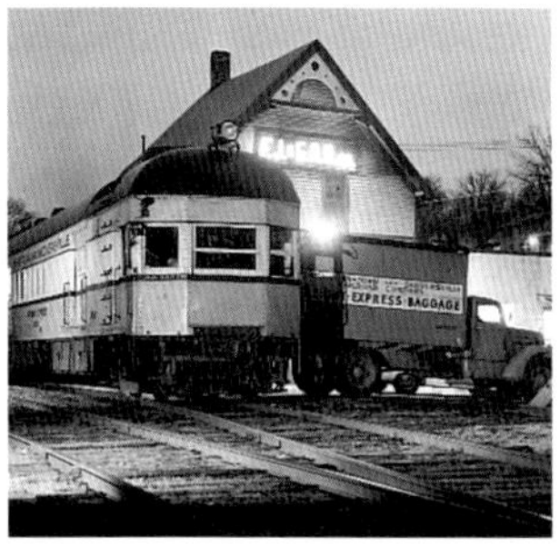

SIERRA RAILROAD **Mikado #34 waits at Warnerville, California, silhouetted against the night sky in December of 1977.** *Ted Benson*

A BRILL MOTOR CAR, **of the Fonda, Jamestown & Gloversville Railway, unloads parcels and mail on New Year's Eve, 1957.** *Jim Shaughnessy*

passengers waiting on the platform and the locomotive. Anything additional would have destroyed the drama. Gruber relied upon a simple 35mm camera, fast lens, and fast film: street photography from the hip in the finest Garry Winograd or Lee Friedlander tradition insured this level of spontaneity. Taylor's Calwa Yard shot also comes to mind (page 105). Shot with available yard lights and an open shutter for forty seconds, this haunting image conveys the mystery of trains-at-night in a simplified form, reminding us with its Zen-like quality that not everything has to be "seen" in order to convey its essence or beauty.

This seat-of-the-pants style of picture-making, with the photographer and equipment pared to essentials, characterizes the most frequently used approach in *Starlight*. This type of shooting further enhances the excitement of night photography in that, unlike the wired-in-series flashbulb setup (where a Polaroid test is sometimes possible and the results are therefore more consistently determined), it's unpredictable. Oftentimes you don't know what you have until film is processed and the prints made.

Brouws, Delvers, Jensen, Dorn, Depperman, Hand, Shaughnessy, Middleton, and Roskoski also kept things simple. Using 4 x 5", 35mm, and $2^1/_4$" formats and a variety of both color and black-and-white films allowed them to get the shots they needed without much fuss. As for myself, I've employed myriad types of cameras over the years, ranging from 4 x 5" to 35mm, from Hasselblad to Bronica, finding the little Rollei Autocord the best all-around camera for the abuses inherent in the night photography game—whether it be cameras on tripods toppled by fierce winds or a photo session in a Northwest downpour, that little compact camera held up well.

MY LATE FRIEND, Warren Marcus, and I did our single most difficult night photograph in California in 1960. It was of a three-foot gauge West Side Lumber Company Shay locomotive pulling a train across a high timber trestle over the Tuolumne River in the Sierras (page 73). Located in a dark forested area with a twenty-foot-wide river running underneath and no easy access to its far side, the curved trestle, known as River Bridge, proved quite challenging to light and shoot. The shot required hauling 200 feet of wire and two flashbulbs and reflectors up a steep embankment on our side of the water, and carrying my 4 x 5" Speed Graphic, homemade forty-five-volt battery-box, tripod, and assorted accessories to the other side—stringing flimsy household wire across the dark abyss as we went. The wire ran from the two reflectors—which hopefully were pointed where they would light the Shay as it lumbered across the rickety trestle—to the shutter of my camera.

We knew the wooden-beam log cars towed by the train would be empty and barely visible in the final photo. No matter, for we'd hoped that a dramatically lit locomotive and trestle would carry the image. Warren and I sat uncomfortably on the rocky hillside for hours, talking and waiting for the train. At one point, as the wait began to seem interminable, I yelled to Warren, "We're either geniuses or fools, and I don't know which!" He was sitting somewhere above me and I could hear him chuckling in the darkness.

We finally heard the "blowtorch" sounds of a Shay locomotive approaching from the mill. I cocked the Speed Graphic and waited until the locomotive was nearly across the trestle and in position. I triggered the shutter and the flashbulbs went off as planned. We'd been sitting in darkness for so long that their brightness blinded us. But with that momentary burst of lumens we saw the Shay properly placed and knew we had our shot. We shouted a few loud cheers into the night as the Shay's exhausts faded off into the distant woods.

The shot, however, wasn't complete. Since it was such an enormous structure, we had to return to work. Needing to light the trestle, particularly the lower and nearer portions that hadn't received illumination from the two powerful flashes, I opened the shutter again. With the same sheet of film still in camera, we walked beneath the timbers and fired several "open flashes," careful to hide our bodies from the lens. It was muddy and slippery; my dog fell into the river. The shutter remained open for quite a while but eventually, with several hundred thousand lumens of additional light, we had the shot we had envisioned.

It would have been a better photograph had the train been descending the grade with logs, but it would have been daylight by then. At the time, we didn't realize we'd never be able to do this picture again. Several months later we learned this had been, in fact, the last revenue run into the woods for the West Side Lumber Company. It wasn't a perfect setup, but Warren and I were both willing to let stand what we had accomplished.

AS THE TWENTY-FIRST CENTURY DAWNS, it would appear that even with the onslaught of new technologies, from the Internet to DNA research, the railroad will prevail. The strong relationship that still exists between railroads and the people of our present civilization is a subject obviously not dead. It has persisted and is actually enjoying a resurgence. Traffic levels on the freight carriers, thanks to the deregulating Staggers Act of 1980, have returned to historic highs with ton-miles exceeding their former World War II peaks. Vacationers are once again rediscovering the pleasures of rail travel, as first-class accommodations return to name trains like the Coast Starlight.

The burgeoning tourist steamline trade and preservation movement, best exemplified by the California State Railroad Museum in Sacramento, the Steamtown facility in Scranton, Pennsylvania, the Cumbres & Toltec Scenic Railway of Chama, New Mexico, or smaller operations like the mostly volunteer diesel-operated Naugatuck Railroad in Connecticut, is much in the news and charging full-speed ahead. It only stands to reason that as older styles of railroading recede and are supplanted by other, more contemporary forms of modernity, we will welcome these repositories of rail history as a tether to past eras of industrial brawn and earlier ways of living. This is the place where railroads and trains resonate in our hearts.

Forty years ago we feared that paving over the land with one hundred billion dollars worth of interstate highways would rid the rails of trains. But we were wrong. Unless we want to go broke as a nation, our children's children will continue to enjoy the excitement of trains rushing through the night on their fuel-efficient errands; will continue to enjoy the immense aural beauty of a three-chime steam whistle blowing for a lonely crossing; will still beg to stand trackside, transfixed, as the California Zephyr or the Sunset Limited streaks by; will find beauty as starlight falls on the rails at eventide. You know it's so.

Richard Steinheimer
Sacramento, California

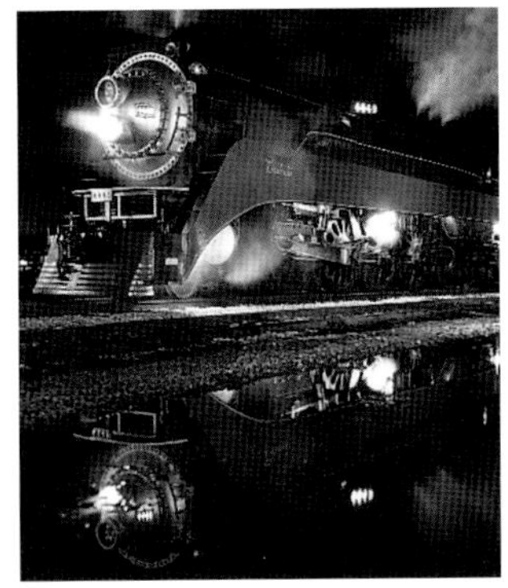

A LATE-NIGHT DOUBLE image of Southern Pacific's GS4 4-8-4 #4449 is reflected back at the photographer in San Luis Obispo, California, in the mid-1980s. *Paul Lukens*

overleaf:
PHIL HASTINGS' camera captures for all time the despair of a railroad preparing for the end. The Oneida & Western, a thirty-eight-mile rail line, succumbed to chronic financial problems in the mid-1950s. The engineer and fireman walk somberly back to their locomotive—the diminutive 2-8-0 #2—to resume the dismantling of a railroad and a way of life in the hills of central Tennessee. *Philip Hastings / CSRM*

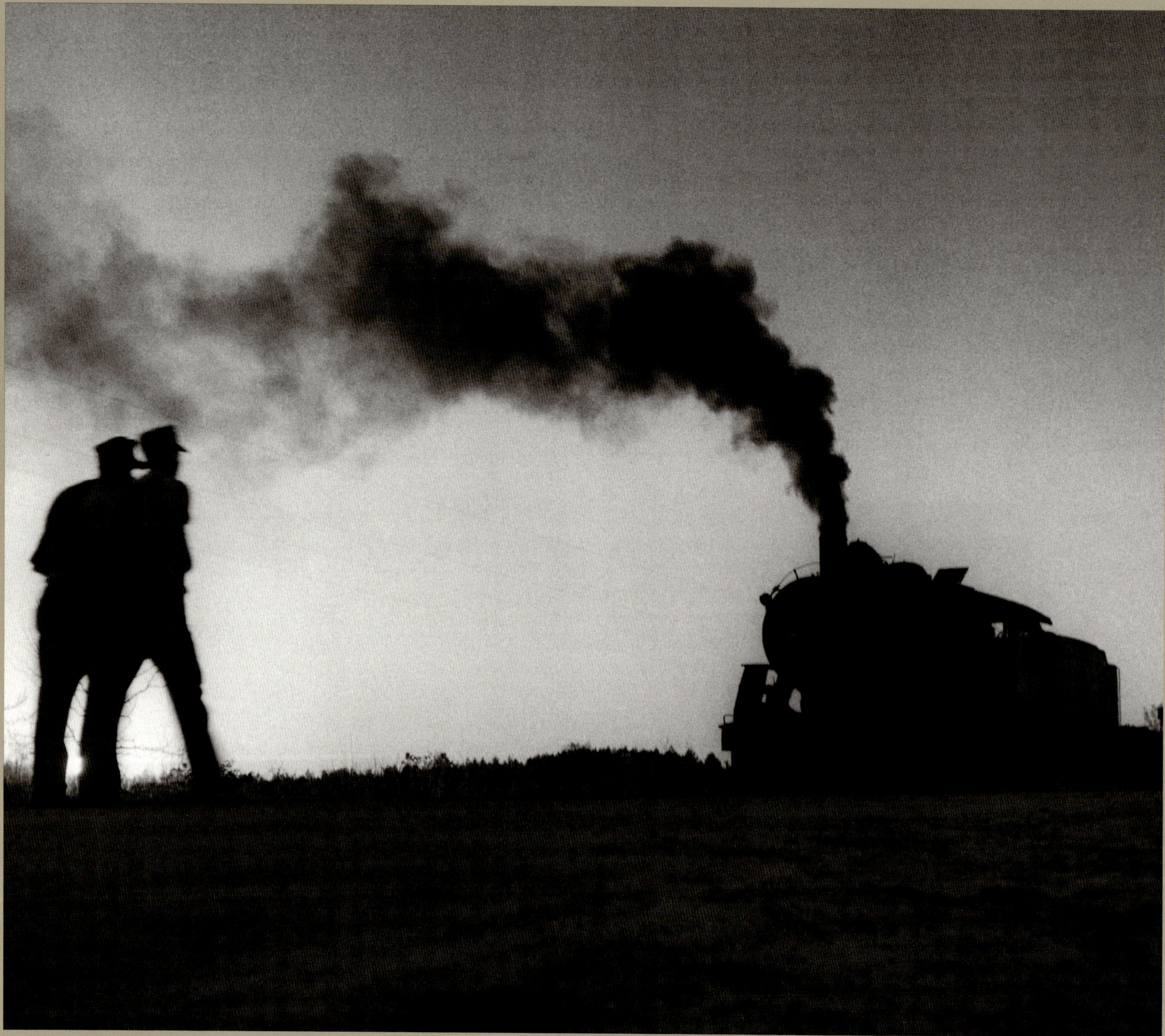

Chapter One TOWARD NIGHTFALL

TOWARD NIGHTFALL

The Railroad at Sunset

Hunkered down against the back bulkhead of a gondola filled with steel pipe, we hide from the wind's cold bite. Our car, cast among four score of its metallic brethren, is tied tightly to a fast freight bound for Northwest destinations. We speed, out past Lodgepole and Robbers Creek and all the lonesome unknown sidings. The flanks of the box-cars ahead, set afire by the sun's setting rays, stand out in bright relief against the darkening backdrop of pine and fir. The Plumas National Forest spreads beyond our vision. We are traveling toward night-fall on a rolling rocket of shooting steel—7,600 tons of unstoppable momentum.

It has been a long, dusty ride from Oroville up through the Feather River Canyon. While we thrill to the adventure, the harsh realities of riding freight trains isn't lost on us: at one point, as our train brakes for a curve, a shifting load slams against the bulkhead, just inches from where I was standing a moment before.

Later, we enter the small yard at Bieber as the last light drains down from the west, leaving watercolor washes of magenta and purple. The train slows and we become warmer, out of the knifelike wind. The glimpse of a distant campfire tucked in near the periphery of the tracks warms us further

SUNSET AND A WESTERN thunderstorm gather above the double track Southern Pacific mainline near Rose Creek, Nevada, on a hot August afternoon in 1984. Following a route virtually unchanged since the fall of 1868, the trains today still ply the desolate miles across the Great Basin on America's original transcontinental railroad. *David Styffe*

with its suggestion of comfort and camaraderie. Around it we find a circle of hoboes with tired, worn faces. As the flames illuminate their eyes I imagine the fire also highlighting the darker, more shadowy sides of their stories—tales undoubtedly with a dramatic edge—told by men who hadn't taken their lives through typical moments, but who chose instead to chance all and ride a different road into the night.

Now, with the light all but gone—and Orion and the Pleiades anchored in the black firmament above—darkness comes and a cool dampness settles over this railroad earth.

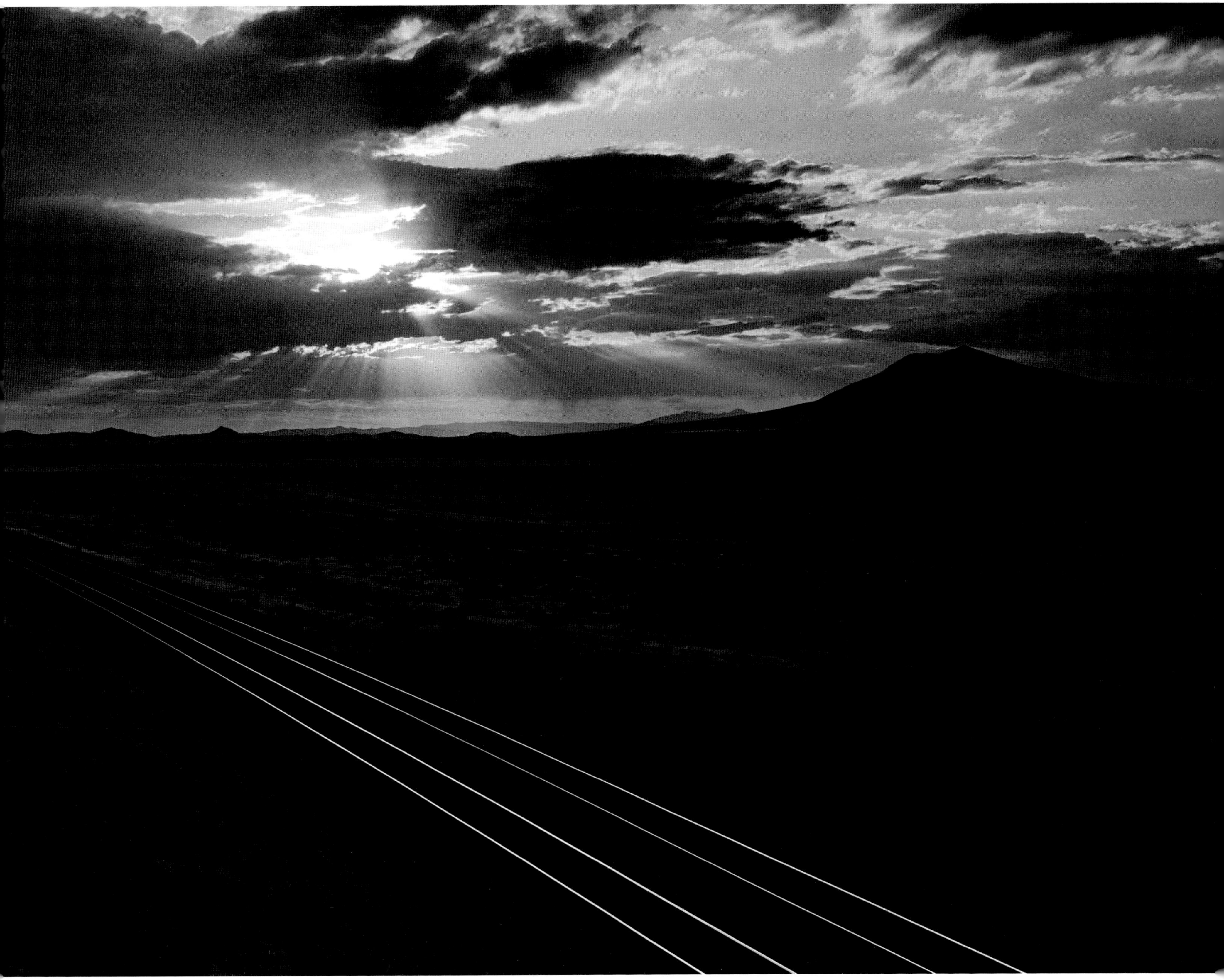

AESTHETICALLY SPEAKING, the railroad environment at sunset offers the observer an opportunity to witness the interplay of shadow, shape, and contrast. This was especially true during the steam era, when billowing clouds of pungent coal smoke were silhouetted against the darkening sky, and the massive industrial forms of water columns and coaling towers towered over mere mortals. At dusk, in Hamilton, Ontario, a lone hostler takes on water for his thirsty 0-8-0. The engine, viewed from the head end, is an inky shadow of headlight and steam. Trundling across a trestle, opposite, over the moraines of Wisconsin, is a CMStP&P 4-6-0 with a work train and sidedoor caboose in tow. The time is the early 1950s. *All, Philip Hastings / CSRM*

middle right:

UPPER QUADRANT semaphores stand tall against an impending sunset near Wapato, Washington, 1977. *Dick Dorn*

top right:

UNION PACIFIC'S Challenger 3985 crosses the Utah salt flats on a fan trip in 1981. *Mel Patrick*

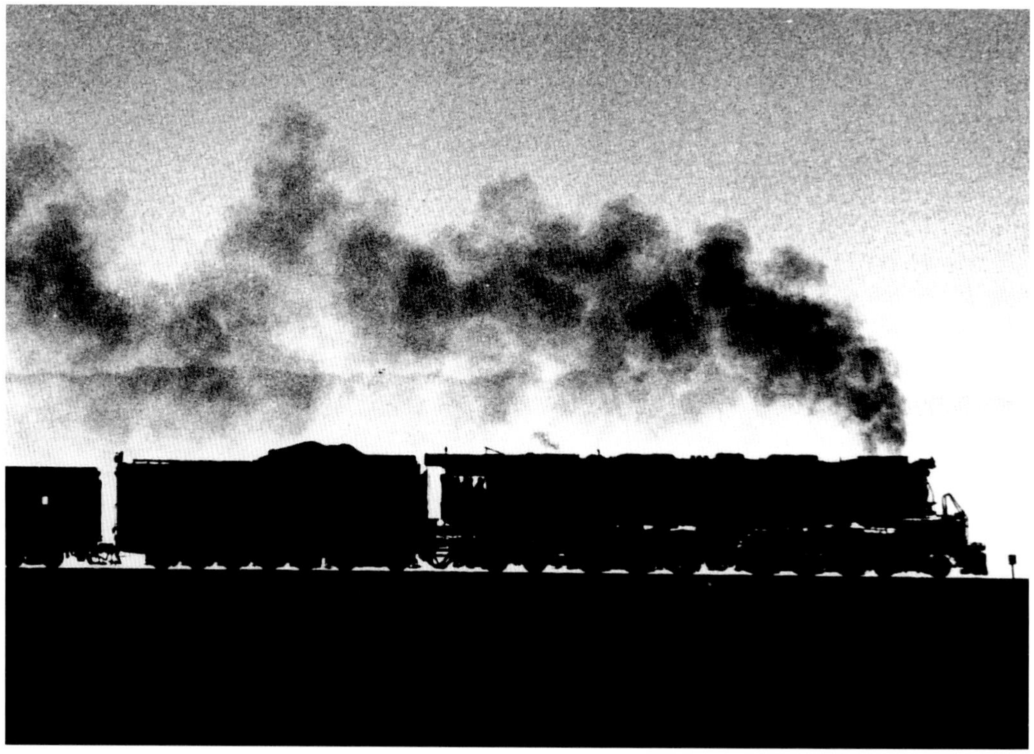

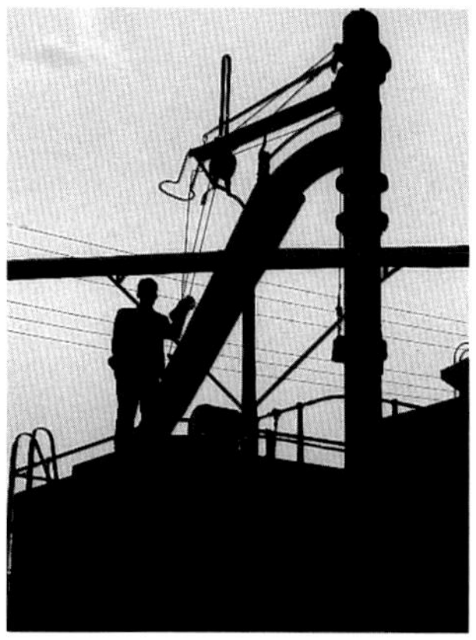

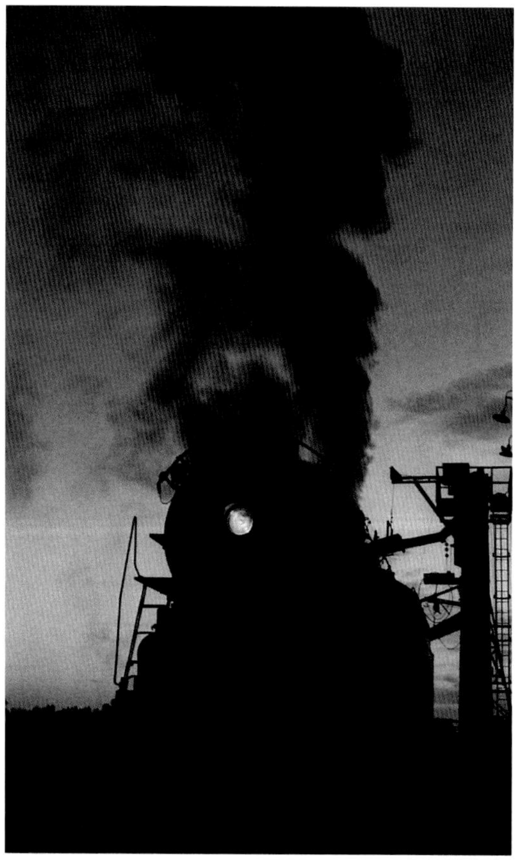

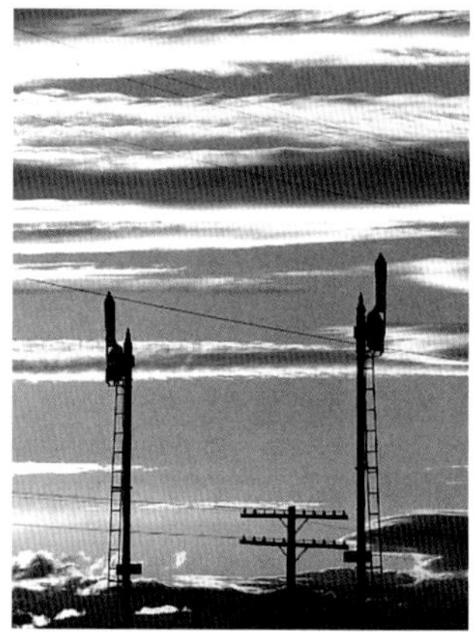

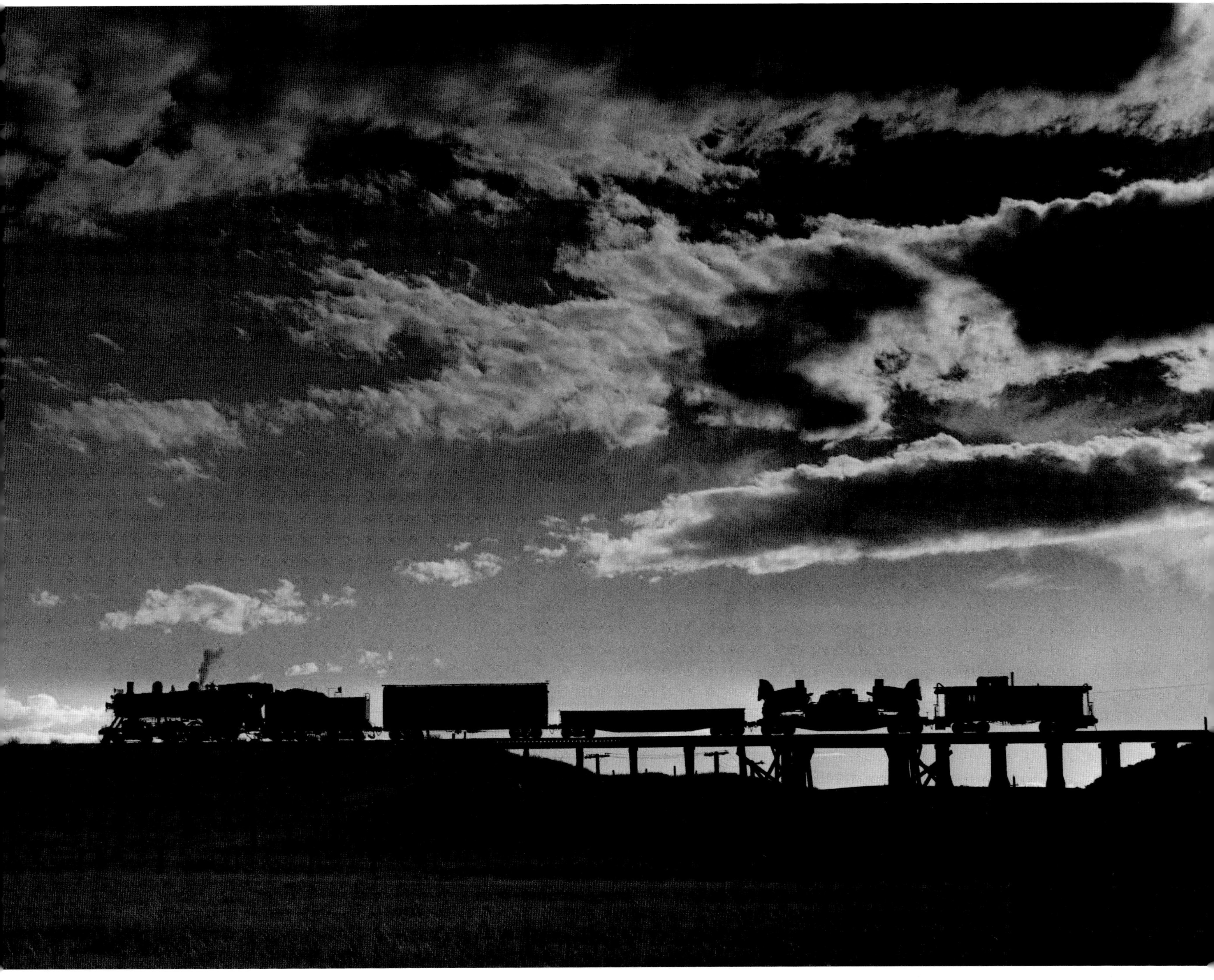

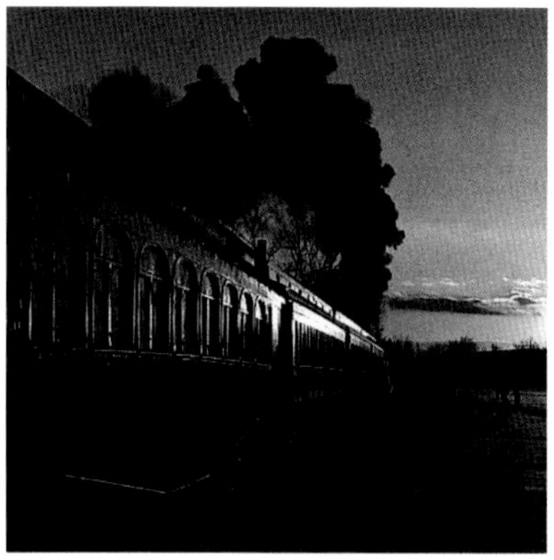

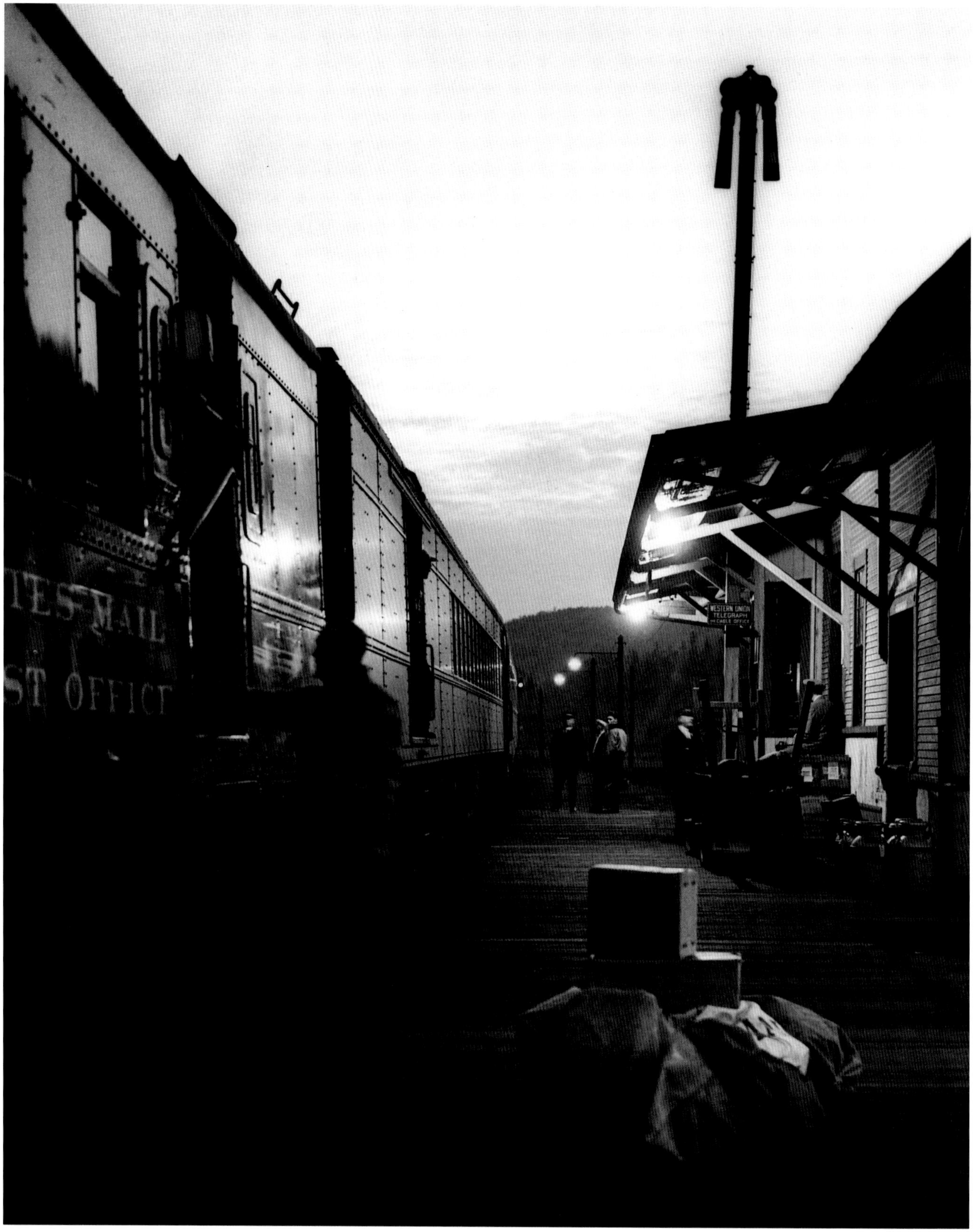

above:

MID-CONTINENT Railway Museum's Chicago & North Western 4-6-0 #1385 heads into a winter sunset during the annual "Snow Train" festivities at North Freedom, Wisconsin.

right:

ON AN OCTOBER eve in 1948, the station agent helps unload the Railway Post Office Car on a Boston & Maine local at Bradford, Vermont. RPO service—first instituted in 1862 during the Civil War—was how the nation's mail moved for over a hundred years.

far right:

CANADIAN NATIONAL'S train #75 sits in the gathering dusk waiting for passengers to board at Cochrane, Ontario, in 1972.
All, Philip Hastings / CSRM

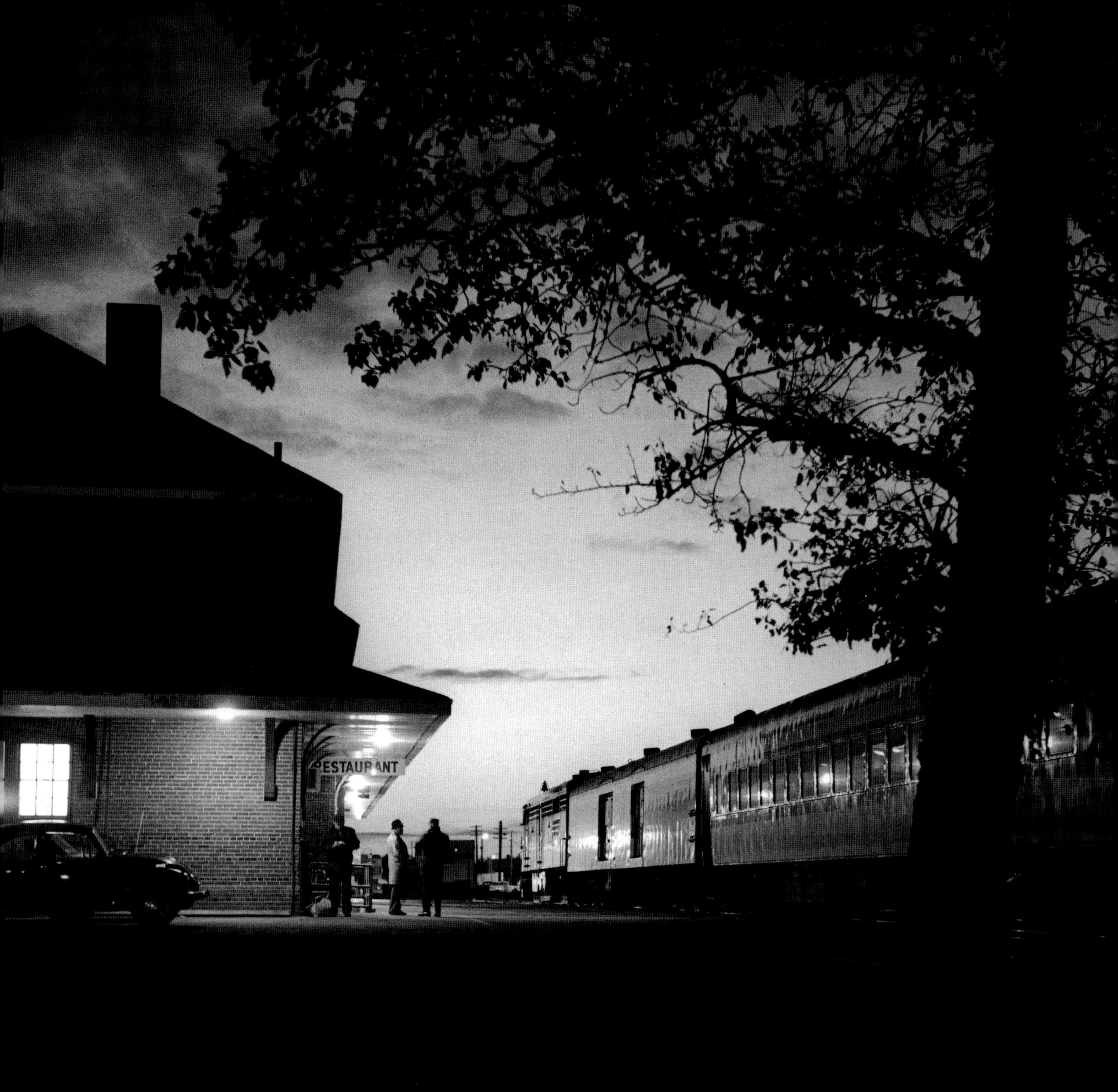
ESTAURANT

A STRING OF PACIFIC Fruit Express refrigerator cars sits silently on the wye at Surf, California, on a late November afternoon in 1984. Ominous skies, portending stormy weather, almost block out the bright disk of the sun. With the wind blowing incessantly and the tides pounding the coastline beyond the cut of cars, the scene is evocative of a film-noir set.

Sudden, Surf, and Honda: all are place names and one-time station stops on the Southern Pacific's Coast Route running between San Francisco and Los Angeles. Each had its share of history and mysterious tragedy. In 1907, train #21, the second section of the Coaster, a Shriner's Special, derailed at Honda, killing thirty-six. Sixteen years later, at Sudden, and billed as the worst nautical disaster in California history, seven Naval destroyers, whipped by the natural forces of wind and wave and a grave navigational error, ran aground in heavy coastal fog. The Espee, in a grand humanitarian gesture, sent special trains throughout the night and the following day to help transport survivors and the dead. Then, in 1983, heavy winter rains washed out a bridge near Surf, paralyzing the railroad. The line remained closed for seven days as bridge and building crews watched a relentless procession of Pacific storms hamper their around-the-clock efforts to reopen the mainline.

The facing photograph captures, in silver-gelatin, a reminder of these events.
Jeff Brouws

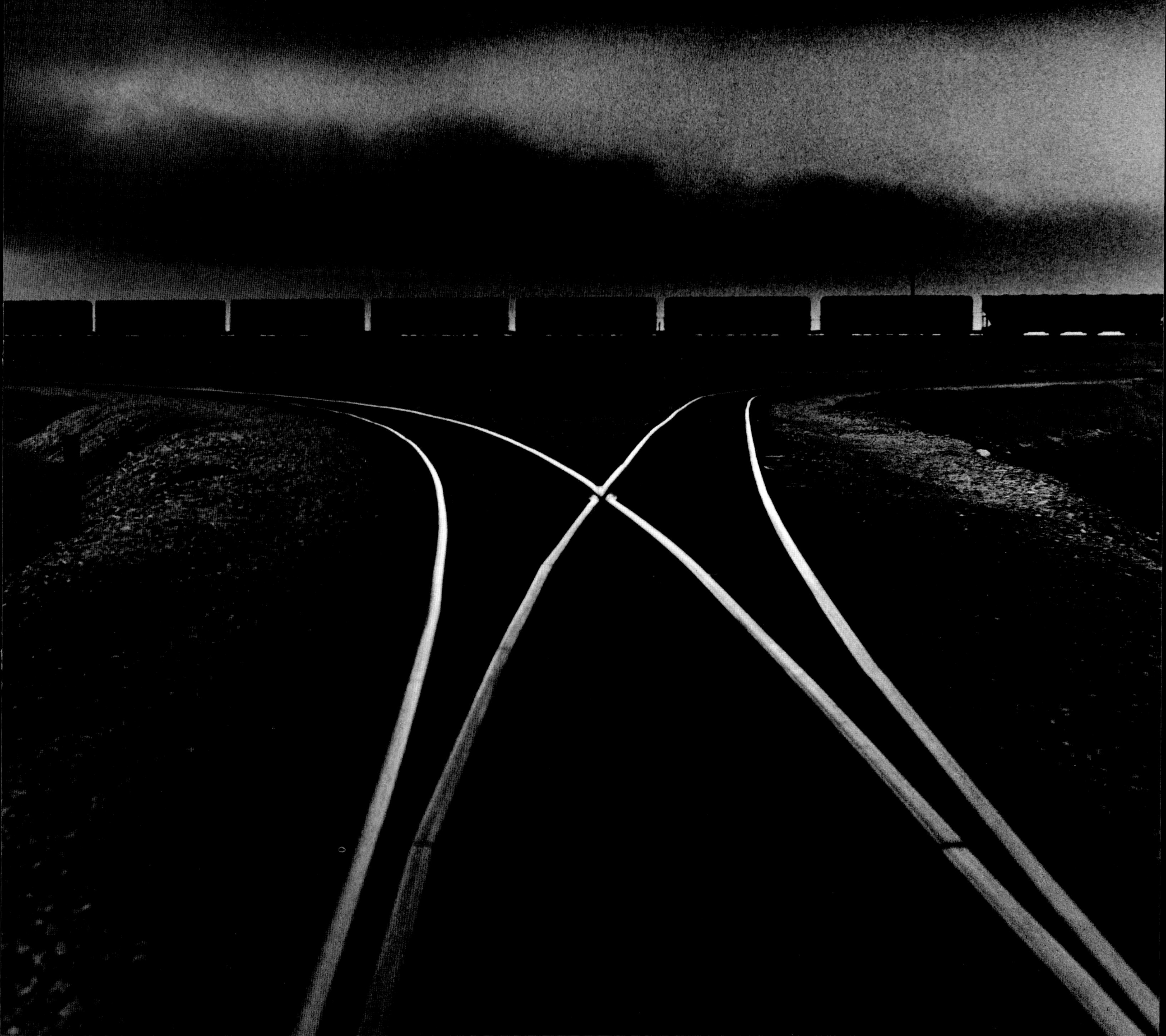

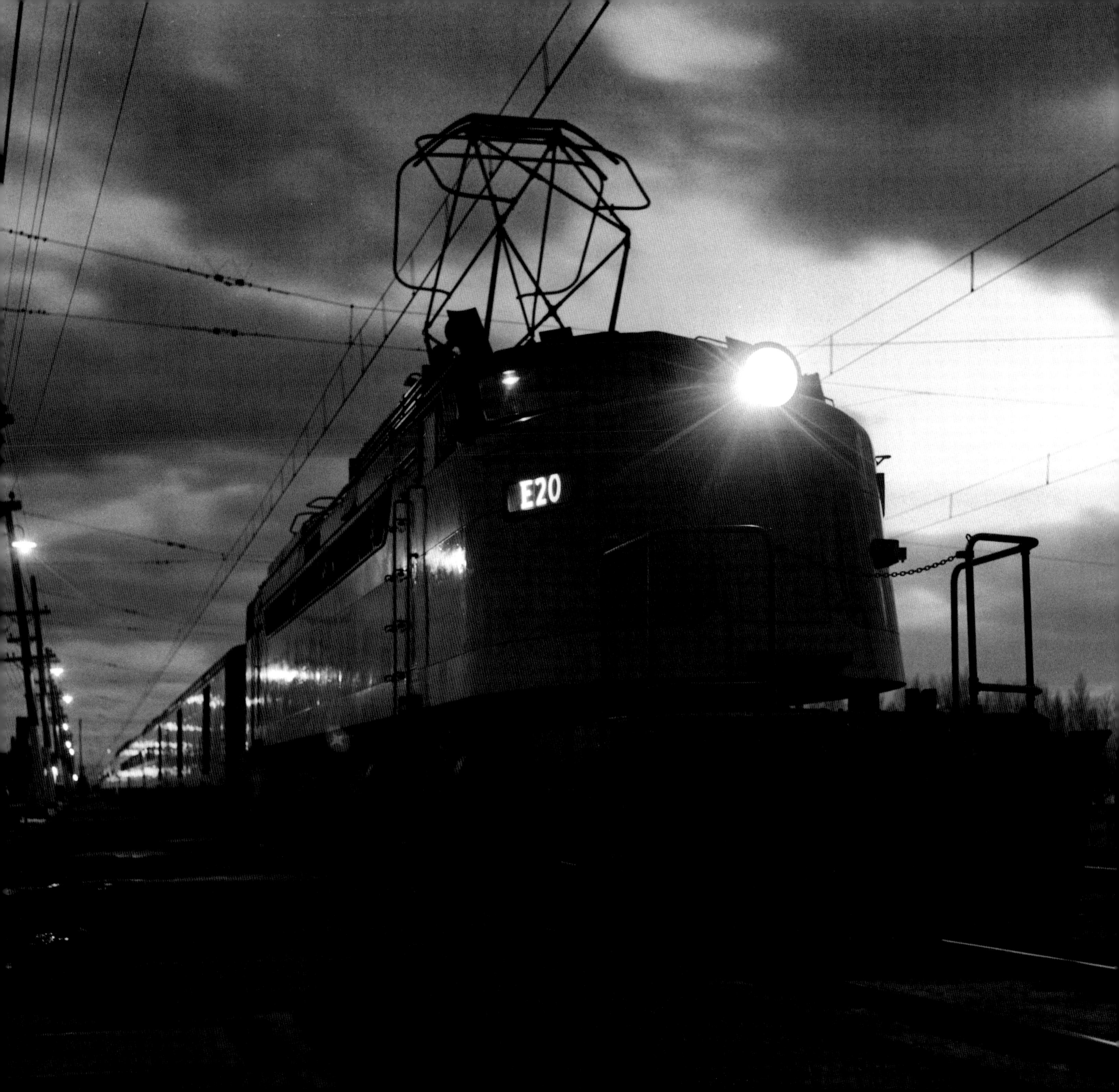
E20

LITTLE JOE E20 pauses momentarily in Deer Lodge, Montana, with the Seattle-bound Olympian Hiawatha in 1953. The "Joe," named after Joseph Stalin, was part of a locomotive order placed in 1946 by the Russian government with GE but never delivered. With mounting Cold War tensions following WWII, Harry S. Truman embargoed strategic goods to the USSR; twelve of the units were eventually purchased by the Milwaukee Road at the "fire sale" price of a million dollars.

The Hiawatha series of passenger trains inaugurated in May 1935, between Chicago and the Twin Cities, was the CMStP&P's response to its competitors' streamlining efforts. The later addition to the train sets (after 1948) of the stylishly sleek lines of the Brooks Stevens–inspired Skytop observation car was the ultimate example of industrial design and modern aesthetics.
Richard Steinheimer

IT'S 9:05 P.M. by the accuracy of the photographer's watch as the Coast Starlight winds through the Cascade Range at Cruzatte, Oregon, with a ragtag collection of streamlined equipment gathered from the various railroads that joined Amtrak in 1971. The final light of day glints off the fluted stainless steel siding of this seventeen-car consist, turning it momentarily into a serpentine figure cleaving the oncoming darkness. Gliding southward over the Natron Cutoff, #11 will soon stop at Klamath Falls, Dunsmuir, Redding, and other points on the Espee's Shasta Division. Tomorrow, Amtrak's most popular train will continue its descent, spanning the broad longitude of the Golden State, with Los Angeles its destination.
Dick Dorn

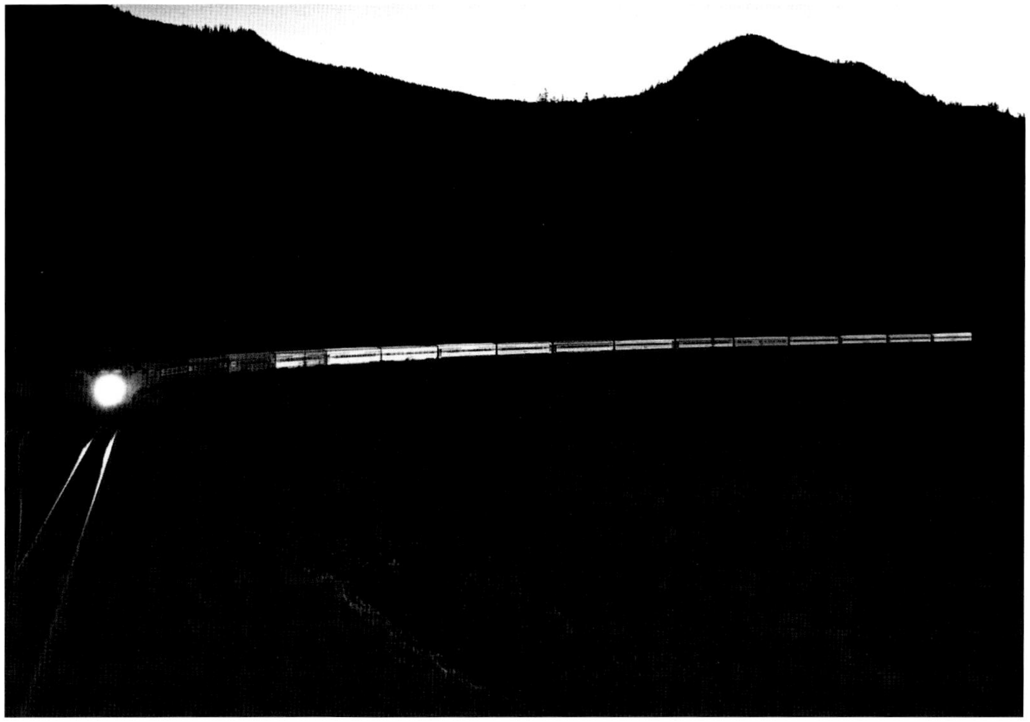

right:

OUT IN THE FLAT PRAIRIE landscape of Iowa, a Rock Island conductor hoops up train orders at dusk.
Philip Hastings / CSRM

far right:

IN A TIME-EXPOSED blur of neon and headlights, Amtrak's Coast Starlight rolls through the industrial backyard of Burbank, California, on the last leg of its 1,190-mile journey from Seattle. Los Angeles Union Passenger Terminal is fifteen minutes and ten miles away on this October evening in 1982.
Jeff Brouws

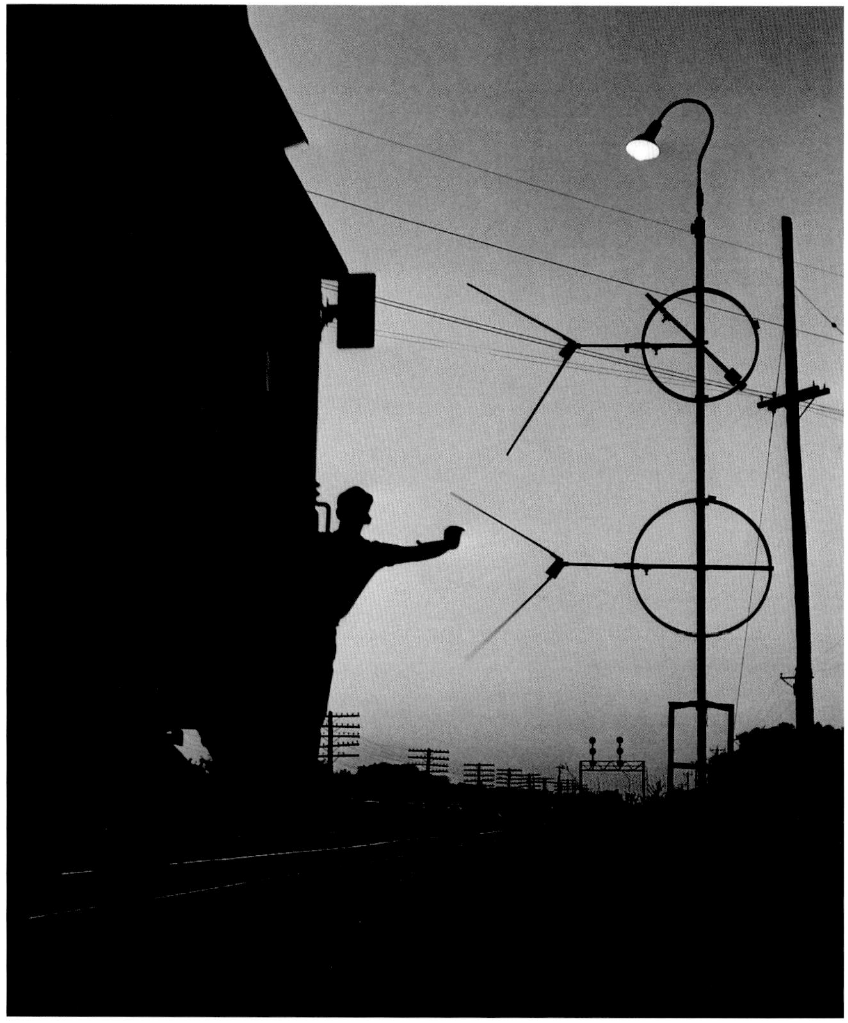

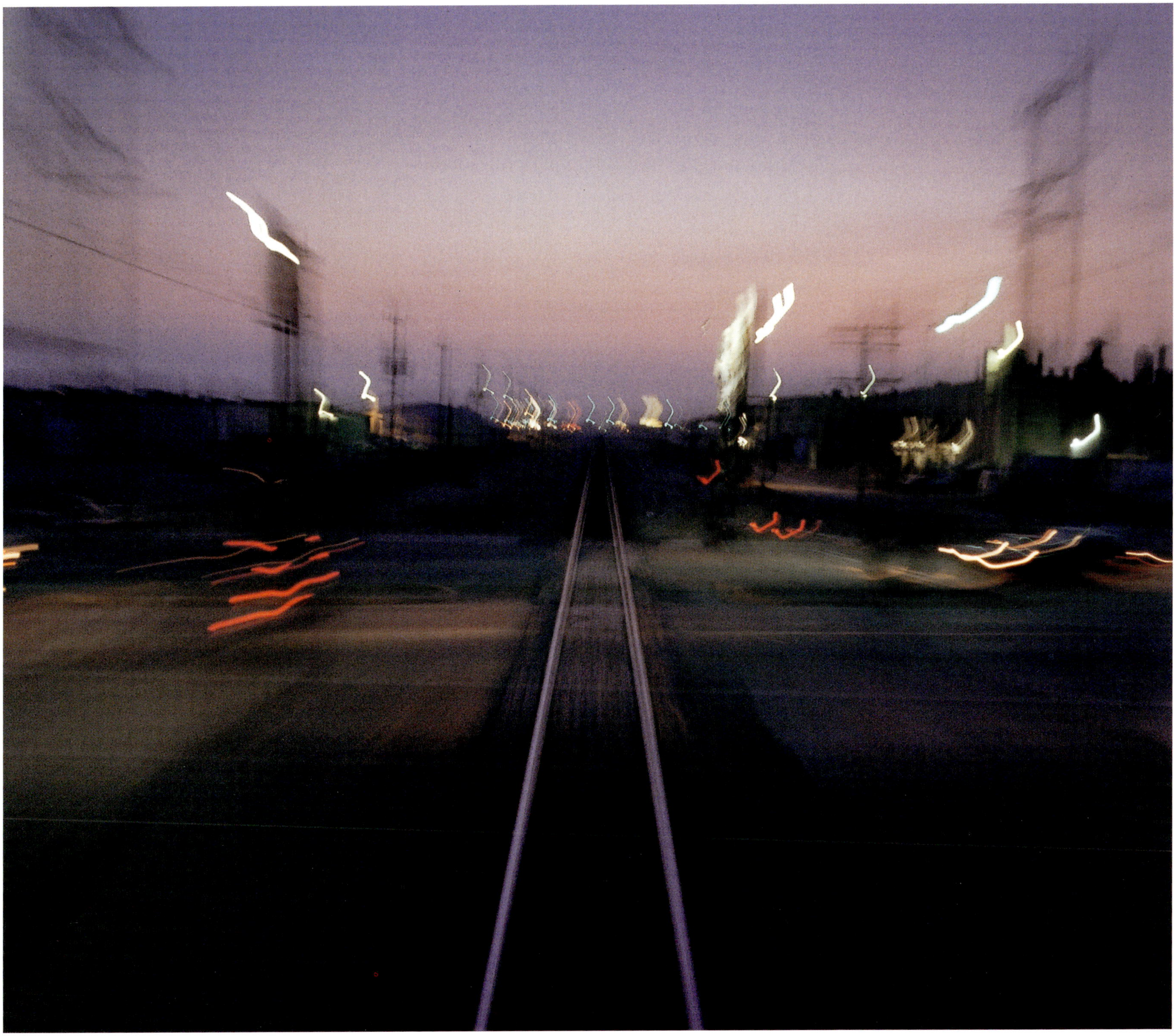

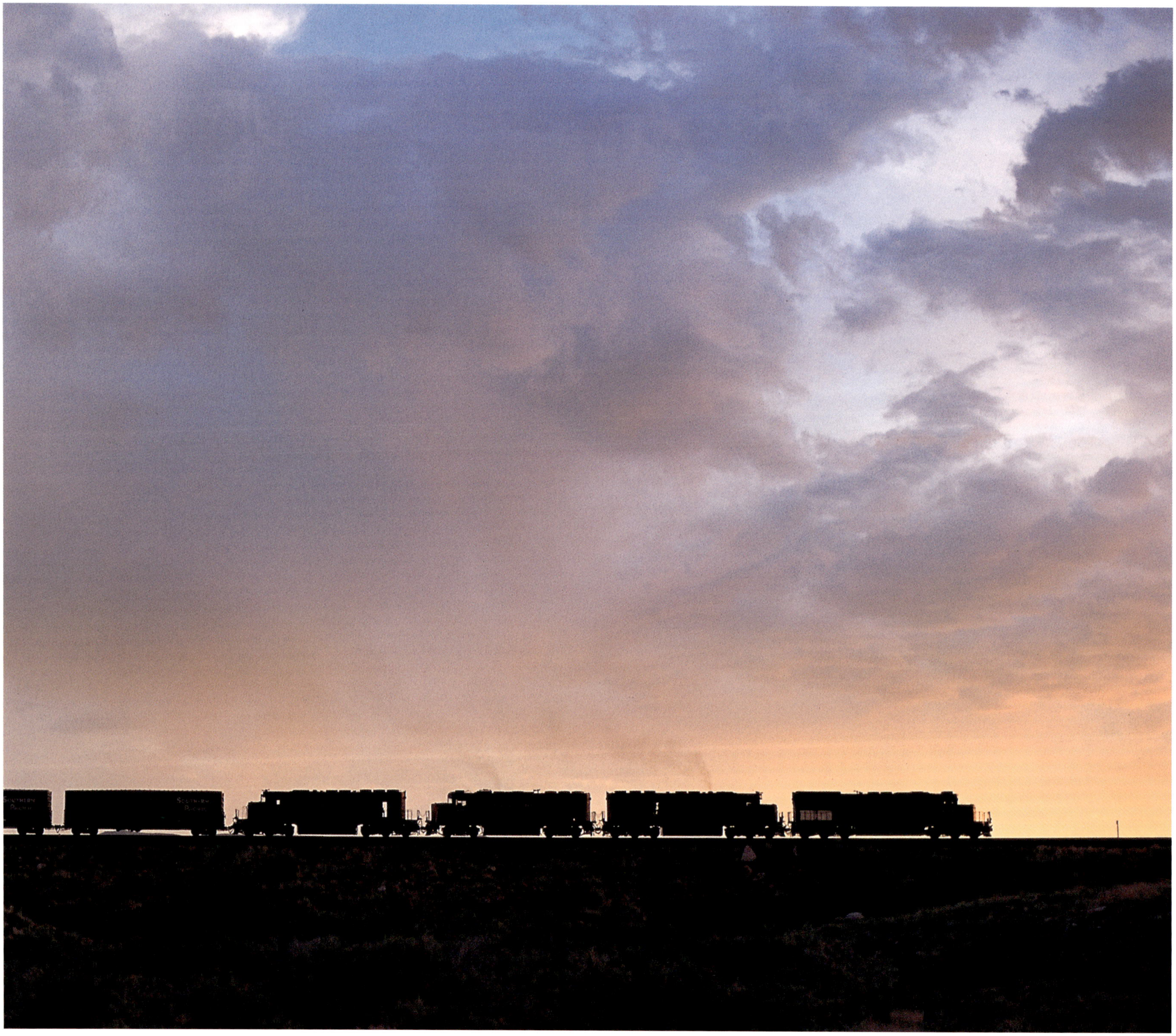

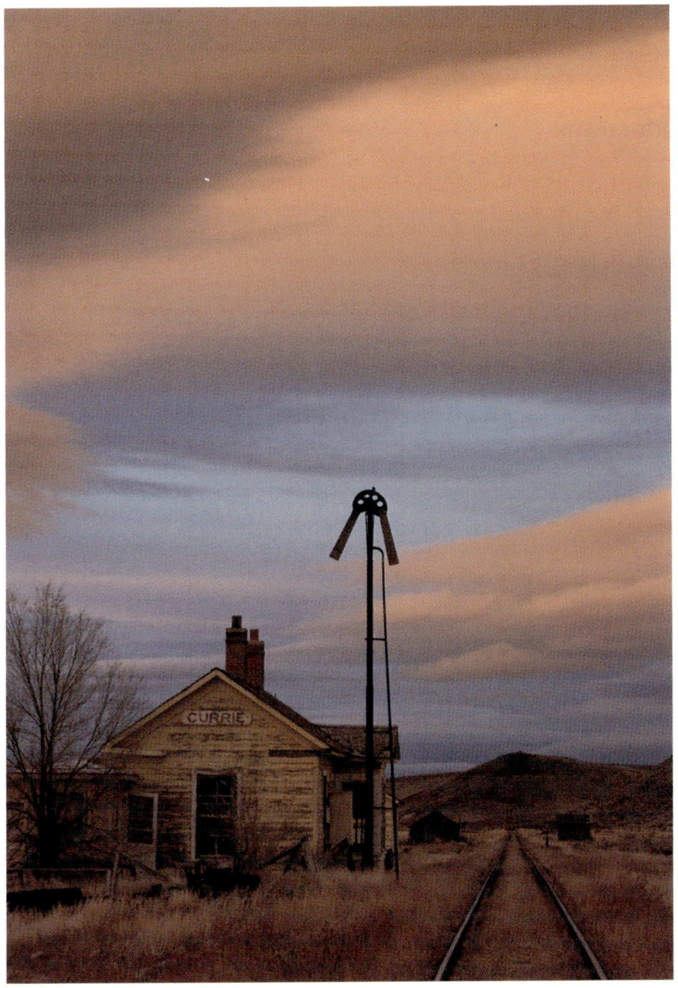

far left:

SET AGAINST A colored backdrop reminiscent of a Turner landscape painting, a Rio Grande tunnel motor leads a quartet of diesels off the Rocky Mountain Front Range near Arena, Colorado, 1995.
Mel Patrick

left:

FORLORN AND seemingly forgotten, the train order board at Currie languishes in the "all clear" position beside the former Nevada Northern weed-encrusted right-of-way. The harsh desert environment of the Great Basin slowly reclaims the abandoned depot as a brilliantly muted sunset unfolds over the Steptoe Valley north of Ely.
Joel Jensen

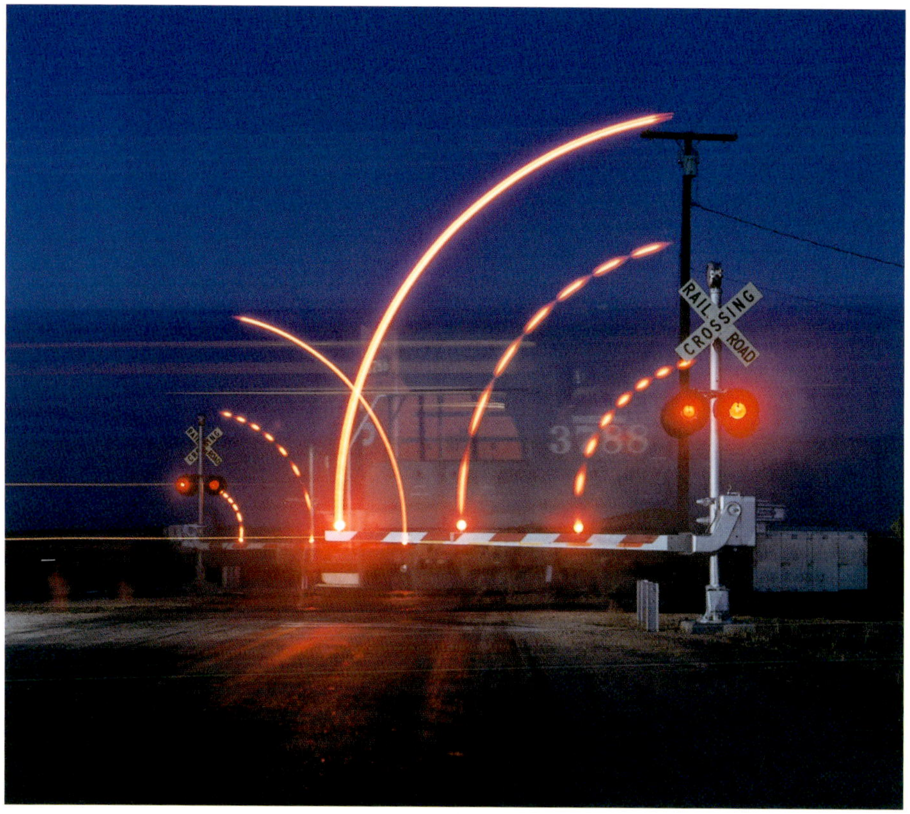

WITH LIGHTS BLINKING and the clamor of bells ringing, the lowered crossing gates of Searles Station Road trace graceful arcs of color as Espee GP9 3788 sets out cars at Searles, California. In the morning, a pair of venerable Baldwin AS-616 locomotives of the Trona Railway, with their cactus emblems, will appear at the Espee junction with loaded hopper cars to be swapped for empties. Once the switching moves are made, the train will return to the Kerr-McGee potash plant located in the remote and desolate Argus Range.
Ed Delvers

AN APPLICATION OF the air-brakes creates incredible sparks as the eastbound Grand Canyon Limited slows for the curves at Hesperia, California, on its daily run between Los Angeles and Chicago in the early 1960s. Inaugurated in 1929, this popular Santa Fe vacation train offered its clientele a direct link, via Williams, Arizona, to one of the most scenic wonders of the world.
Richard Steinheimer

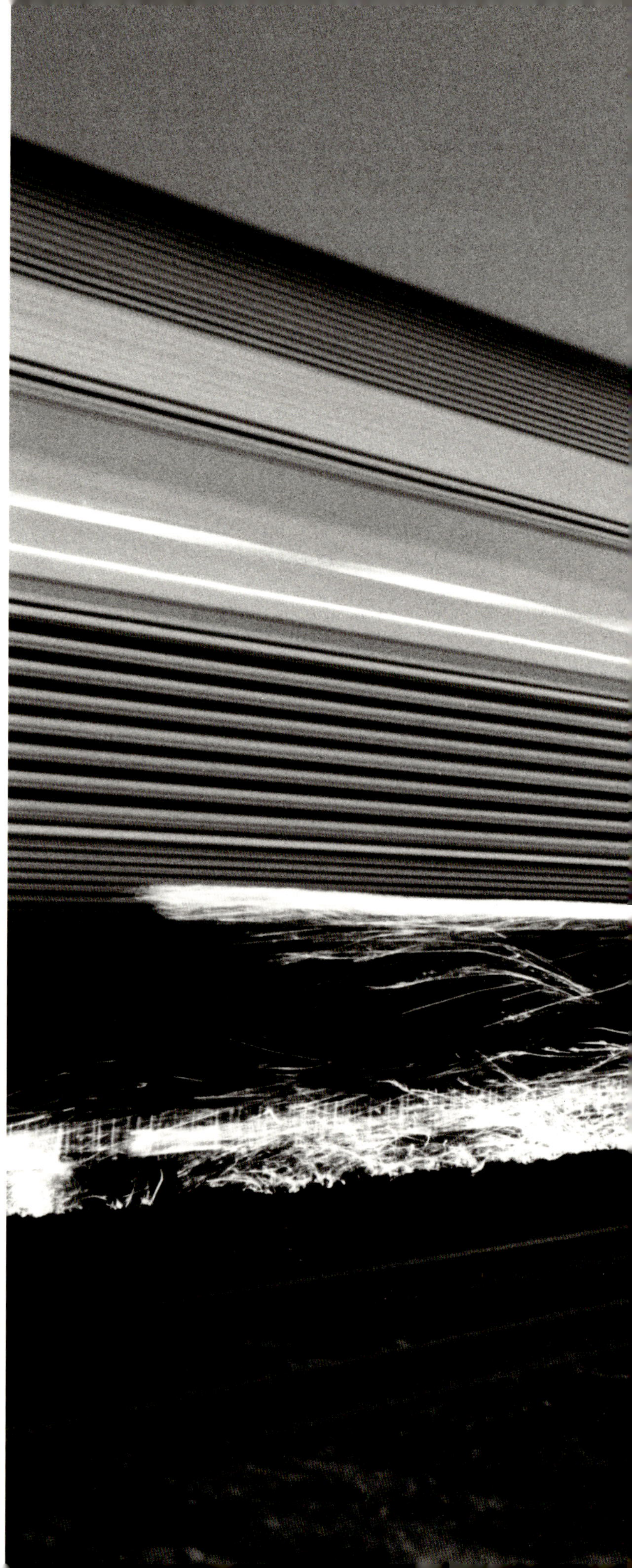

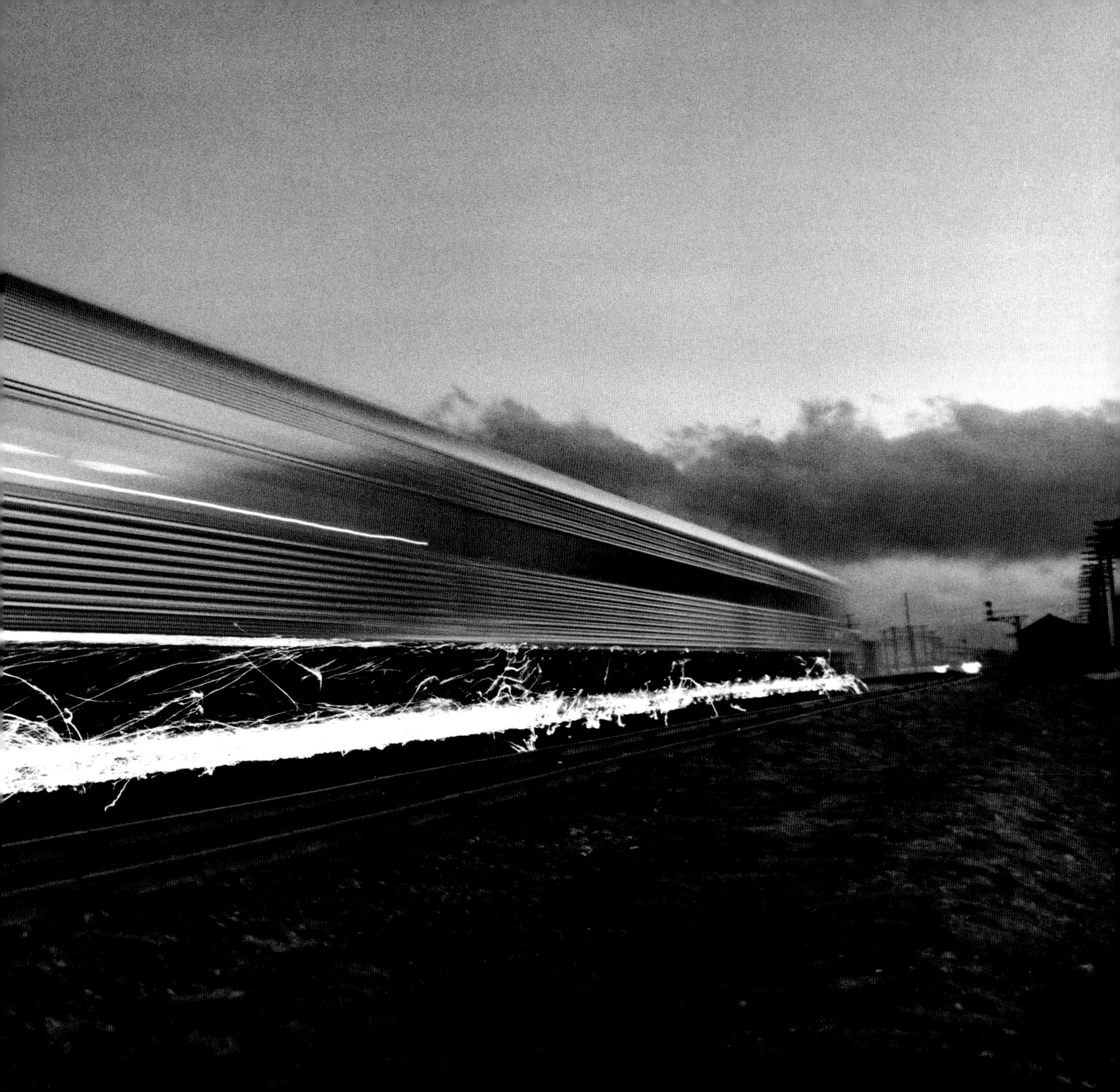

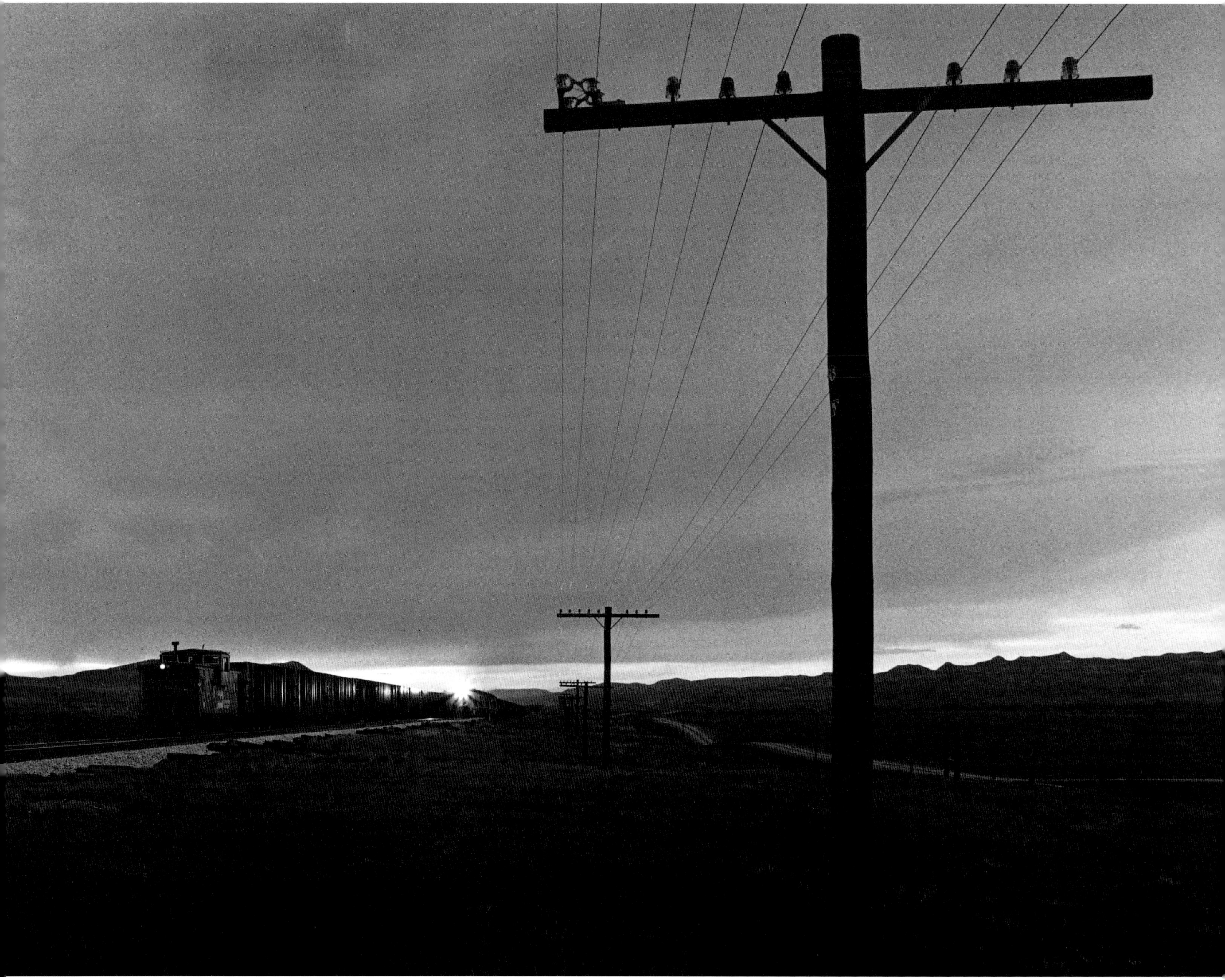

AT ECHETA, on the Wyoming prairie, the twilight plays host to the passage of two Burlington Northern coal trains in the summer of 1982. Running across the "Everywhere West" landscape made famous by the slogan of its Chicago, Burlington & Quincy predecessor, this BN mainline crosses territory a short distance from where General Custer and the Seventh Cavalry succumbed to Sitting Bull at the Battle of Little Big Horn in 1876. Today, BNSF freights still rumble across the Powder River Basin, transporting millions of tons of "black diamonds"—230 million in fiscal 1998 alone—enough to generate electricity for 10 percent of all homes in the United States.
Richard Steinheimer

right:

CONDUCTOR AL MORENO takes a few minutes on the rear platform of his caboose to survey Sierra Railroad's Oakdale-bound freight in the late 1960s, as it winds its way down Canyon Tank Grade. Located in the foothills of California's Mother Lode, the Sierra, incorporated in 1897, is the oldest continuously operating shortline in the state. Having a dual personality—that of diesel freight hauler and steam excursion railroad—the SRR finds itself the common carrier for cut lumber and wood chips during the week, then historic steam locomotive park at Jamestown on the weekends. Many of its steam engines have been the favorites of Hollywood, taking a supporting role in such classic western films as *High Noon, Duel in the Sun,* and *Rage at Dawn.*
Thomas L. Taylor

overleaf:

THE NEON SIGN "Go By Train" beckons to passing travelers at Union Station in Ogden, Utah, in 1953. The Plymouths and Chevrolets decorating the parking lot portend the changes to come: America's love affair with car culture and the interstate is about to begin. Around future's corner, the great passenger trains will fall into public disfavor as the automobile, and the independence it engenders, becomes the passion of a nation.
Richard Steinheimer

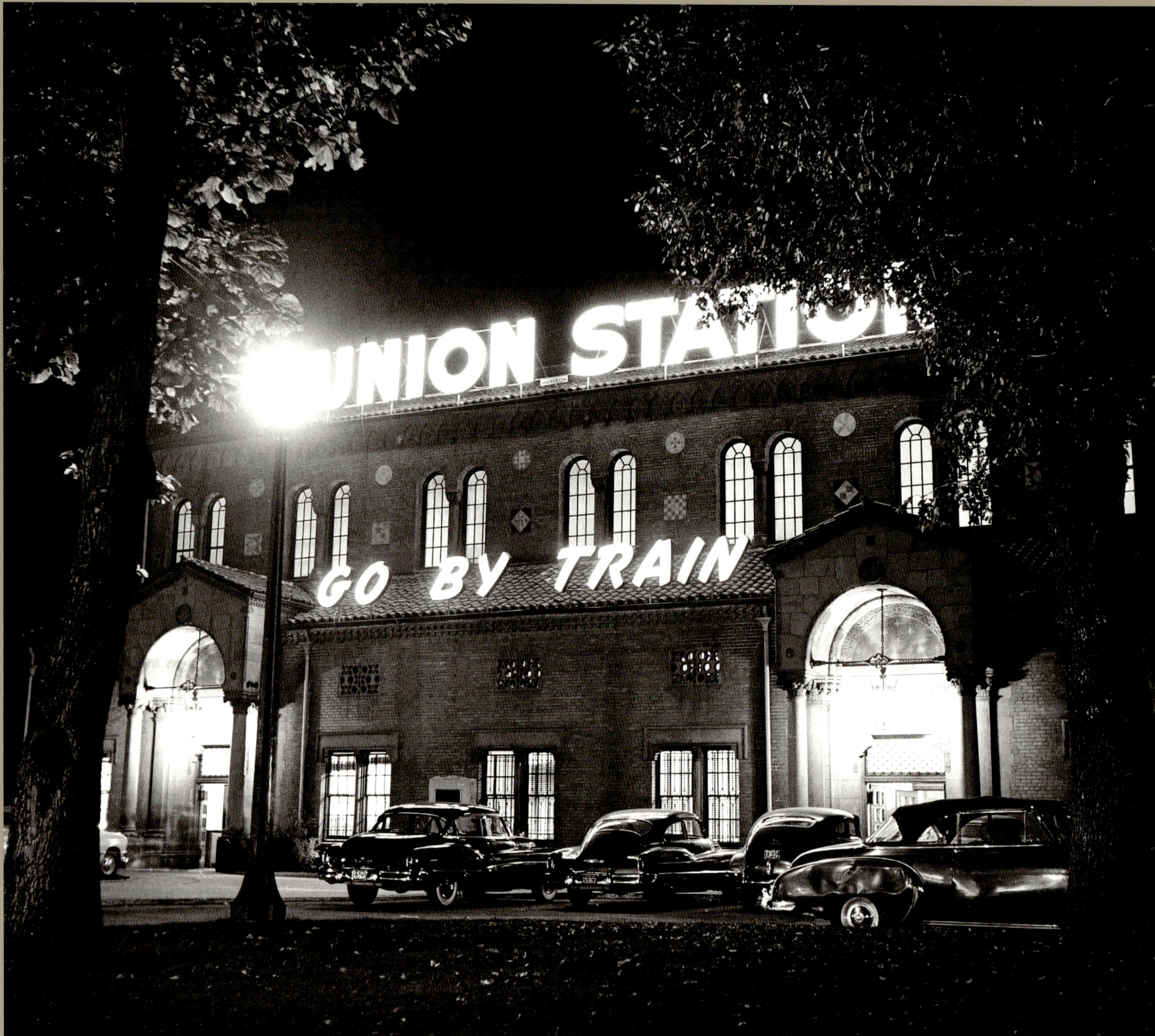
UNION
GO BY TRAIN

Chapter Two SENTIMENTAL JOURNEY

Down at the Depot

Union Station in Los Angeles at 2 A.M. seems a little more like a deserted cathedral made for prayer and contemplation than a point of arrivals and departures. It's quiet now; the ceilings seem to draw the sounds up from below and one feels compelled to speak in whispered tones. But it wasn't always this way. Fifty-five years ago, when the passenger train was the way people got to where they were going, this was a busy, crowded, thriving place—a place as yet untainted by automobile culture, free-ways, and the demise of mass transportation in America. For now, imagine your great-aunt down from the San Fernando Valley bringing her sister to catch the Southern Pacific's Morning Daylight, just one of sixty scheduled trains. Dashing into the crowded Harvey House cafe for a cup of coffee prior to train time, they sit at the U-shaped counter, bantering with the waitresses and stealing a few intimate moments to say goodbye. Their parting, since they see one another infrequently, is always very poignant.

You might also see yourself as a child, nine or ten years of age, coming here to leave on your first train trip aboard the overnight Lark to the Bay Area. You remember the taxi ride to the station, the endless waiting, anticipation building, until

IN A SCENE REMINISCENT of a Hitchcock film, passengers await the arrival of the C&NW's Rochester 400—a through train to Chicago—on a very cold winter's night at Blair Street Station in Madison, Wisconsin, 1963. *John Gruber*

porters threw back the doors, revealing those long, cavernous, subterranean tunnels leading to the platforms above. Once there, you hear the dynamos whine on the 4-8-2 Mountain coupled to the head end. She'll carry your train through Chatsworth and Ventura, skirting the edge of the Pacific Ocean's travel brochure scenery all the way to Pismo.

Thin veils of light pouring from the sleepers' windows beckon with suggestions of comfort. You find your room and settle in. The 9 P.M. departure approaches. A muffled "all aboard" sounds beyond the glass and the train moves forward, gaining a slow momentum. Your journey has begun.

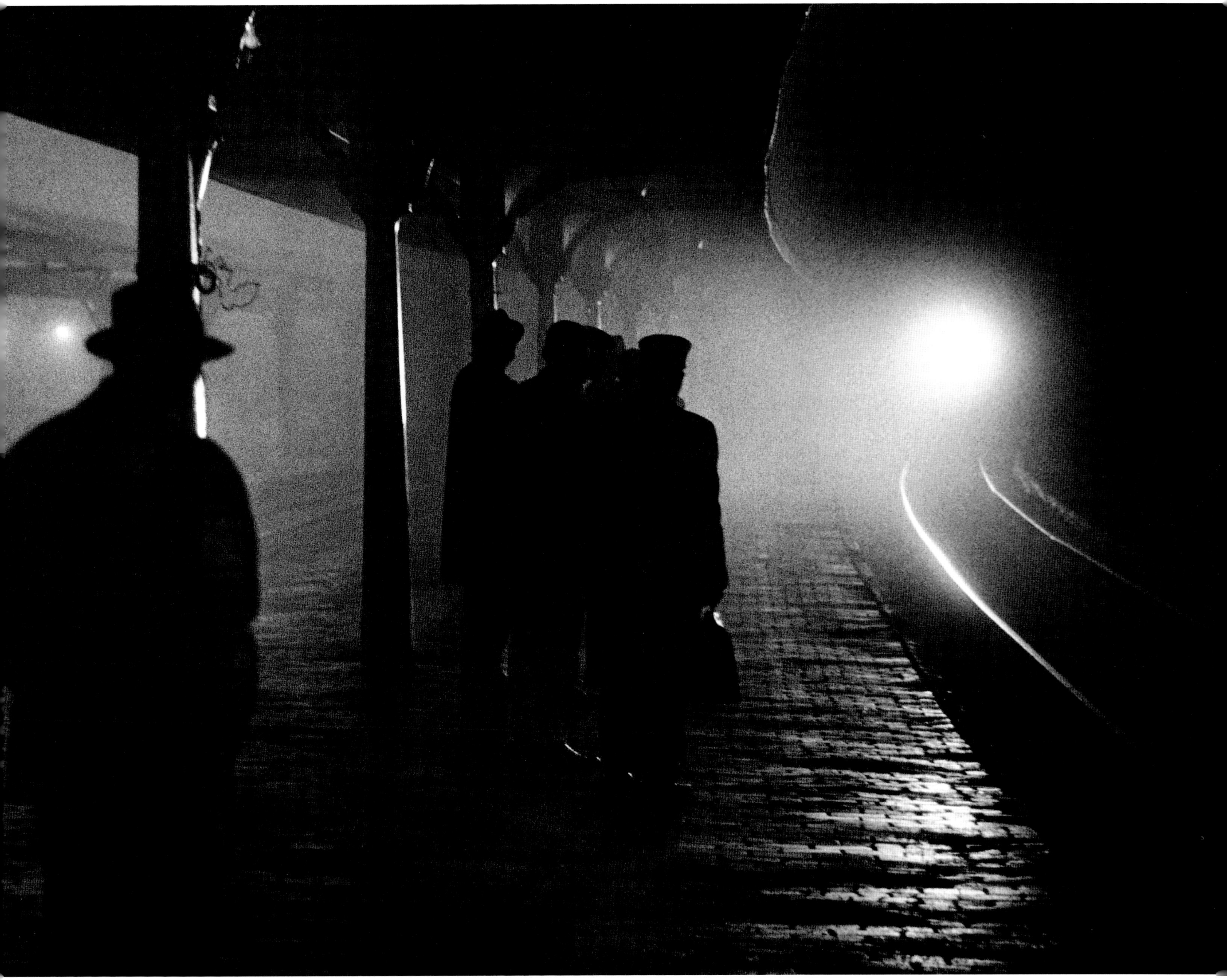

NEW YORK CITY'S Grand Central Terminal, a Beaux-Arts masterpiece, was designed by Warren and Wetmore in 1913 at a cost of $43 million. Traffic peaked in 1947, when sixty-five million passengers walked to their trains beneath the constellation-studded ceiling. The station fell into severe disrepair in the late 1960s and almost saw the wrecking ball, until preservationists convinced the Penn Central not to demolish it. Although name trains like the 20th Century and Empire State no longer call here (Amtrak routes its traffic through Penn Station), more than sixty million commuters a year ride the daily Metro North lines into New York City. Presently undergoing a major renovation and rededicated in 1998, GCT is once again a grand destination. This elegant marble stairway leads to the lower level and the waiting commuter trains, bearing silent witness to the multitudes that have passed this way for nearly nine decades of daily life.
Ed Delvers

below:

EMPTY BAGGAGE CARTS wait for the onrush of porters and the arrival of late night trains at Spokane Union Station in 1973.
Wayne Depperman

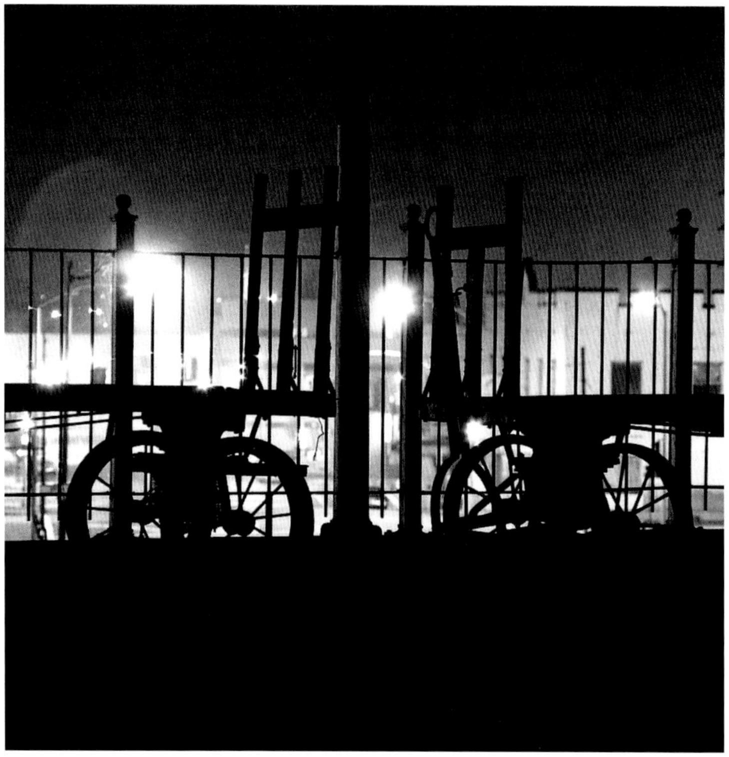

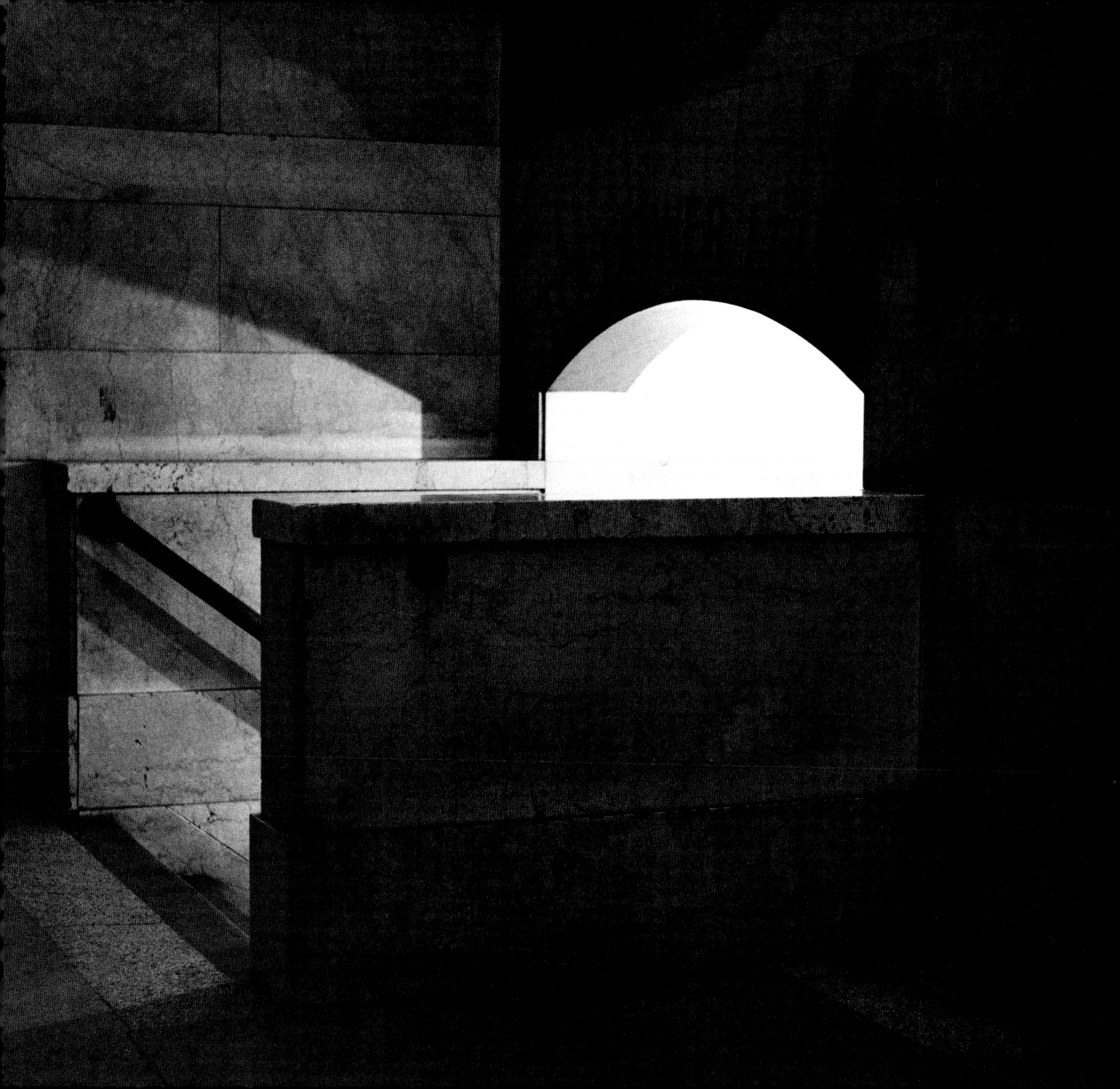

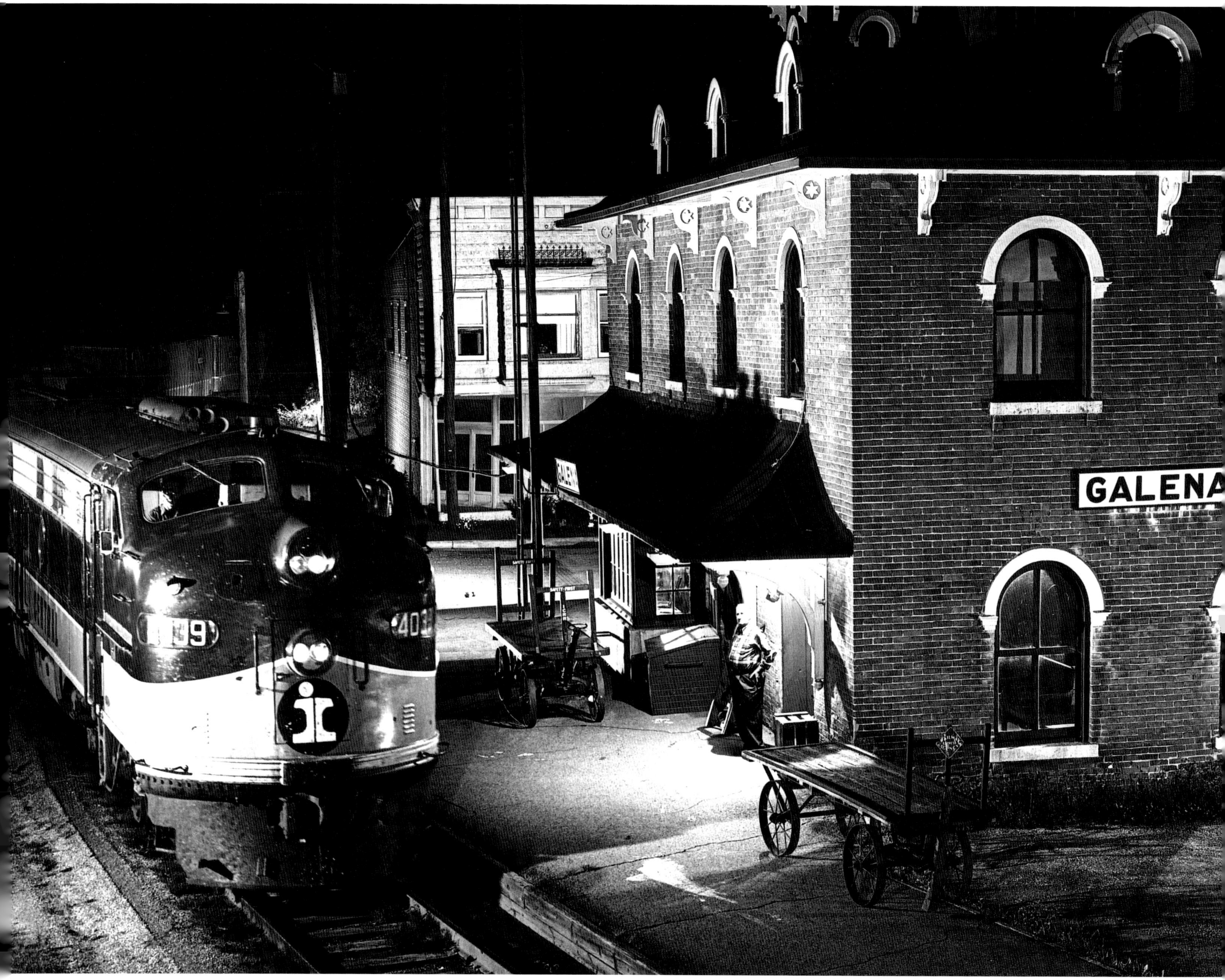
GALENA

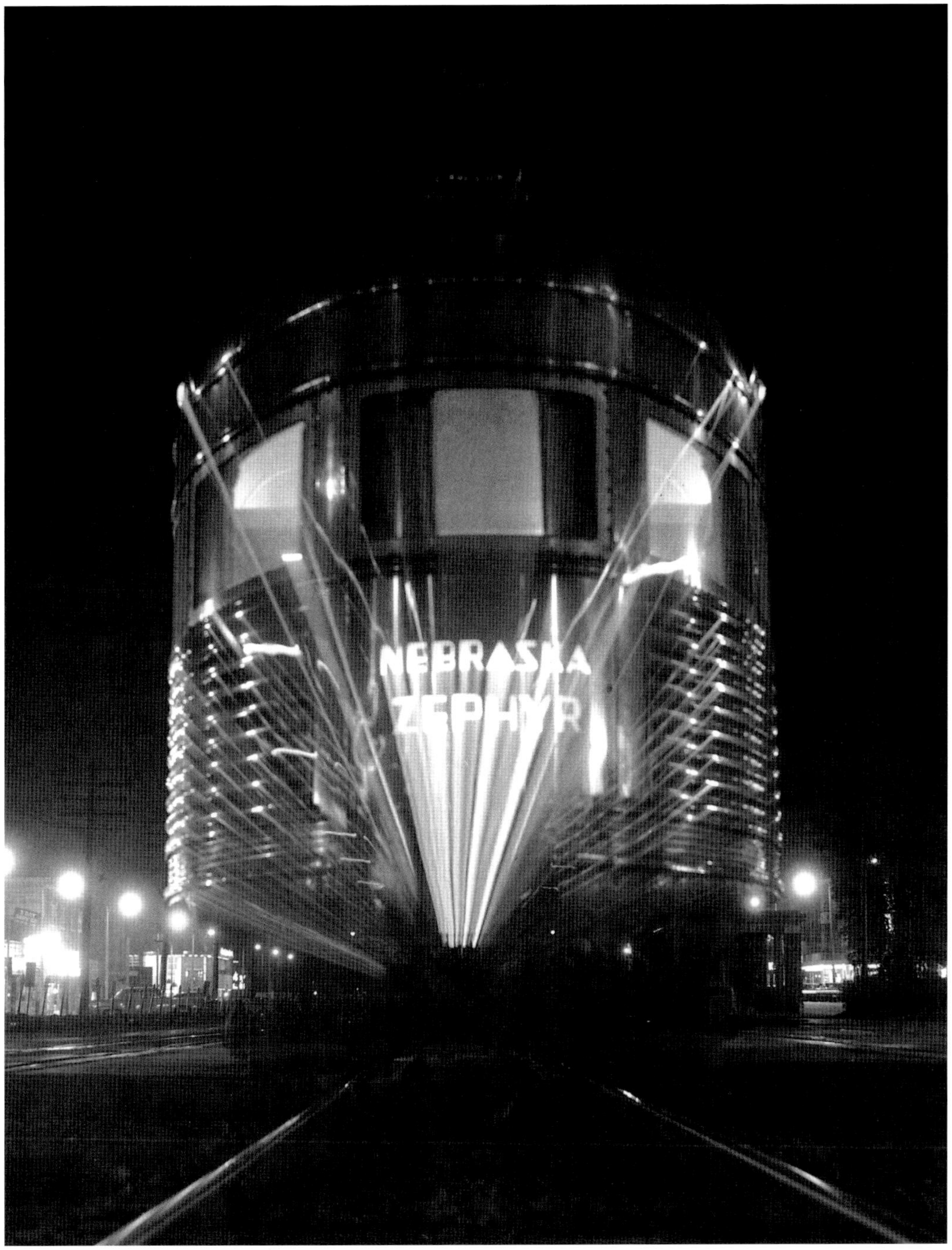

GALENA, ILLINOIS, population 3,647, and the birthplace of U. S. Grant, bears more resemblance to a model railroad diorama than to a real location in America. Nineteen flash bulbs, wired remotely and in series, light up the town's main street and the pre-midnight passage of Illinois Central train #11, the Hawkeye. A pair of battered, aging E9's guide the head end trailer-on-flat-cars (TOFC), filled with mail, past the quaint red-brick, two-story depot built in 1857. Local resident of fifty-two years Patrick J. Hatter looks on, conducting the age-old ritual played out in many places across "the Mainline of Mid-America": watching the nightly parade of trains whistling through town.
Mel Patrick

AN ARTFUL time-exposure accentuates the streamlined contours of the Chicago, Burlington & Quincy's Nebraska Zephyr as it departs from La Grange, Illinois, on its final lap into Chicagoland on a crisp fall evening in 1966. This train set, dating from 1936, was one of the articulated varieties used by the ever-modernizing Burlington for its Chicago-St. Paul service. The CB&Q, under the leadership of President Harry Murphy, whose tenure lasted from 1949 to 1965, remained a railroad dedicated to providing quality passenger service, registering more than 820 million passenger miles in 1964 alone—evidence of a unique attitude among Class 1 railroads of the era. Later management would not look so kindly on the fate of the Zephyrs, as Louis Menck, Murphy's successor at the helm, dismantled the CB&Q's passenger program shortly after his arrival.
Mel Patrick

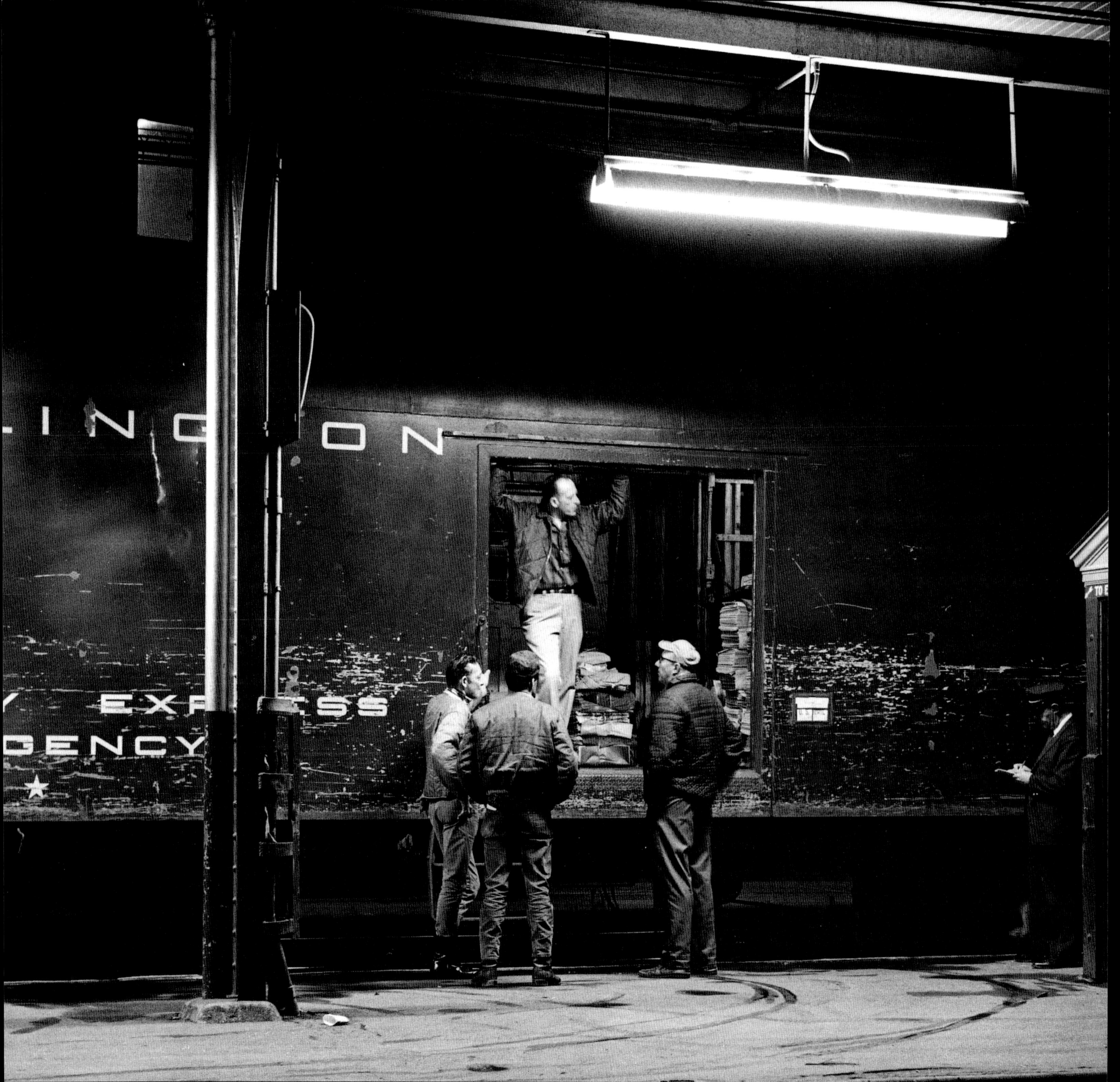

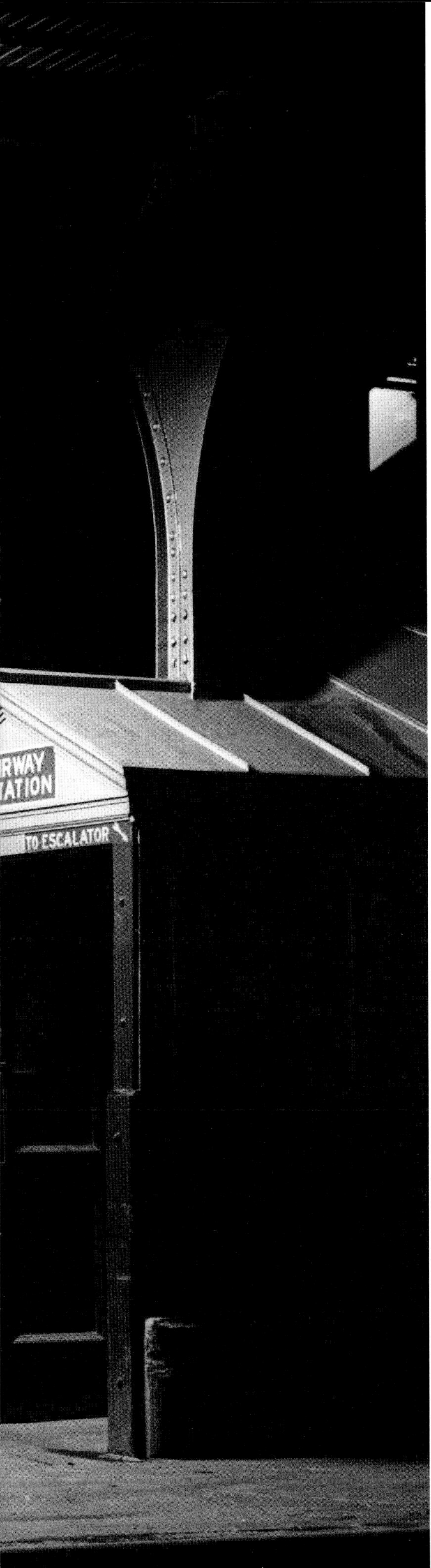

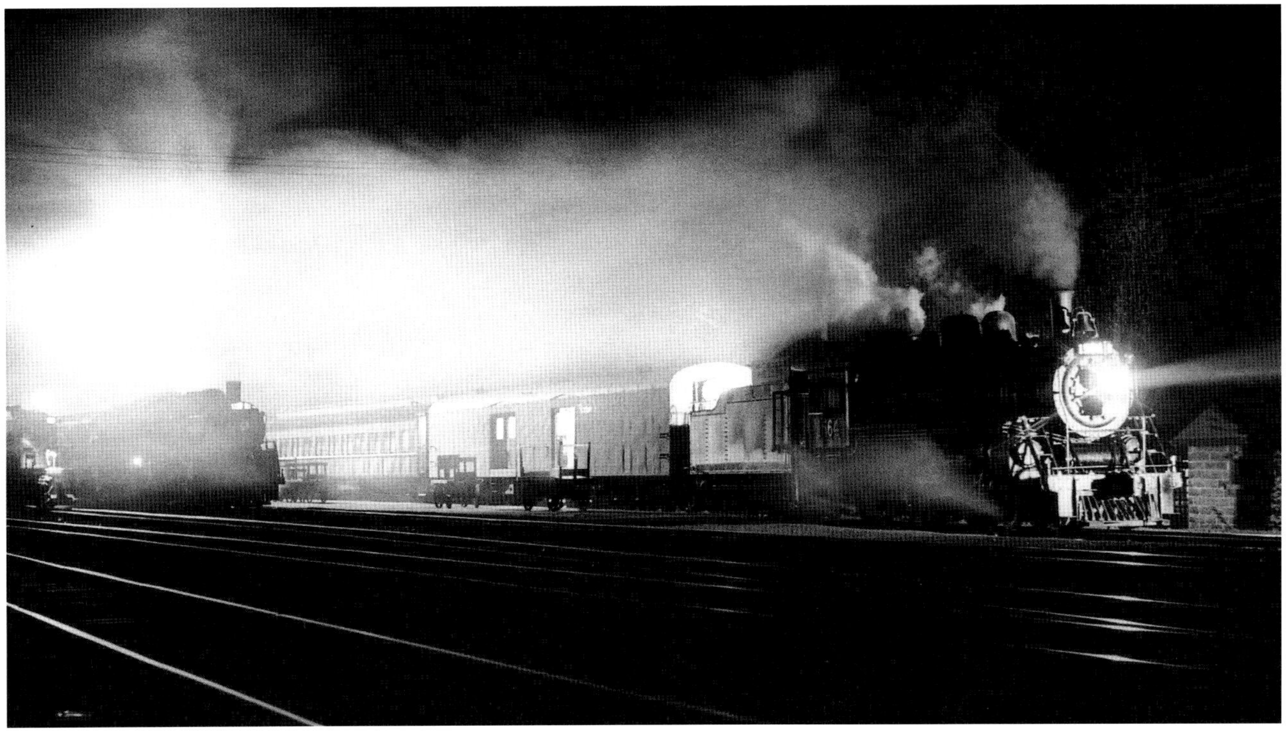

AN REA CLERK STRETCHES and shoots the breeze with fellow railroad workers during a station stop of CB&Q's Ak-Sar-Ben Zephyr at Omaha, Nebraska, in the early 1960s. The Railway Express Agency, in operation between 1850 and 1975, moved packages across America prior to the advent of the United Parcel Service and FedEx; its ubiquitous green trucks were a familiar sight near stations and depots across the continent. The conductor eyes his train orders and timetable in ritualized fashion; the railroad worker's poses are studies in arrested motion. Anxious anticipation and an eagerness to be on the move—across the expansive prairie landscapes of the Midwest toward a 3:35 A.M. arrival at Burlington, Illinois—are in the air.

above:

CANADIAN NATIONAL 4-6-0 #1564 pauses with its train at Palmerston, Ontario, en route to Owens Sound and Toronto in this 1958 view. Less-than-carload freight and express packages are being loaded into the baggage car behind the Ten-Wheeler as cylinder cocks and pop valves bleed, sending streams of smoke and steam up into the midnight Northland sky. *All, Philip Hastings / CSRM*

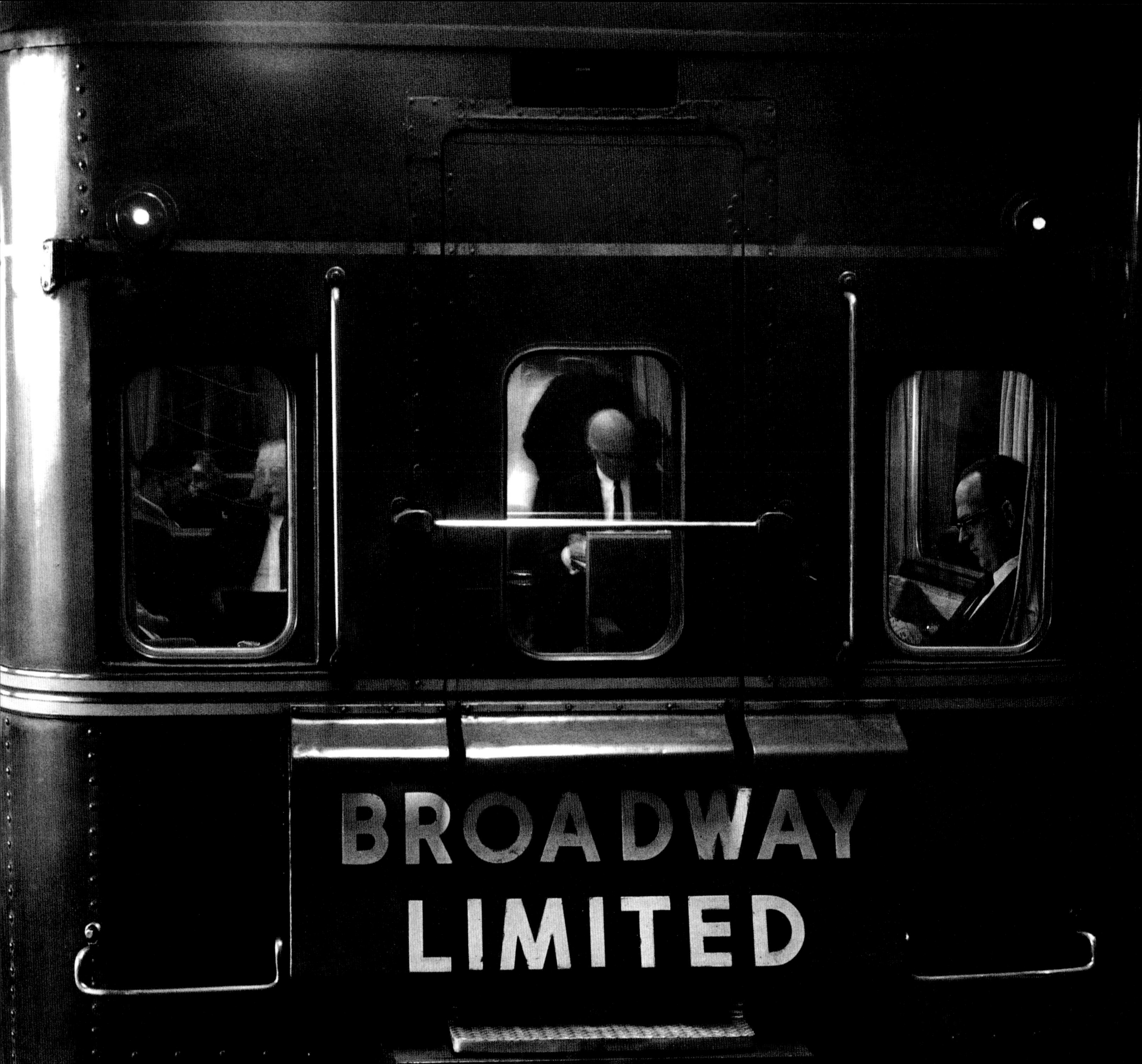
BROADWAY
LIMITED

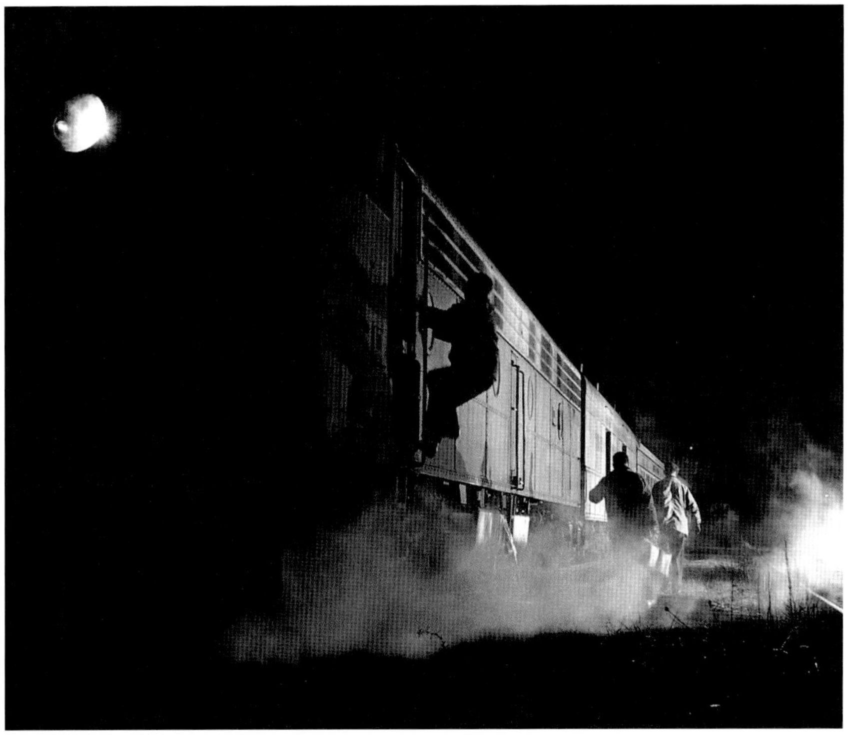

THE BROADWAY LIMITED, Pennsylvania Railroad's train #26, awaits its 5 P.M. departure from Chicago Union Station in 1966. The all-Pullman Tuscan-red consist catered to an elite clientele used to such first-class amenities as on-board telephones, gourmet meals, and a rear observation car with bedroom and shower. Often considered the finest passenger train in the U.S., the Broadway Limited was inaugurated in 1902, streamlined in 1938, and run under the auspices of Amtrak until 1995. Passengers seen through the rear windows read the afternoon Chicago papers with final New York stock quotes, while sipping chilled manhattans and sampling hors d'oeuvres before dinner.
Mel Patrick

above:

A HEAD-END CREW change takes place on Amtrak #363 at Niles, Michigan, December 1972.
Mel Patrick

IT'S TRAIN TIME in Niles, Michigan, as Amtrak #363, the St. Claire, reenacts what could be a scene from the lonely prose of Richard Ford's novel *The Sportswriter*. This was once the route of such New York Central Chicago–Detroit trains as the *Twilight Limited* and *Motor City Express*, trackage that belonged first to the Michigan Central, then the New York Central, then the Penn Central.

A half-dozen passengers detrain and the conductor, silhouetted in his impatience, waits on the platform to give the highball. It's a cold December in 1972, and only nineteen months have passed since the National Railroad Passenger Corporation and Amtrak took over the conveyance of travelers on the nation's railroads. Many doubt the potential of this quasi-governmental operation.

Twenty-eight years later, amid ever-tightening fiscal constraints and yearly budget battles before Congress, Amtrak has held on and revitalized train travel in America. With 1999 ridership at all-time historic highs, revenues covering 80 percent of operating costs, and the introduction of first-class accommodations on the Coast Starlight, California Zephyr, and Sunset, the environmentally conscious vacationing public seems ready to reembrace the notion of luxurious travel by rail, leaving their cars at home. Witness also the inception of the North American Orient Express, the Talgo commuter trains in the Northwest Corridor, and the reemergence of MetroLink commuter lines (over several former Pacific Electric right-of-ways) in the autopian landscapes of Los Angeles. In short, the future seems assured for passenger trains as mass transportation once again moves to the forefront in urban planning policy.
Mel Patrick

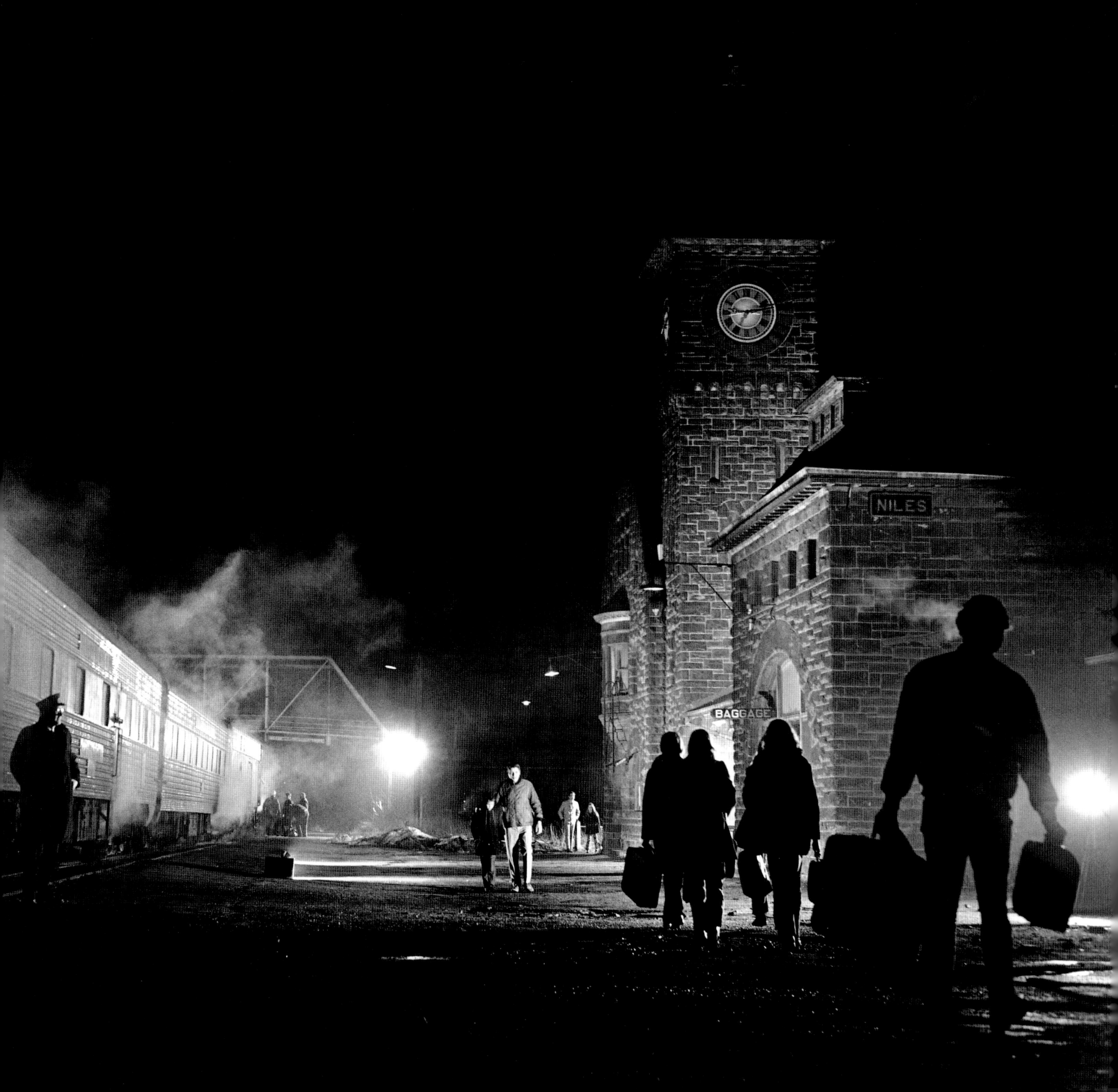
NILES
BAGGAGE

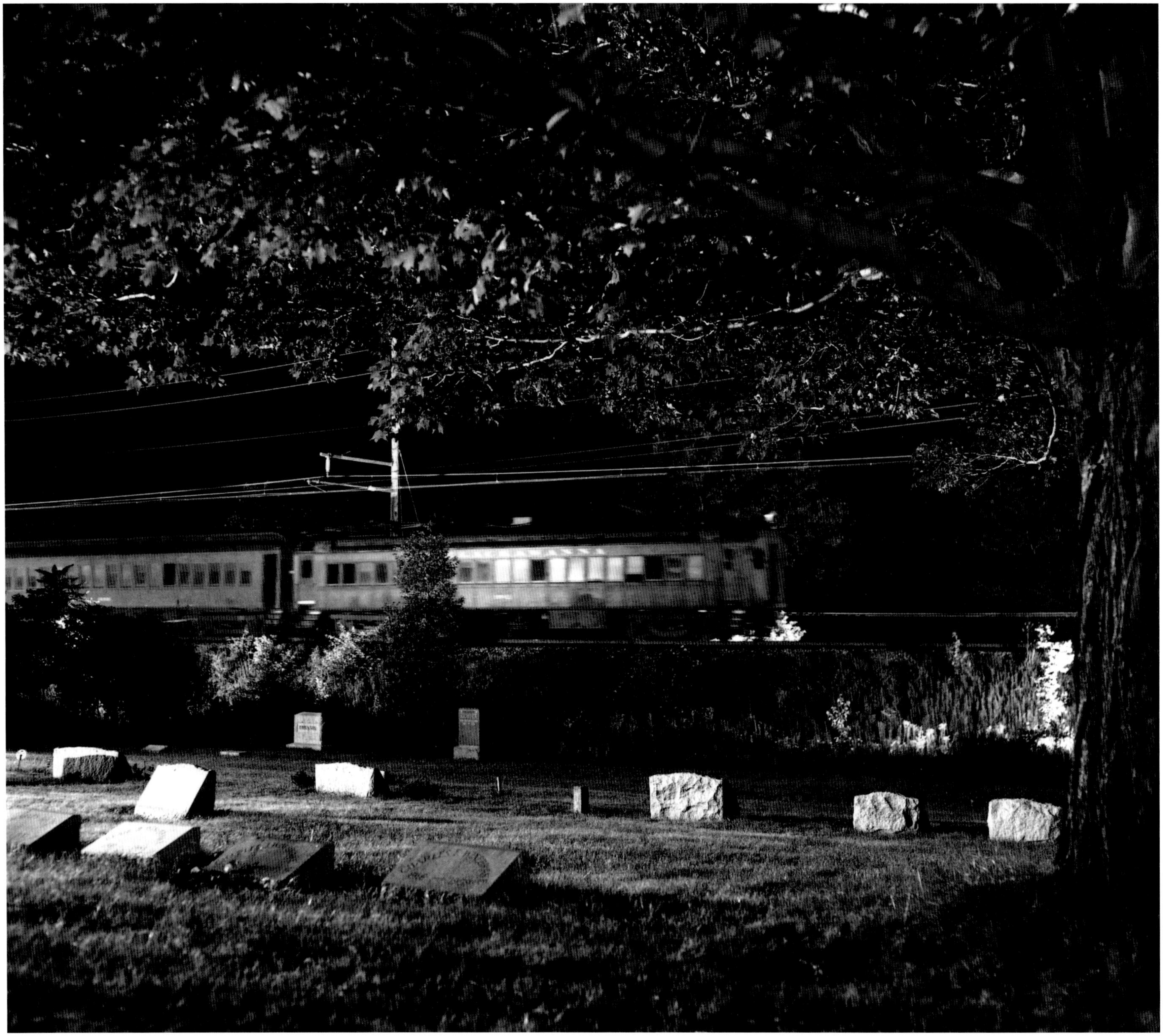

THE SYMBOLISM is obvious as a Delaware, Lackawanna & Western commuter train coasts past the cemetery at Basking Ridge on its way to Summit, New Jersey, in 1984: it's the last month of operation for the elderly fleet of multi-unit cars. Thomas A. Edison, inventor of the incandescent lamp and champion of electricity, operated the throttle of the first passenger-carrying DL&W electric train to leave Hoboken terminal in 1930.

The single-track Gladstone branch, with its bucolic atmosphere, was the last remnant—along with the South Shore in Chicago—of early-twentieth-century interurban lines to last into the 1980s. Both were examples of a once vast network of transit systems that crisscrossed the nation before the auto, tire, and oil cartel—led by GM, Firestone, and Standard Oil with their NCL Bus Lines—conspired to eradicate them from city streets and private right-of-ways during the Depression. Once they were eliminated, the growth of automobile ownership and the build-out of the country's highway system were imminent and unimpeded.
Rails After Dark

THE PANTOGRAPHS are down as several DL&W multi-unit cars sit beneath the overhead wire at Gladstone, New Jersey, on August 24, 1984, the last day of 3,000-volt DC electric operation on the Lackawanna. Come morning, new Arrow III cars will take the place of the venerable "Edison Fleet," with 25,000 volts of modern AC power.
Rails After Dark

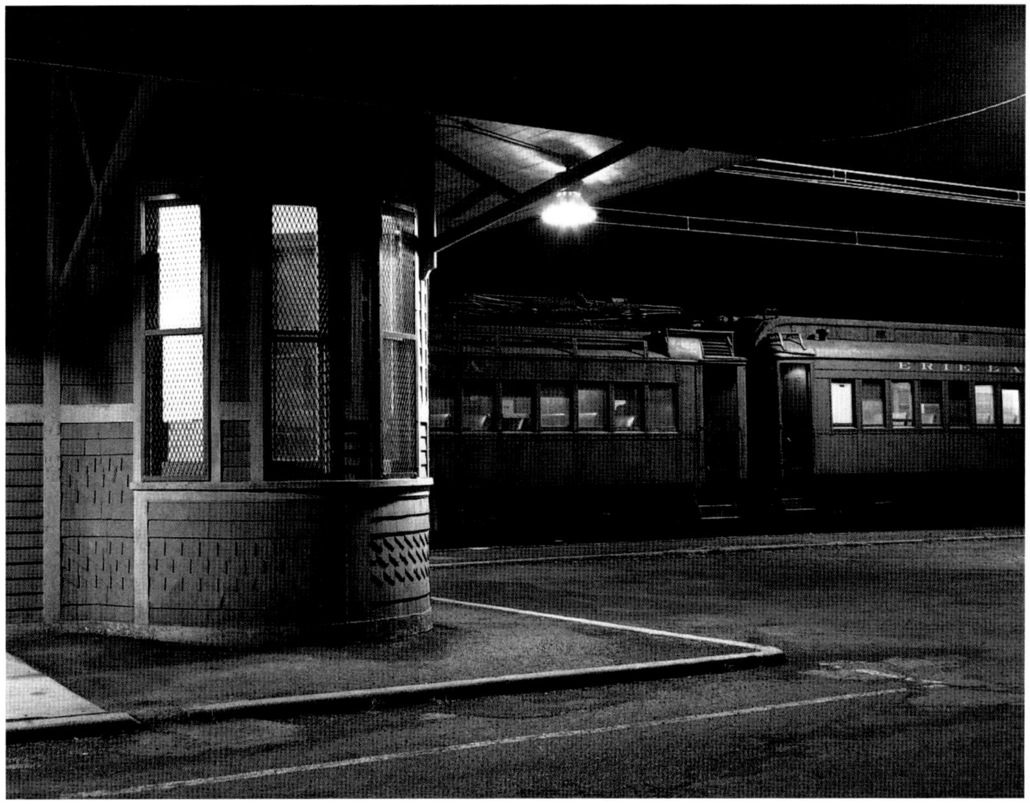

below:

MOTORISTS WAIT beside the Milwaukee Road station at Channing, Michigan, in 1964, as passengers detrain from the Chippewa-Hiawatha.
John Gruber

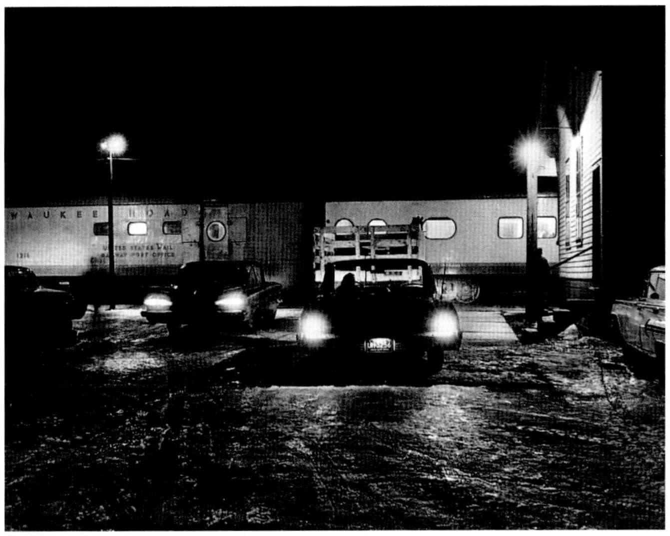

following pages:

A WHITE-GLOVED station attendant oversees the safe and timely departure of a Japanese National Railways semi-express train as it departs Tokyo Central Station in 1982.
Ed Delvers

MIKADO #488 of the Rio Grande runs south out of Alamosa, Colorado, on dual-gauge track to Antonito with an empty equipment train. The time is 1960.
Victor Hand

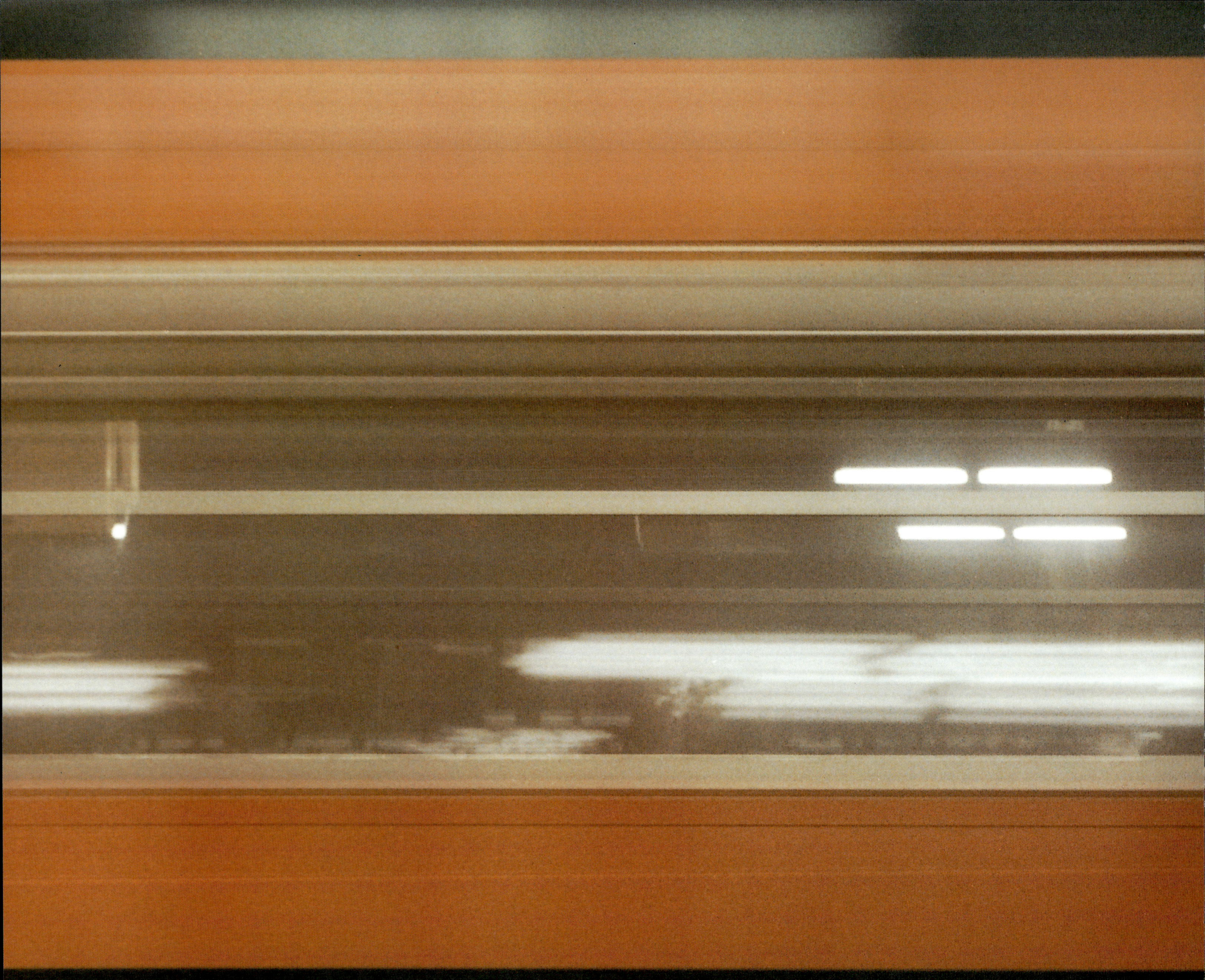

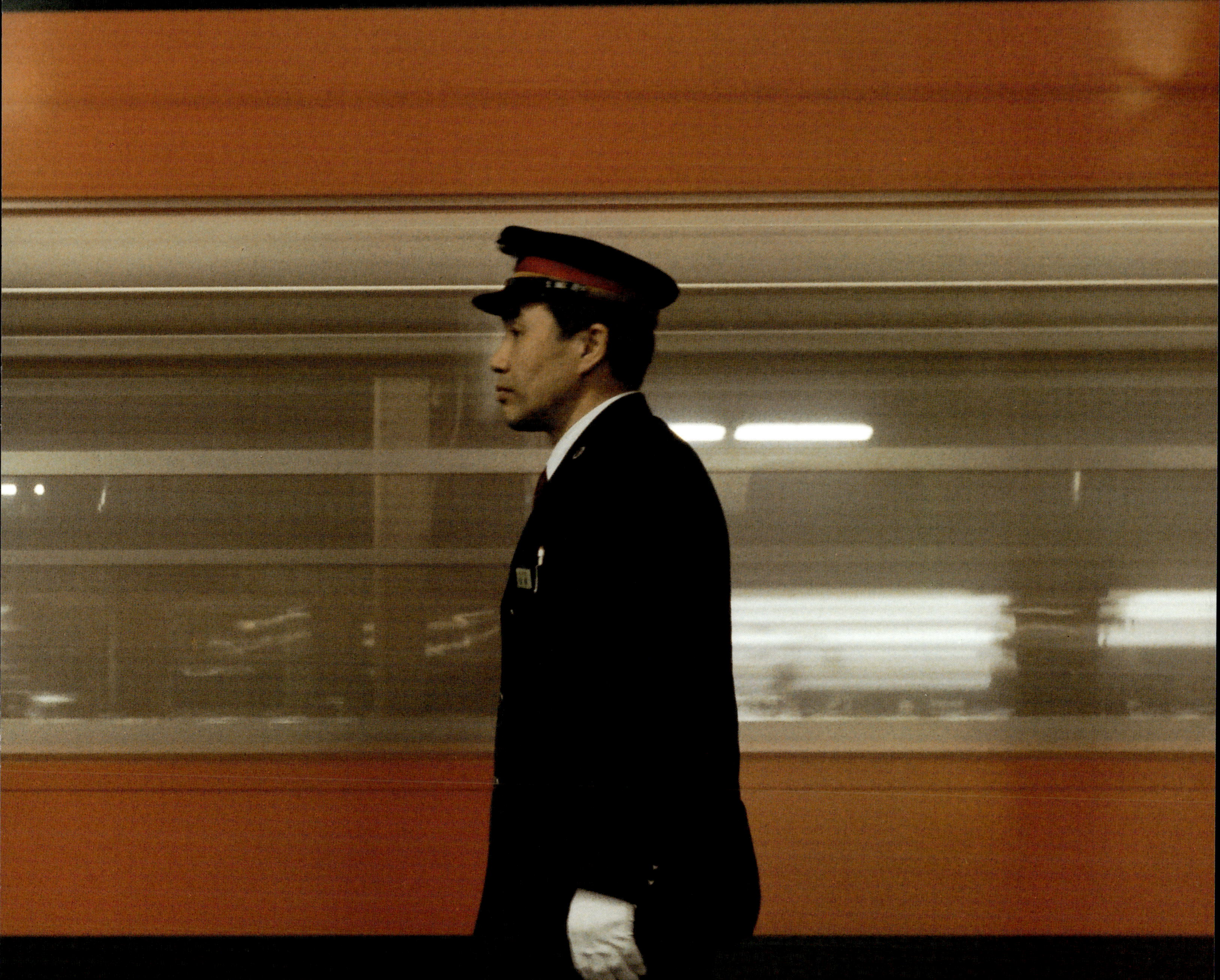

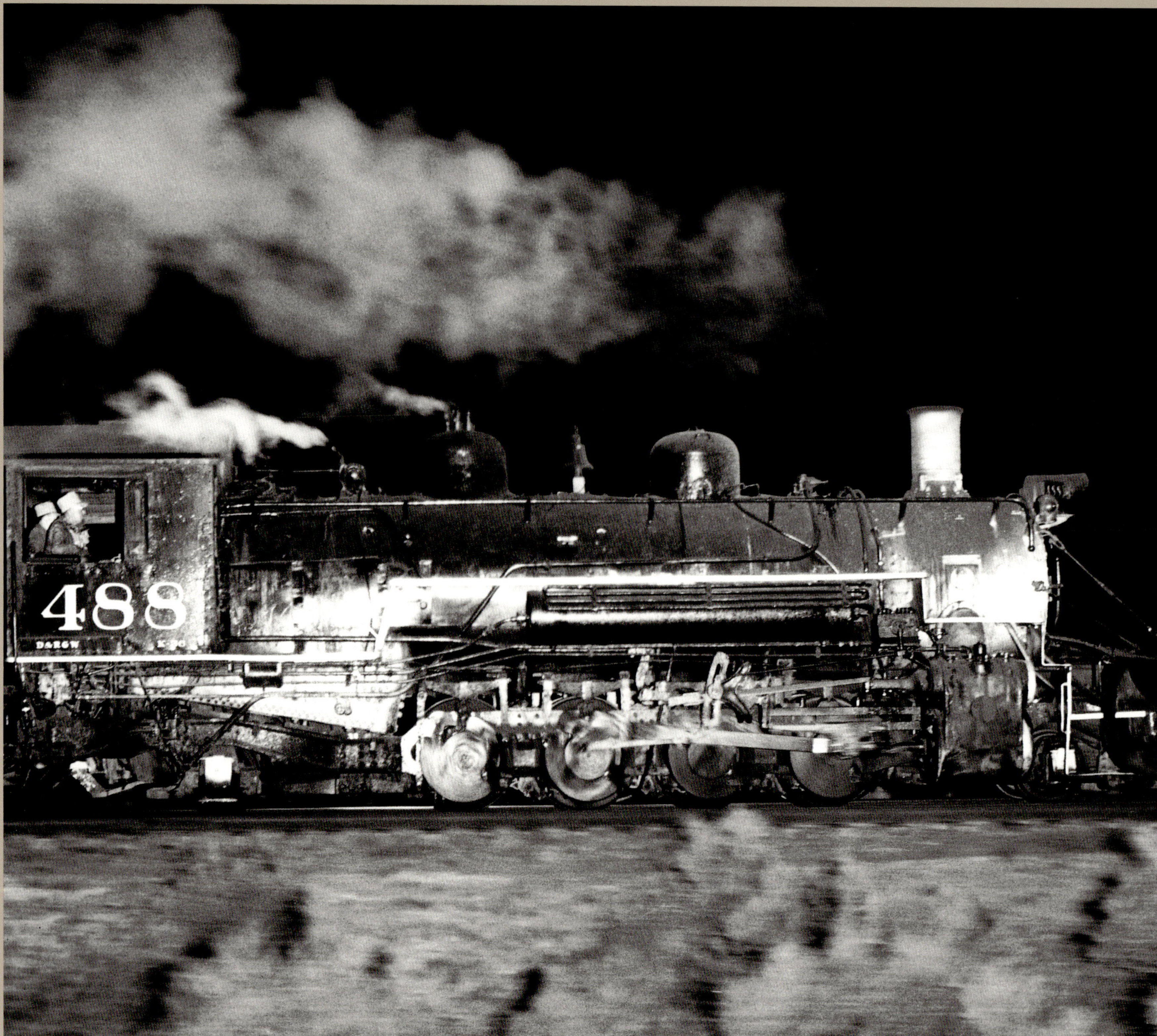
488
D&RGW

Chapter Three CHASIN' THE TRAIN

On the Mainline

Things get better as the black-top roadway reaches Kimball, although the wiper blades have long since stopped working. I am having a hell of a time seeing, but the distorted view of the world through my rain-soaked windshield is a wonderful mixture of color and form.

Just then a Union Pacific freight rolls across the bridge ahead, the lights of the town beyond dancing in mid air as a black coal or hopper or tank car (and the space between them) alternately blocks the view and reveals it. For tenths-of-seconds I catch a glimpse of small-town Nebraska, showing off its charming nocturnal quaintness in a series of vivid kinetoscopic images. I am entranced.

Once under the bridge (train still rolling overhead), I pull my car onto a deserted side street, kill the motor, and sit beneath the lamplights' pinkish glow, listening to the rhythms of the hotshot highballing its consist through the sparse landscape. As the engine's headlight devours the darkness, the Wild West geography of Wyoming and the high plateaus of Laramie lie somewhere off in the future, still 100 mileposts and several hours away. A long night lies ahead for the train crew.

Later, pacing this same freight, the PFX—the Portland Forward Express—on old two-lane U.S. 30,

AMTRAK'S SAN FRANCISCO ZEPHYR drifts down the east side of the Sierras into Reno amid the "bright lights, big city" atmosphere of Nevada's second largest gaming center. Standing on the gangway of a Southern Pacific SDP40, the photographer, in a one-second exposure, captures the essence of big-time mainline railroading after dark in 1980. *Richard Steinheimer*

I seem to be watching something elemental, something historic. Here the highway and the railroad ran in tandem, tracing the original route followed by early settlers. The Platte River Valley spanned two centuries as a major overland transportation/communication corridor, at one time playing host to the Pony Express, the transcontinental telegraph, and the Oregon Trail.

This fast-moving freight, whistling for the crossings, seemed to embody this progress and manifest destiny. It carried with it knowledge of technology, land grants, and the politics that had an impact on this territory's history of human enterprise.

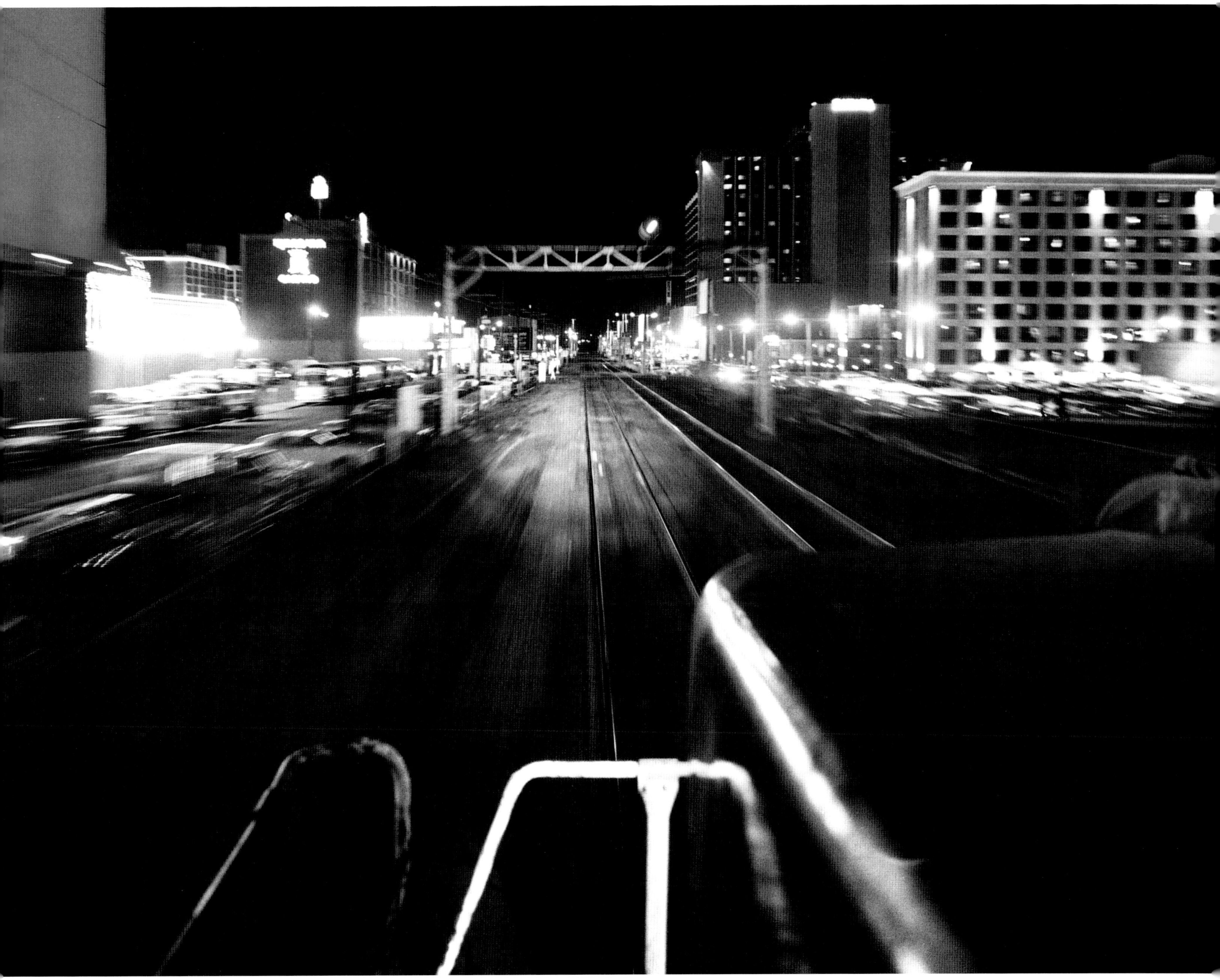

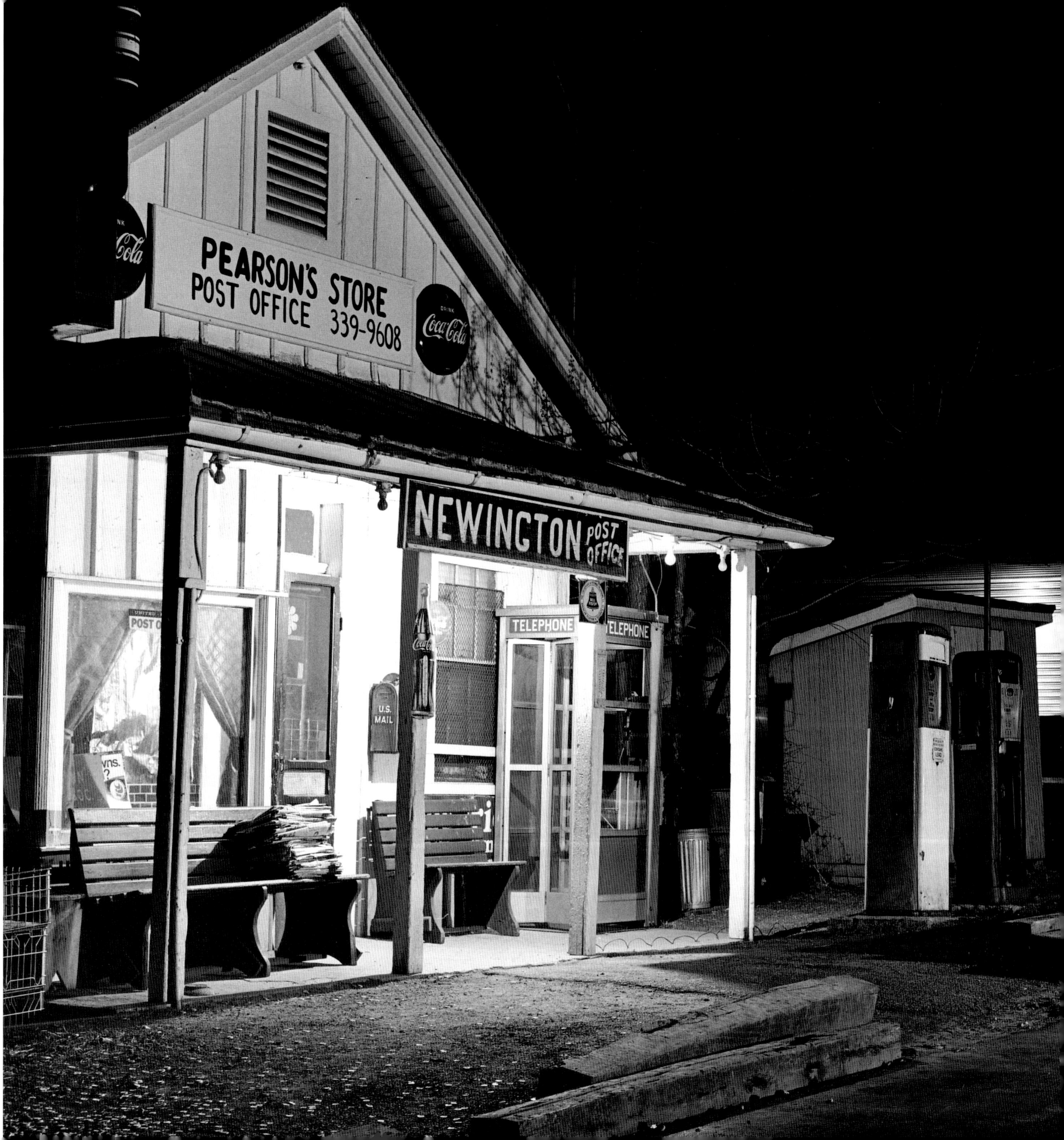
PEARSON'S STORE
POST OFFICE 339-9608
DRINK
Coca-Cola
NEWINGTON
POST OFFICE
TELEPHONE
TELEPHONE
U.S.
MAIL

LOOKING LIKE a tableau advertising small-town America, the general store at Newington, Virginia, has closed for the evening as the Richmond, Fredericksburg & Potomac's seasonal New York-to-Miami varnish, the Florida Special, interrupts the stillness of the southern landscape in this 1971 view. The modernity of Washington, D.C., is twenty miles behind the markers and in stark contrast to the scene outside the train's windows—a scene replete with the necessities of day-to-day rural living. From the solitary pay phone and twin gas pumps to the U.S. Post Office and metal milk crates, this photograph captures a way of life and sense of place vanishing from America's fast-paced, fast-food, shopping-mall style of contemporary culture. *Mel Patrick*

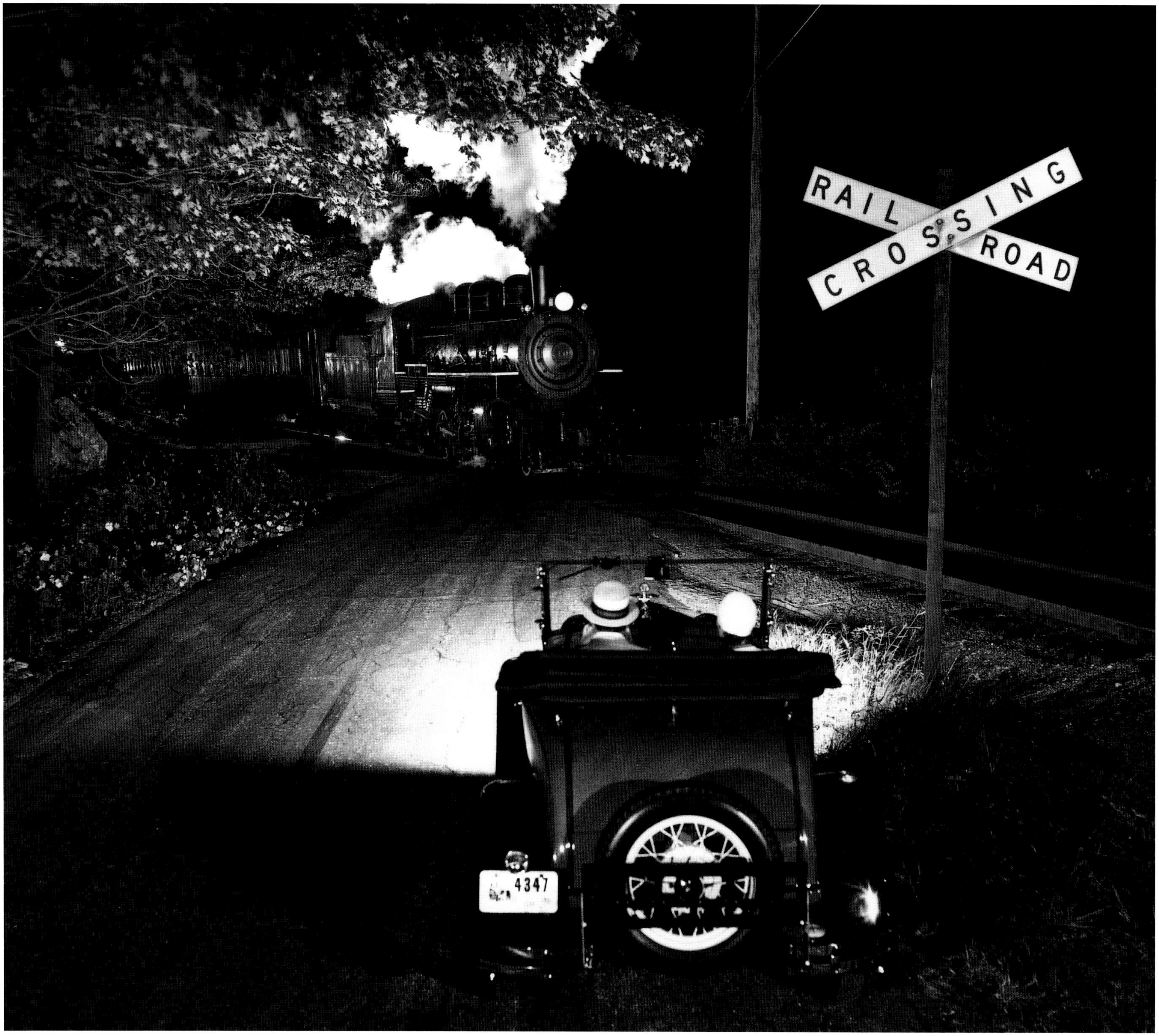
RAIL ROAD
CROSSING
4347

VALLEY RAILROAD 2-8-2 #40 sounds off for the crossing at Old Deep River Road in Centerbrook, Connecticut, while a 1930 Model A Ford awaits its passage. The venerable Mikado started life as a 1920 Alco product whose first home was the Portland, Astoria & Pacific in Oregon. Sold to the diminutive Aberdeen & Rockfish, a North Carolina shortline, in 1935 and operated until 1953, the loco was then acquired by the Valley Railroad in 1977 for $40,000.

Resembling a scene from *Look Homeward, Angel*, this is in fact a re-creation set up by Rails After Dark, a trio of photographers who, in the early 1980s, used elaborate flash techniques inspired by O. Winston Link's historic N&W steam images from the 1950s. Using an array of cameras (including 4 x 5", 6 x 7" and 35mm), hundreds of feet of wire, and a large battery-capacitor synch flash system, each shot required many, often tedious hours to complete.

The Valley Railroad was initially incorporated in 1871 and was rededicated a hundred years later as a passenger-hauling shortline. Operating over ten miles of track near the town of Essex, its rails pass through a Connecticut countryside seemingly unchanged by a century of progress.
Rails After Dark

following pages:
THE RIO GRANDE Zephyr blows past Prospect Junction in December 1972, as blizzard conditions inundate the Denver metropolitan area. The observation car, Silver Sky, a post-WWII Budd design, brings up the markers.
Mel Patrick

2-8-2 MIKADO #499 of the Rio Grande narrow gauge waits at Toltec siding, headlight staring "into the freezing darkness," for the arrival of an eastbound freight descending Colorado's Cumbres Pass in the winter of 1955-56. Operating today as the Cumbres & Toltec Scenic Railway, K-36 Mikes still ride three-foot rails on this last outpost of authentic narrow-gauge railroading in the West.
Philip Hastings / CSRM

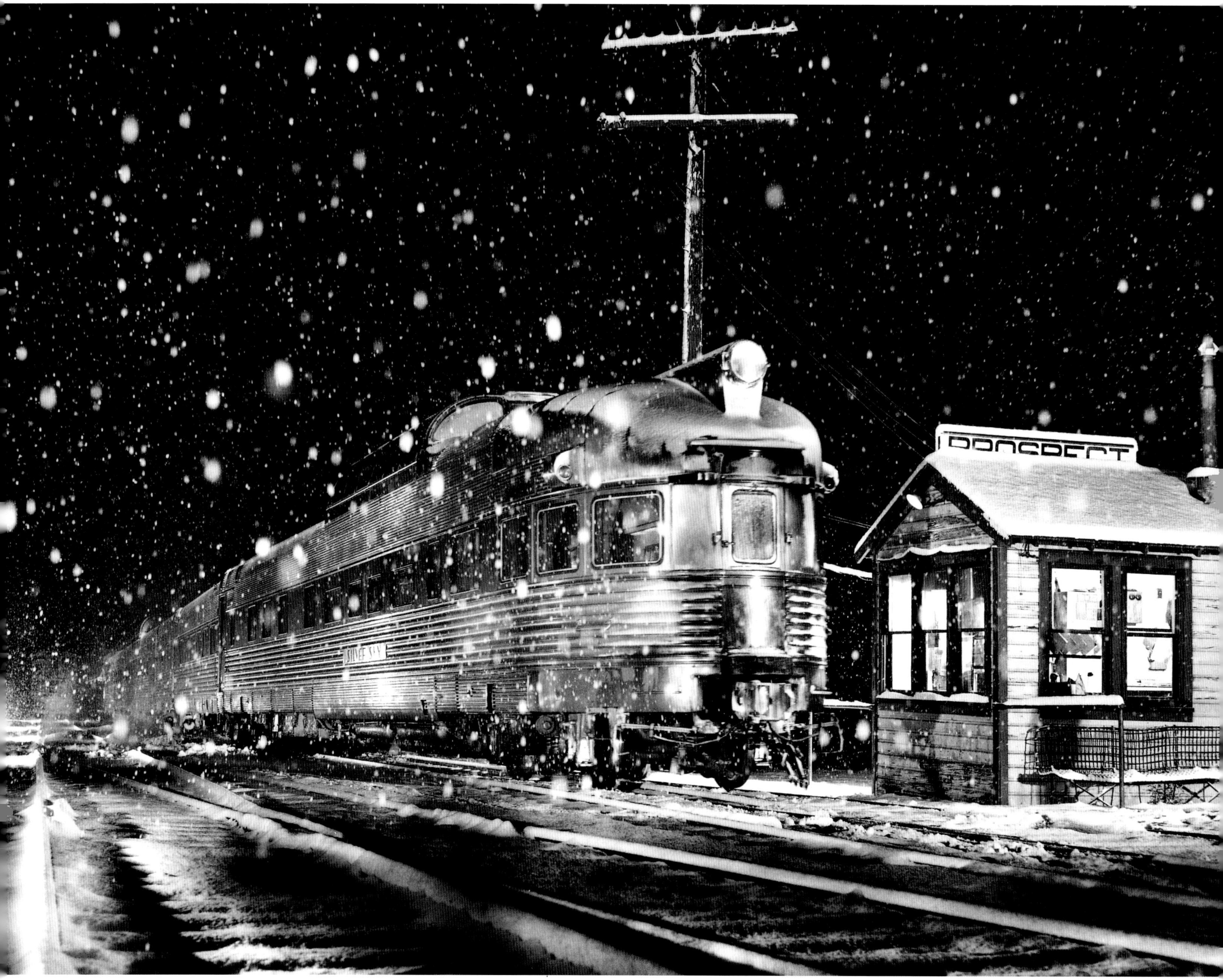

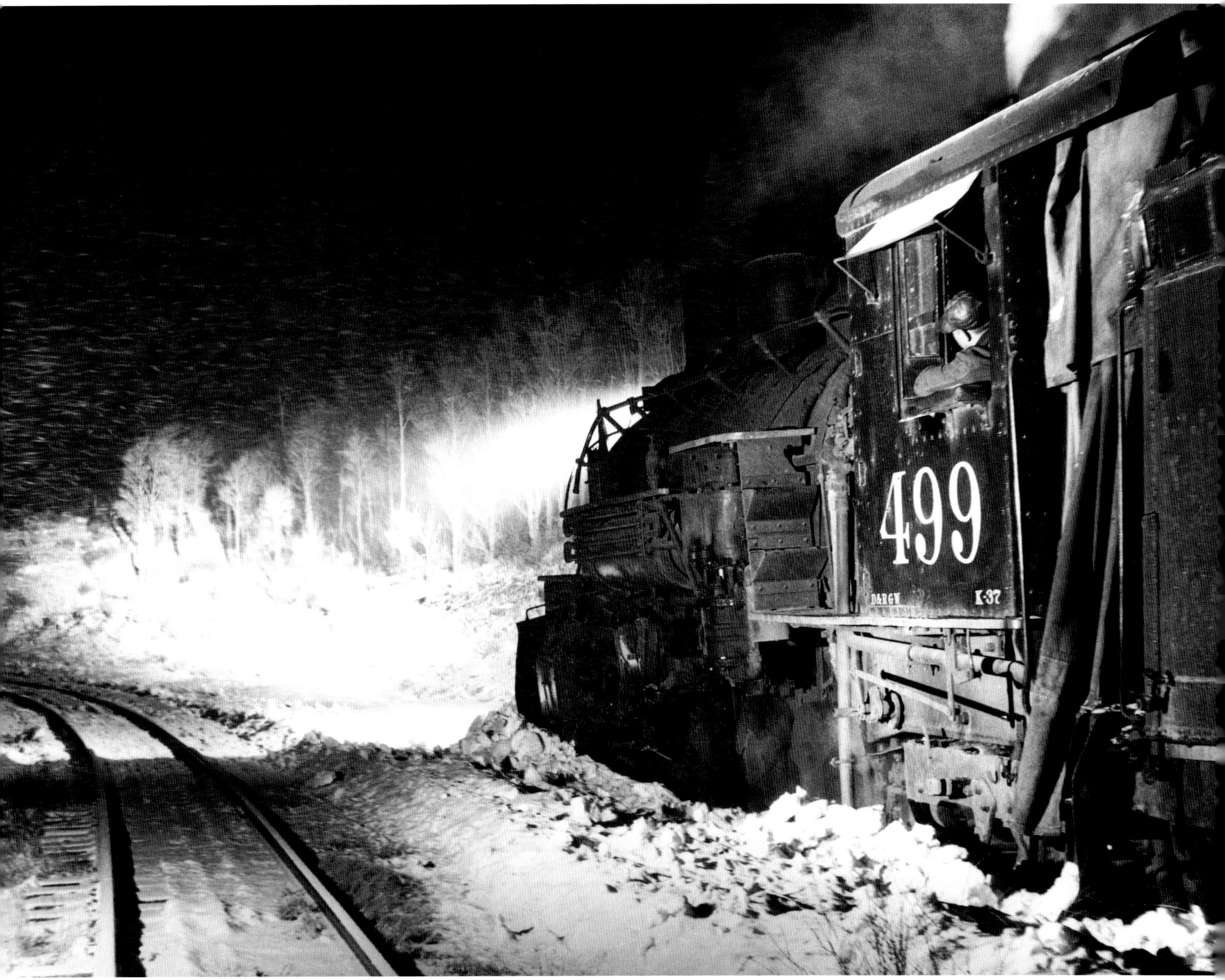
499
D&RGW
K-37

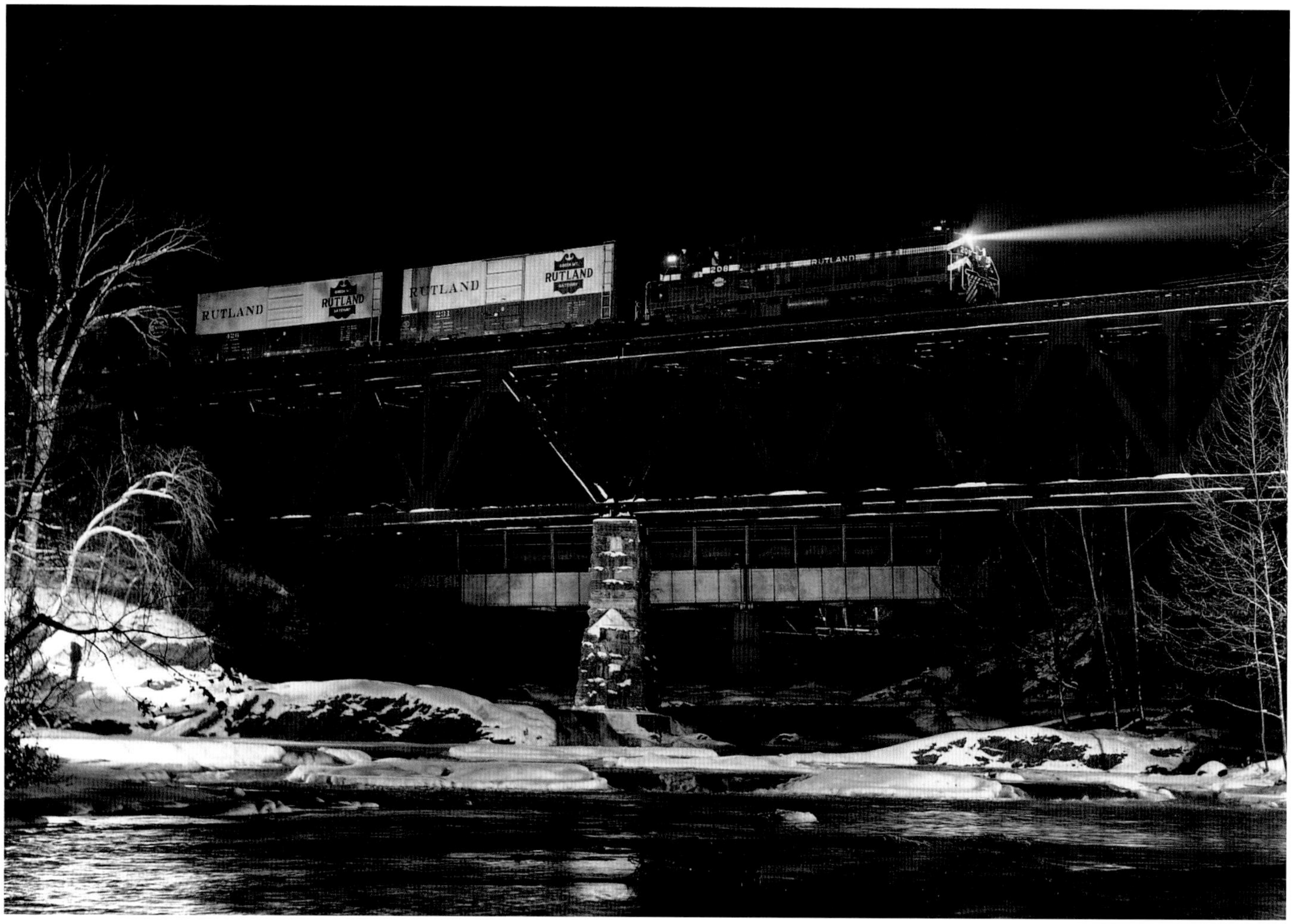

EIGHT #50 FLASHBULBS (the largest ever made) illuminate the passing of a Rutland Railroad milk train as it crosses the Waloomsac River near North Hoosick, New York, in January 1959. The photographer, with the aid of seven men and $1,800 worth of camera gear, conceived the image with the railroad's help. As the train approached the bridge, the engineer was directed by flare to stop his train at the appropriate location. Four photographs were made simultaneously from different locations below the trestle and on the river bank. Camera lenses were set at f5.6 as 744,000 lumens of light were directed toward the scene. After the exposure was made, the engineer was signaled and resumed his trip to Albany. The photographer, in a final gesture of gratitude, raced back to his studio in nearby Troy, processed the film, and developed prints. These were presented to the returning train crew during a stopover three hours later, as they made their way back to Rutland.
Jim Shaughnessy

A WEST SIDE LUMBER Company Shay glides across a trestle overlooking the Tuolumne River as a series of jerry-rigged reflectors with flashbulbs light up the landscape and spindly supports of River Bridge. Camp Clavey, thirty-seven miles up the line, will be its destination tonight as it winds through the Stanislaus National Forest on its last revenue run. The year is 1960, and #8's staccato-like exhaust echoes among the tall pines and Douglas fir, a final encore for narrow-gauge logging in the Sierras.

Having its origins as the Hetch-Hetchy & Yosemite Valleys Railway in 1898, the West Side enjoyed close to a sixty-year existence as a lumber hauler in the California woods.
Richard Steinheimer

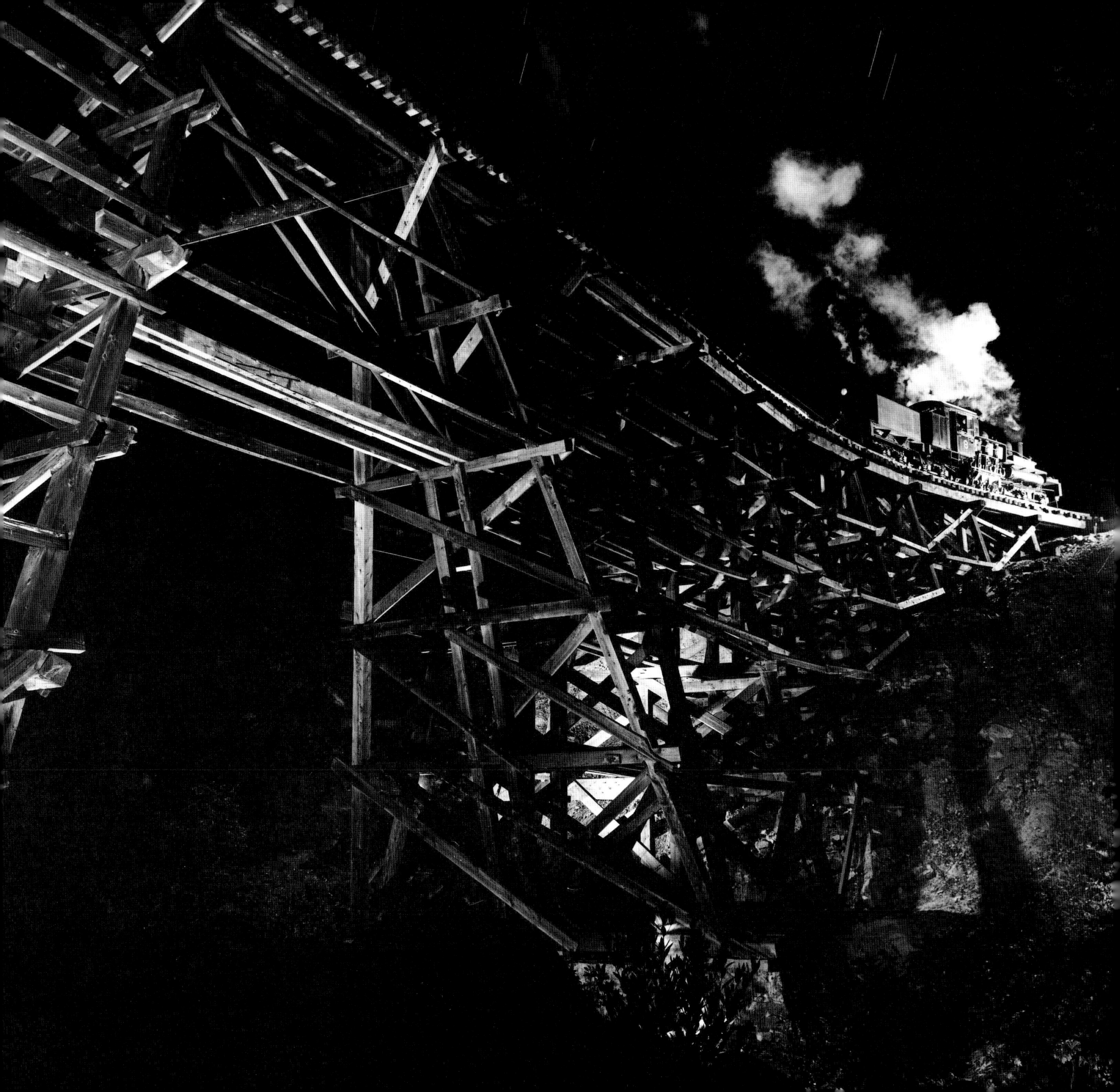

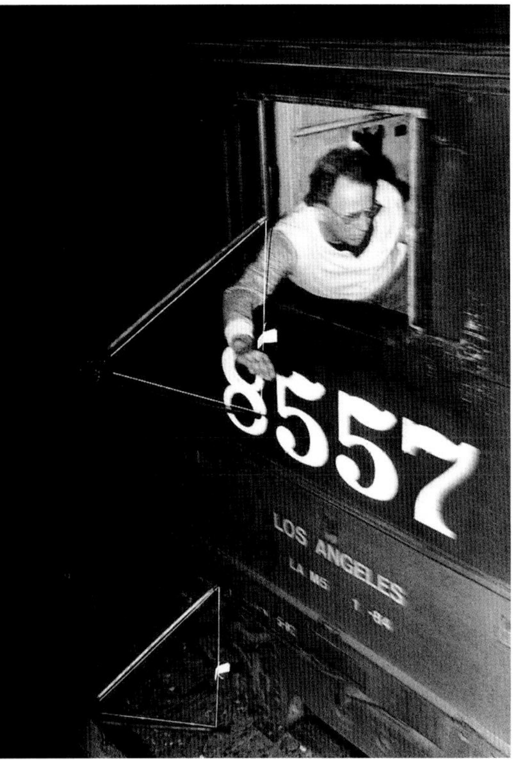

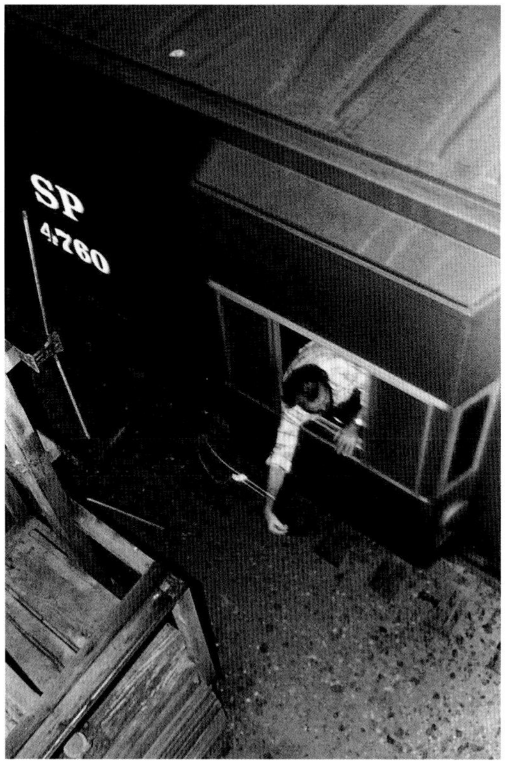

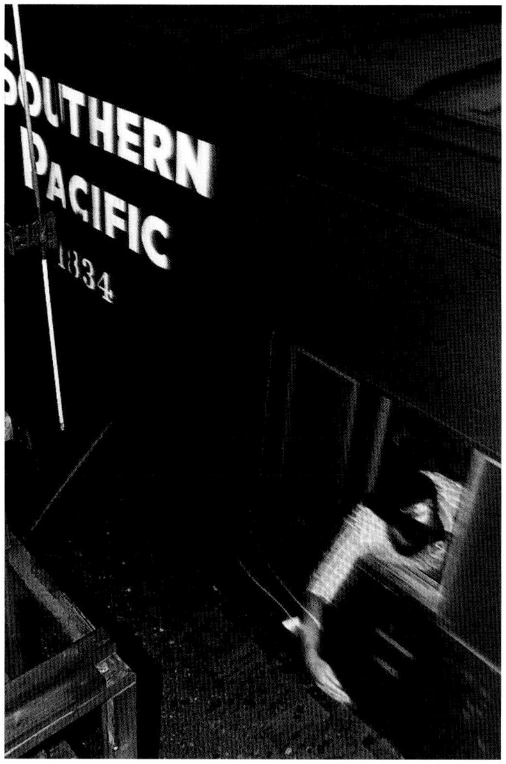

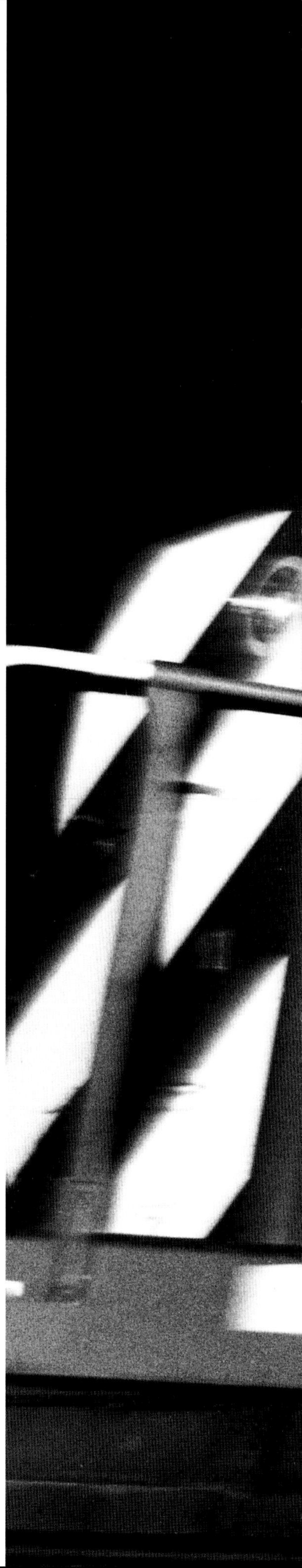

AT THE LONELY outpost of Surf, the photographer has set up his camera in total darkness to record the last vestiges of train-order operation—that is, communication by written messages—on the Southern Pacific's Coast Line. In stop-action frames, the tradition of picking up orders "on the fly" is evidenced by three pictures that capture the essence of this classic bit of railroading drama. It's the summer of 1985, and new DTC block signaling is a few months away from being implemented. Like other aspects of railroading that have disappeared over the last fifteen years—such as the caboose and five-man crew—the train order and station agent will soon be history. Surf will close its doors in August, and the entire California Coast Division will be under radio control by early 1986.
John Roskoski

A BURLINGTON NORTHERN unit coal train slams past the order hoops at Bill, Wyoming, en route to the AMAX Belle Ayr Mine below Gillette. It's 1981, and coal traffic in the Powder River Basin has increased dramatically since the oil embargo of the mid-1970s threatened to choke off an energy-hungry nation.
Richard Steinheimer

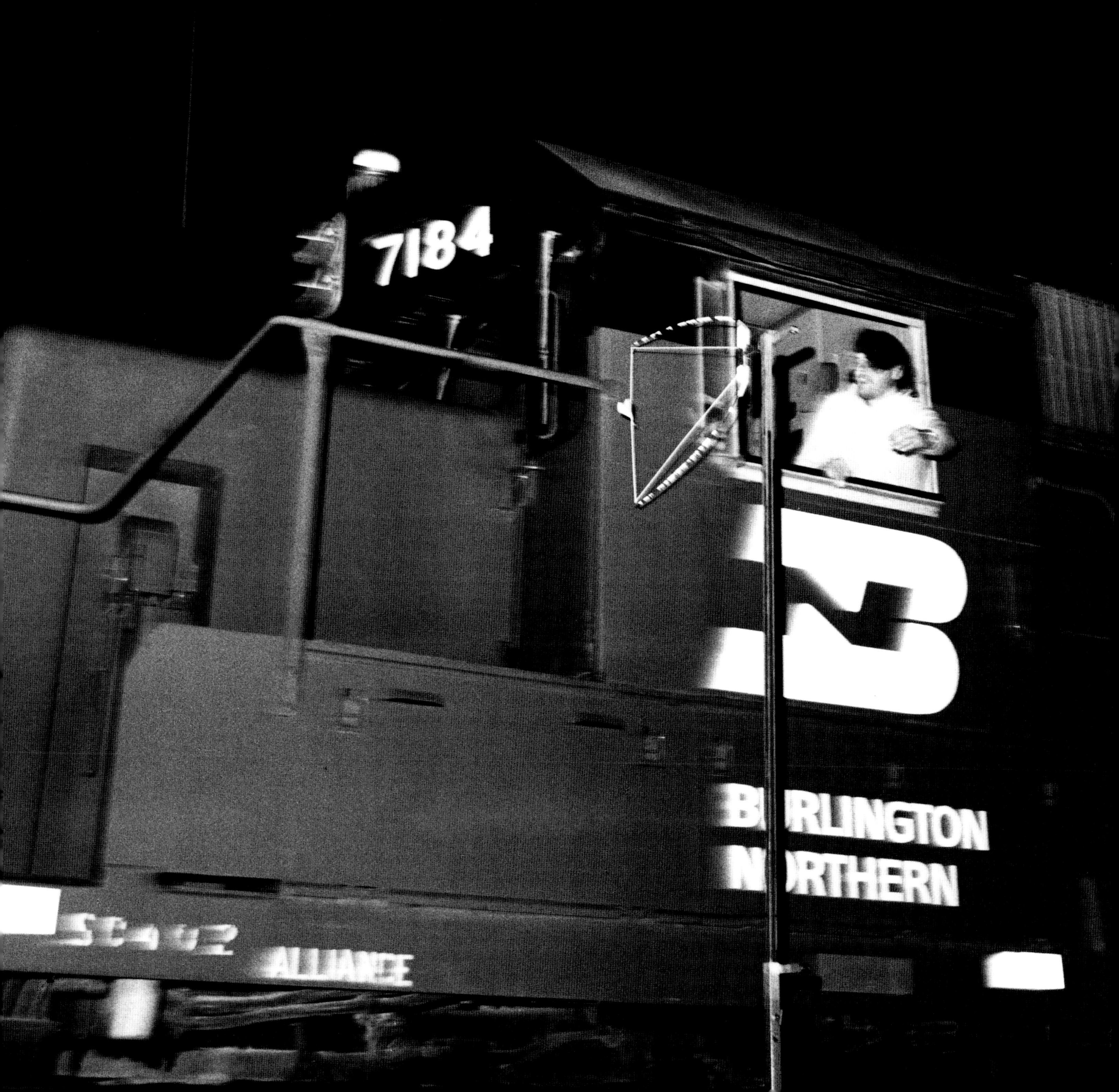
7184
BURLINGTON
NORTHERN
ALLIANCE

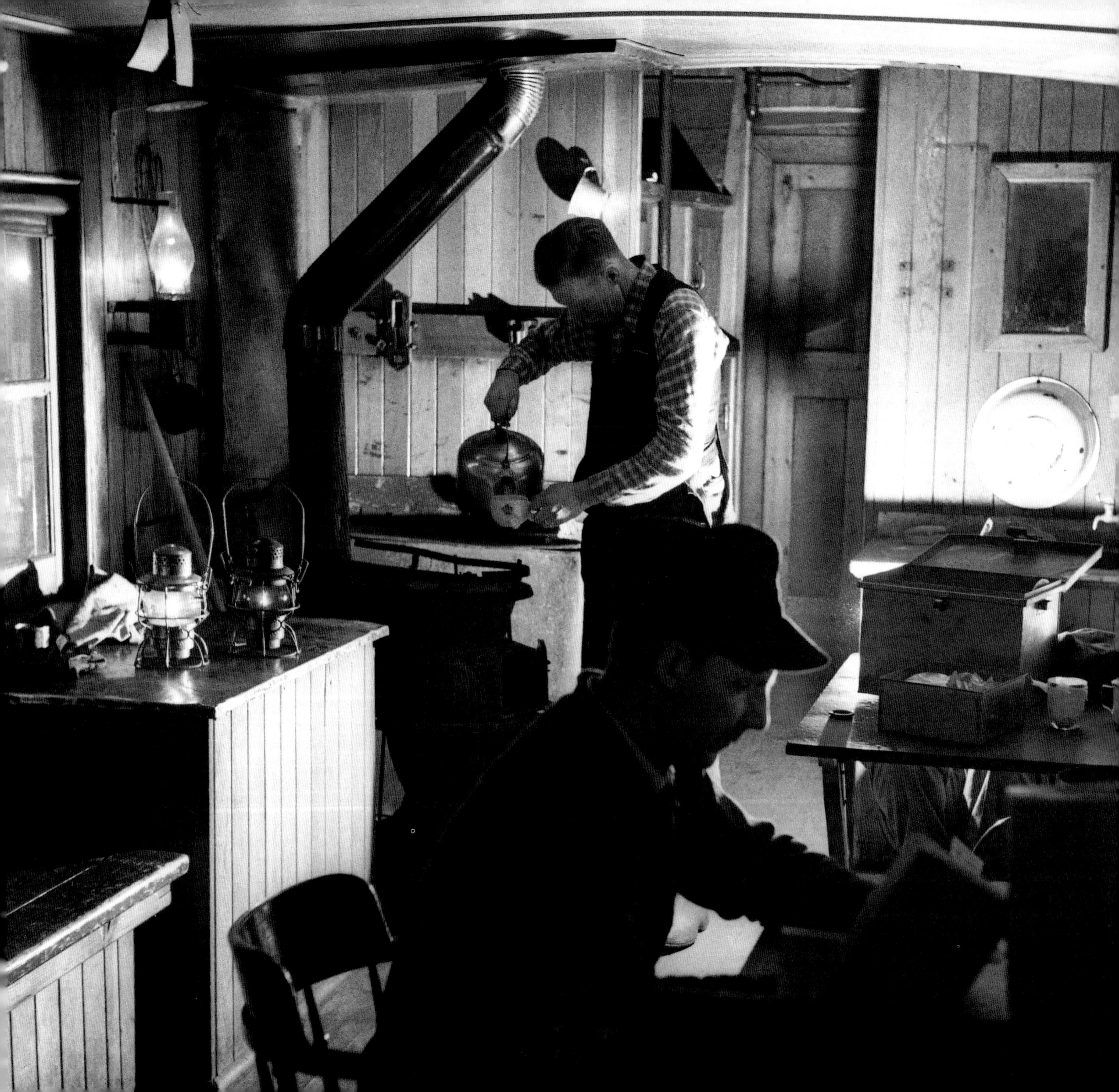

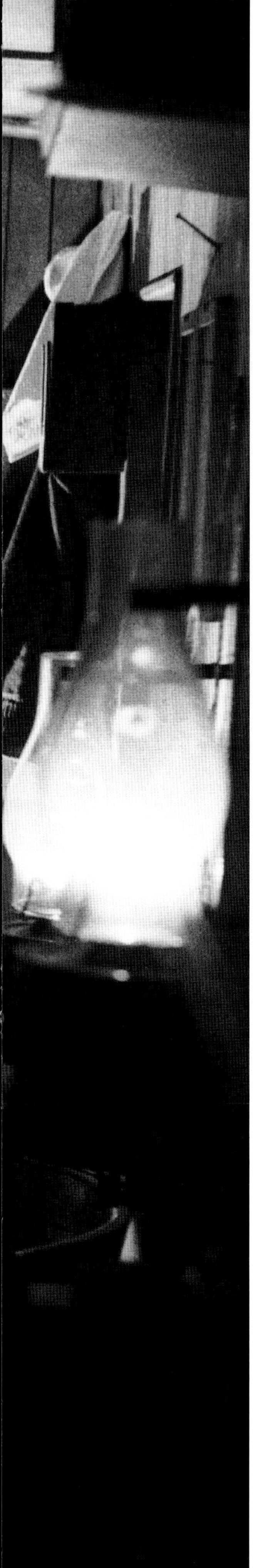

LOOKING OVER wheel reports as his brakeman prepares for tea time, a Canadian National conductor relaxes in the comfort of his caboose—safe, warm, and tucked away from the frigid weather of a wintry night in New Brunswick.

In 1955, during these halcyon days of railroading, the humble "crummy" was more than just a place for work and waybills—it also functioned as a home-on-wheels for the trainmen. Hearty meals were prepared and bunks provided rest for the weary crews after they'd gone dead on the "16-hour law"—the legal number of hours a trainman could work. The late 1980s brought the caboose's final demise as new labor agreements, establishing two-man crews on most freight trains, were implemented.

Today, a flashing rear-end device (known as "fred") placed behind the last freight car has replaced one of railroading's more colorful institutions.

Philip Hastings / CSRM

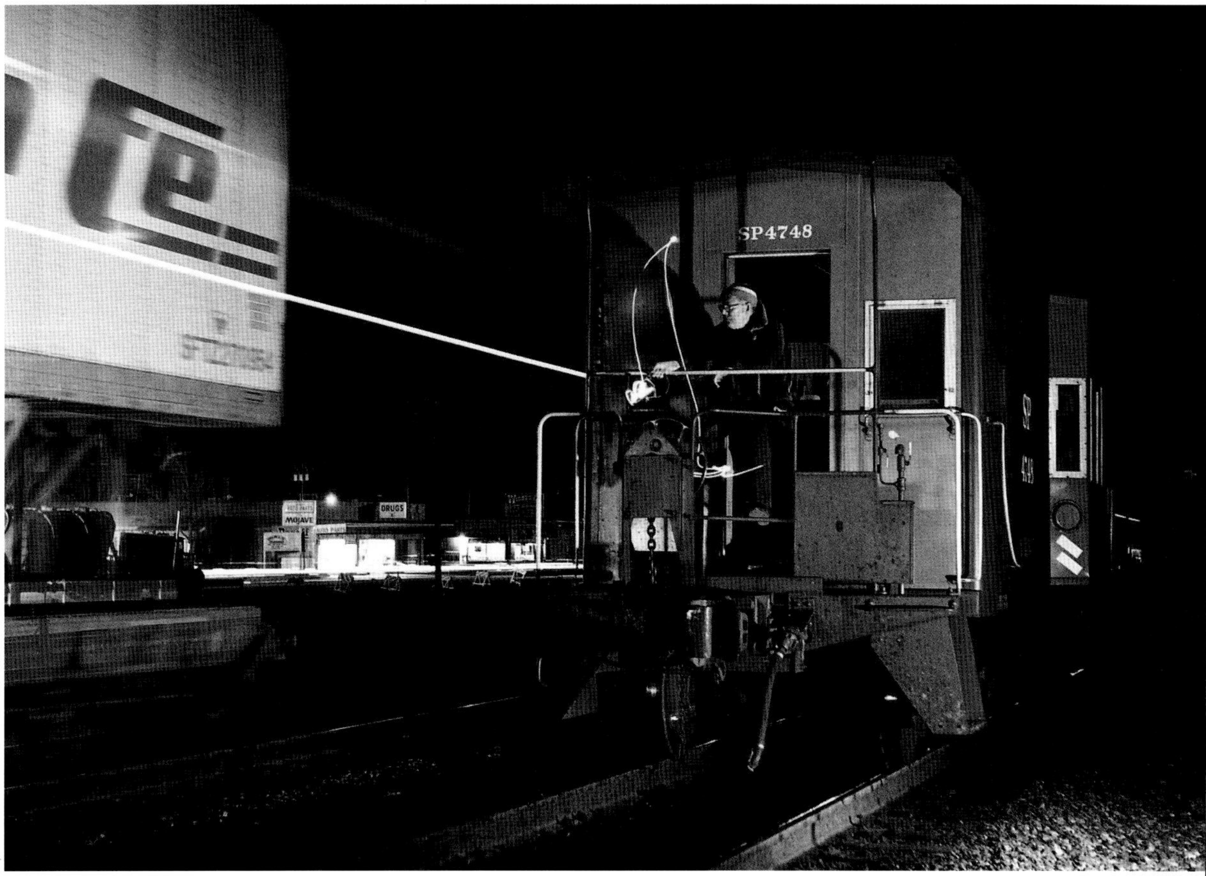

ESPEE AND SANTA FE freights pass one another on joint trackage at Mojave, California, in 1982. The conductor signals an "all black," letting the opposing train crew know there is no dragging cargo or evidence of hot journal boxes, also known as "hotboxes" in the lexicon of the rails.

Jeff Brouws

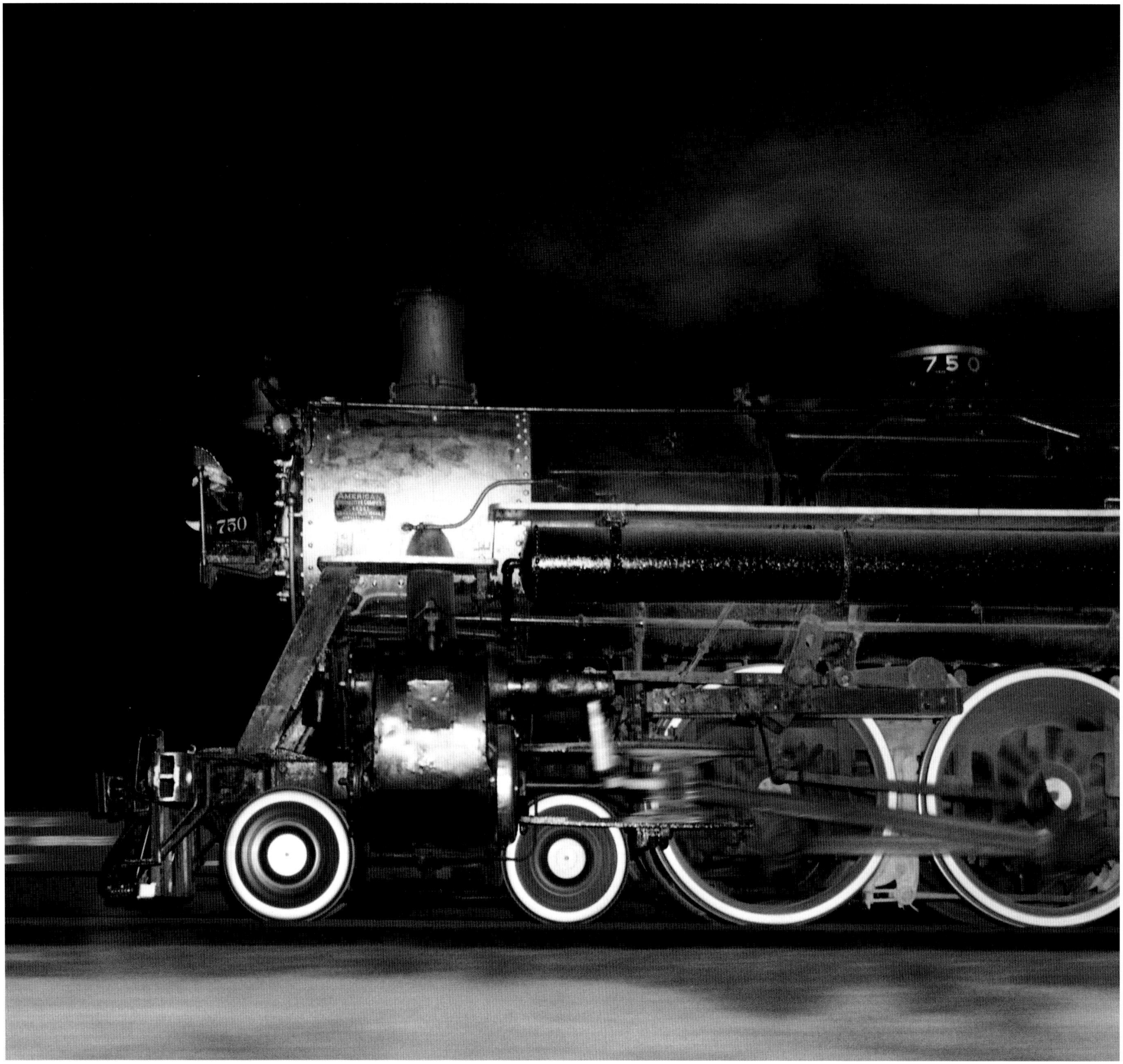
750
750

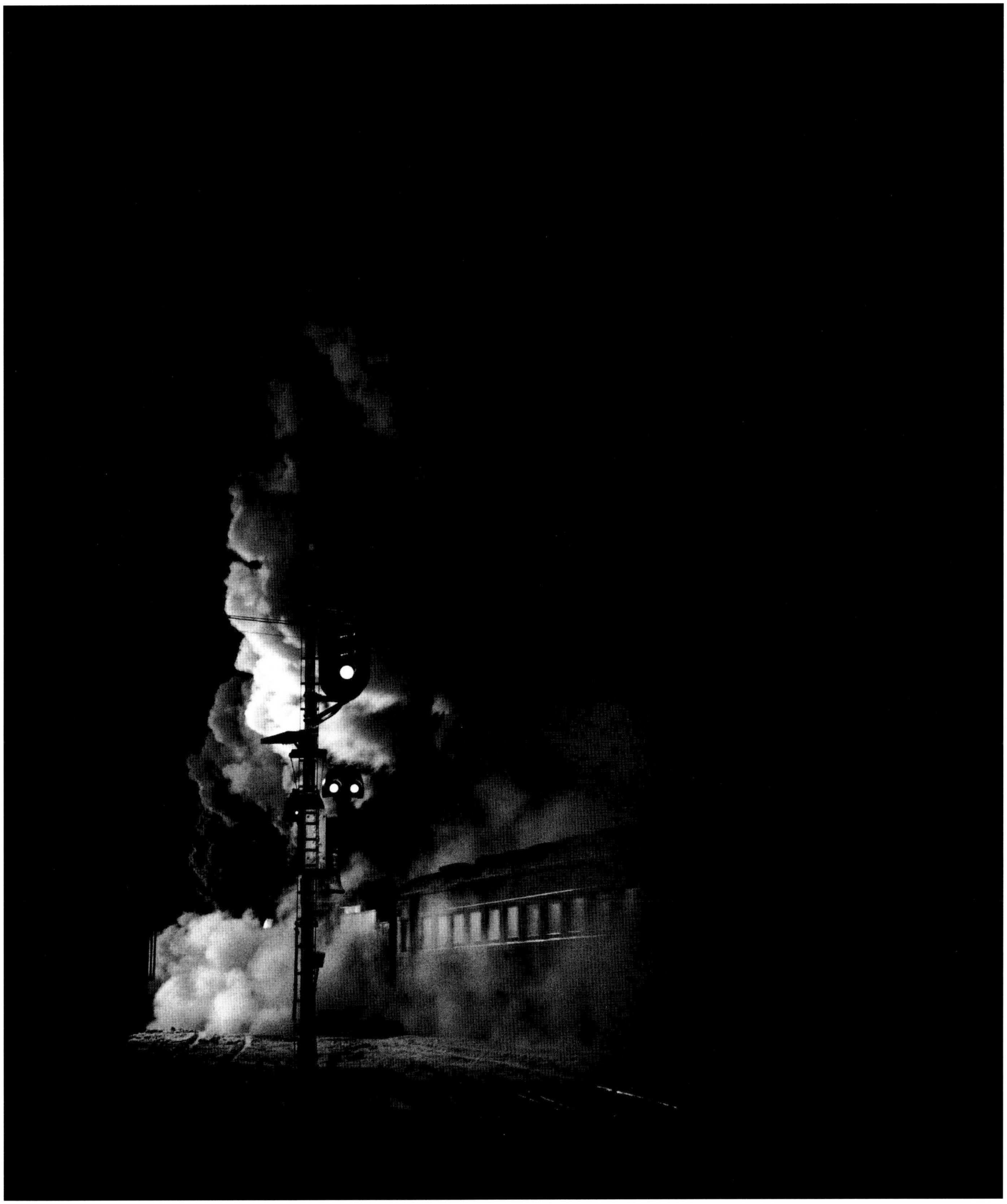

far left:

EX-SAVANNAH & ATLANTA 4-6-2 #750 highballs out of Statham, Georgia, on a fantrip during the glory days of steam revival on the Southern Railway. The train is on an Atlanta-Gainesville circle trip in December 1966.

Victor Hand

left:

IN JAPAN, THE LAST steam-powered express train of the Japanese National Railway was the Limited Express Niseko running between Hakodate and Sapporo, the capital of Hokkaido. JNR's C62 class Hudsons handled the service with additional helpers often assisting the road engine over the mountainous elevations of the Oshamambe-to-Sapporo mainline. Late evening winter departures of these double-headed trains often created spectacular shows of steam and smoke, as seen here in December 1970.

Ed Delvers

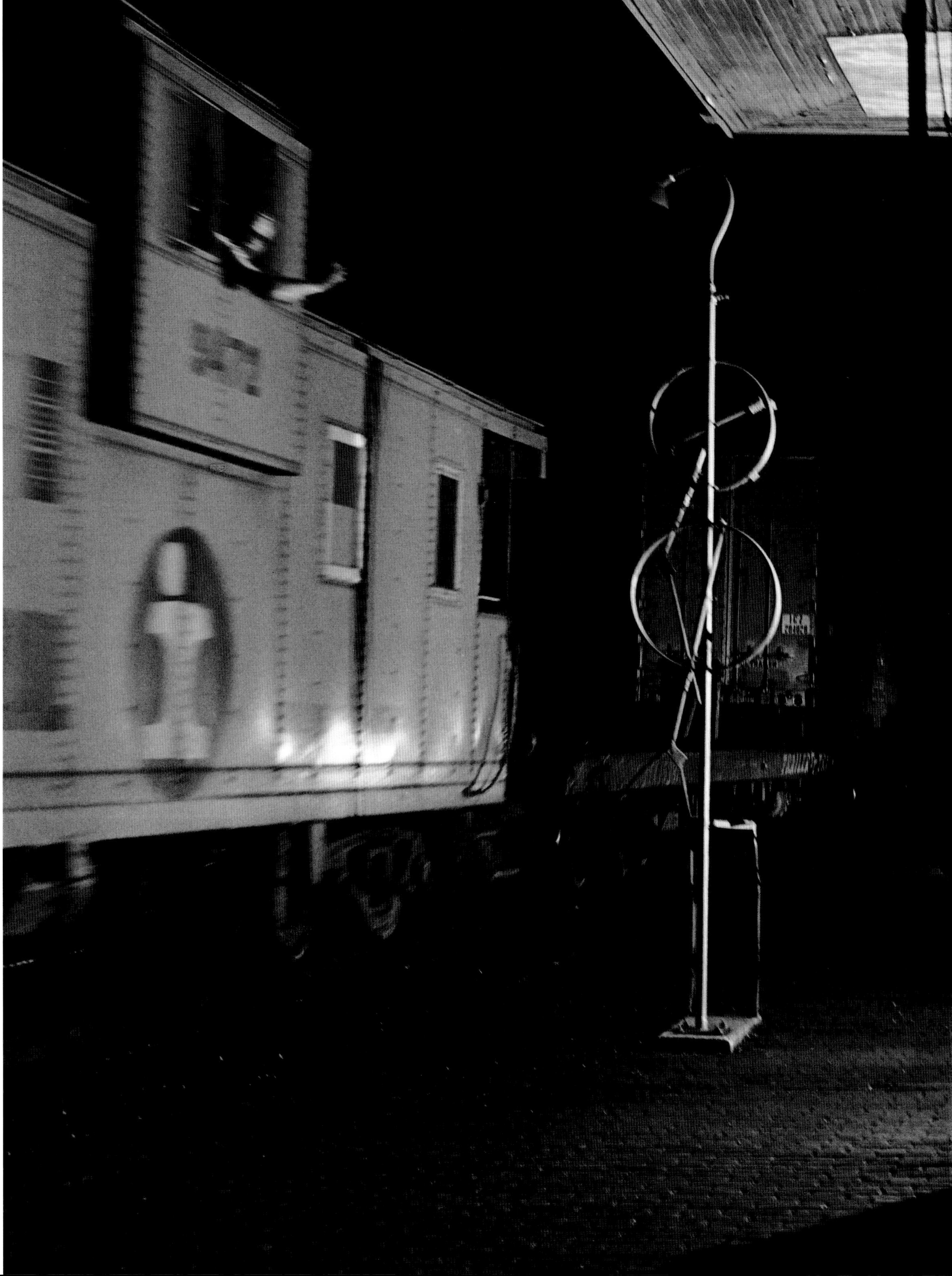

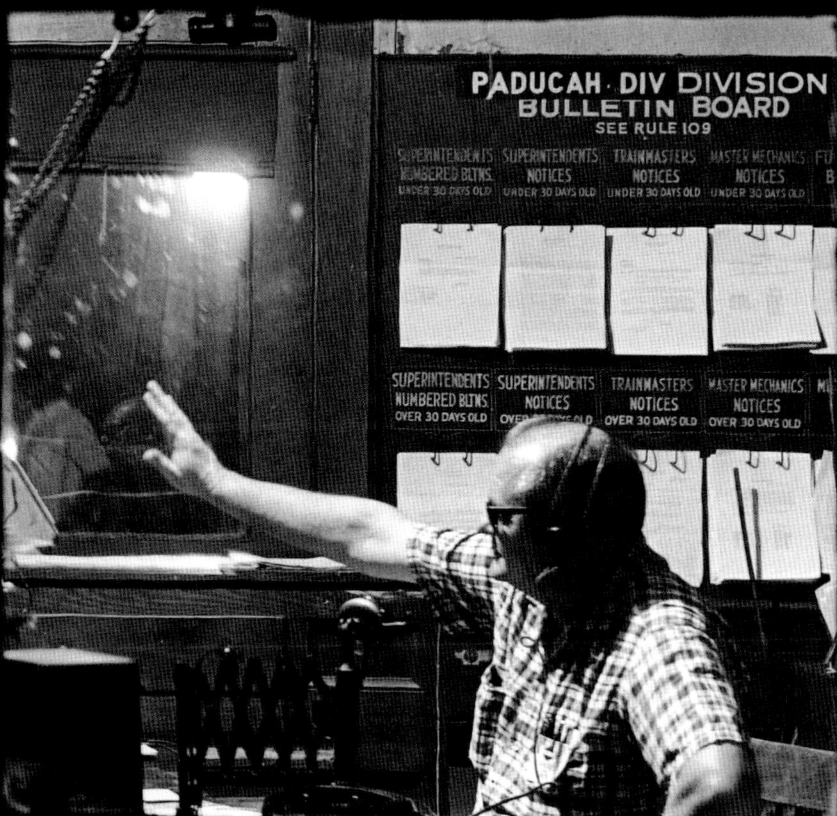

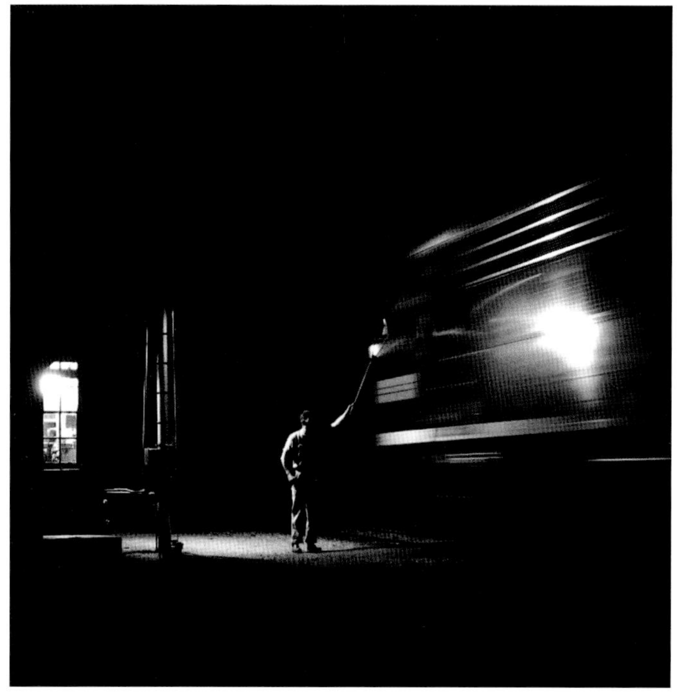

THE MIRACULOUS double exposure capabilities of photography capture a familiar railroading scene in a not-so-familiar fashion. In the first exposure, the station operator at Dyersburg, Tennessee, 450 miles south of Chicago on the Illinois Central mainline to New Orleans, is seen waving from the office. It's 9:50 P.M. July 1971, and the agent, R. A. Fowlkes, is at the end of his shift and ready to go home. With the depot now closed for the evening, the photographer recocks his shutter without advancing his film, waiting patiently in the hot summer darkness. At half past the witching hour, a fast-paced southbound manifest shatters the silence as the conductor waves to the photographer. A second exposure is made, capturing the dramatic interplay between men and machine, film and rail, presence and absence.
Mel Patrick

above:

OPERATOR ROY WILKENSON "hoops up" orders to an eastbound Santa Fe freight, Summit, California, 1962.
Stan Kistler

THE THUNDERHAWK, train 262-2, grinds its way into the frigid Bitterroots wilderness under a full moon in December 1973. The photographer, without the aid of gloves or proper attire, rides the low nose of an SD40-2, balancing his Bronica on the unit's hood to make his shots, attempting periodic exposures between warming his hands and covering his face to prevent frostbite. Earlier in the day, hampered by snow-infested forest service roads, he battled his way into Avery, Idaho, from Alberton, Montana, to make these final images of the Milwaukee Road's Little Joes. Despite long delays, annulled trains, and clearance problems, "Stein" stays cool, perseveres, and goes on to make a series of images that catapults the canon of railroad photography into new realms and immortalize the E77 motor and all of its brethren for a younger generation of MILW railfans.

Initially instituted as a cost-saving measure to compete against the more conventional steam/diesel locomotives of Union Pacific, Northern Pacific, and Great Northern, the power of "white coal" lasted almost sixty years on the Milwaukee Road's Pacific Extension. In the end, the cost efficiencies of electric locomotives couldn't prevent the tide of red ink that washed over the Route of the Hiawathas. The last "juice" was drawn from the catenary on June 15, 1974, and the railroad declared bankruptcy on December 18, 1977. Reorganization and a new Milwaukee Road II emerged two years later.

Richard Steinheimer

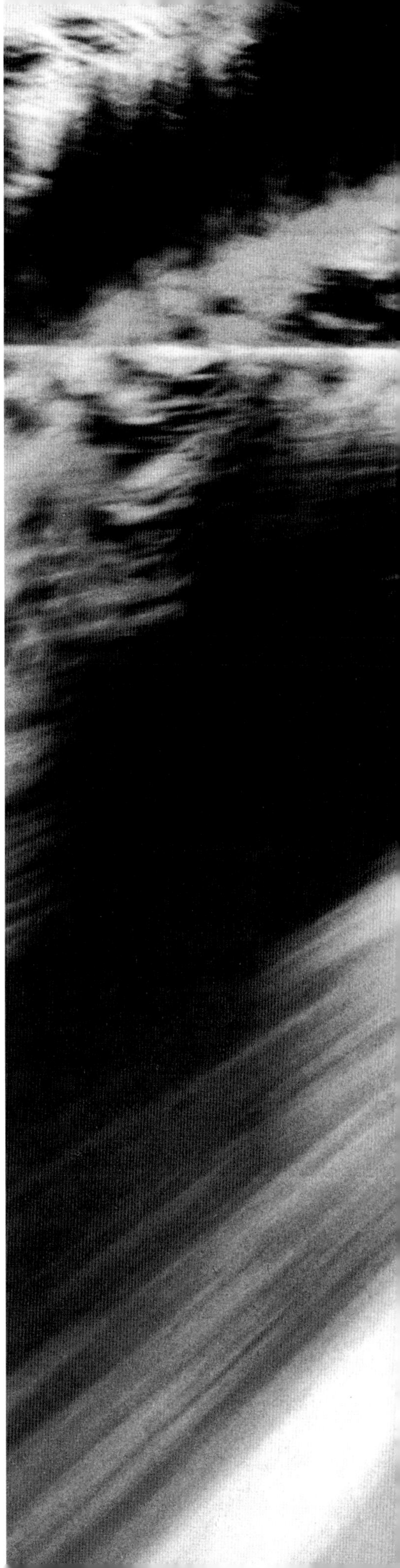

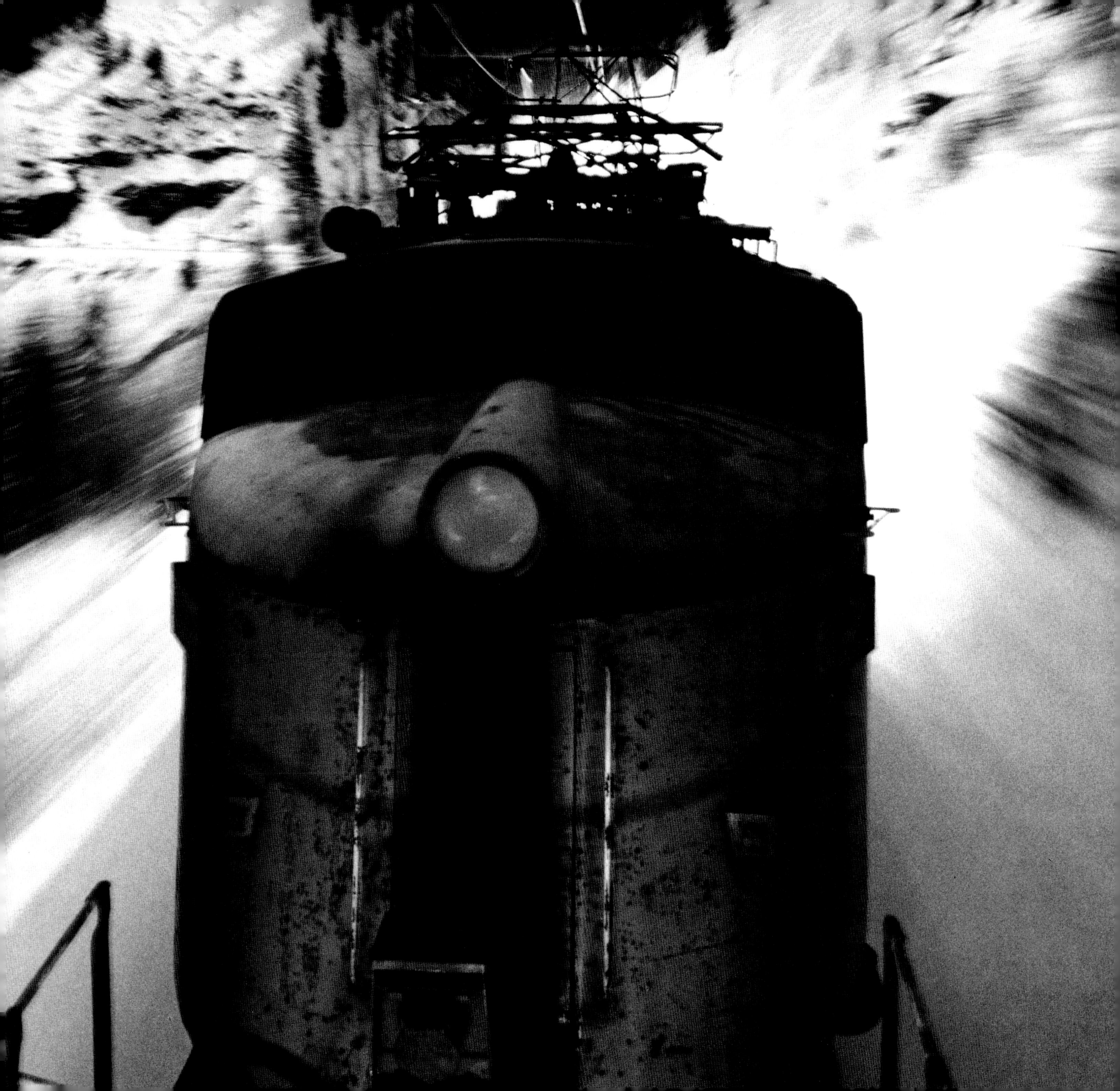

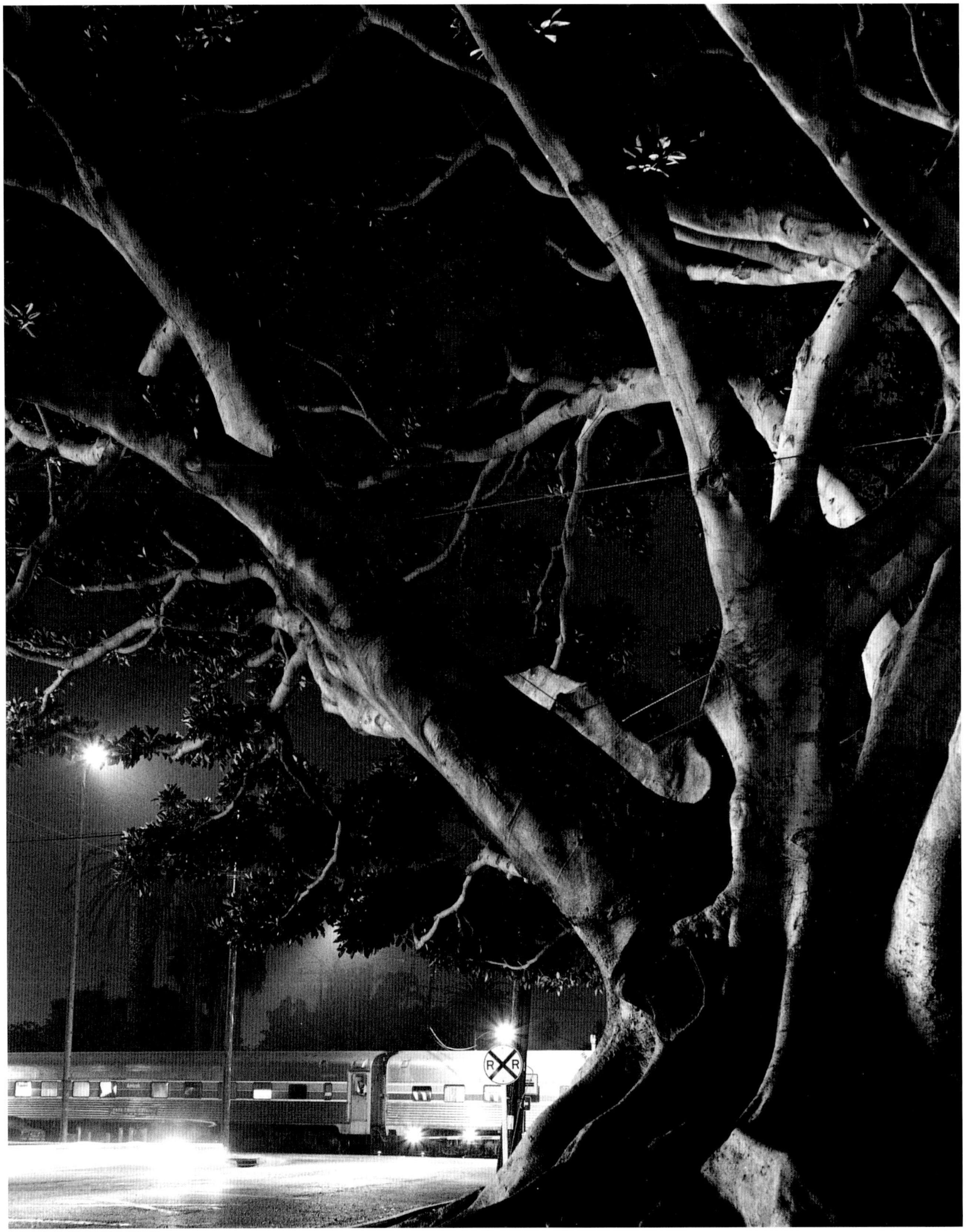

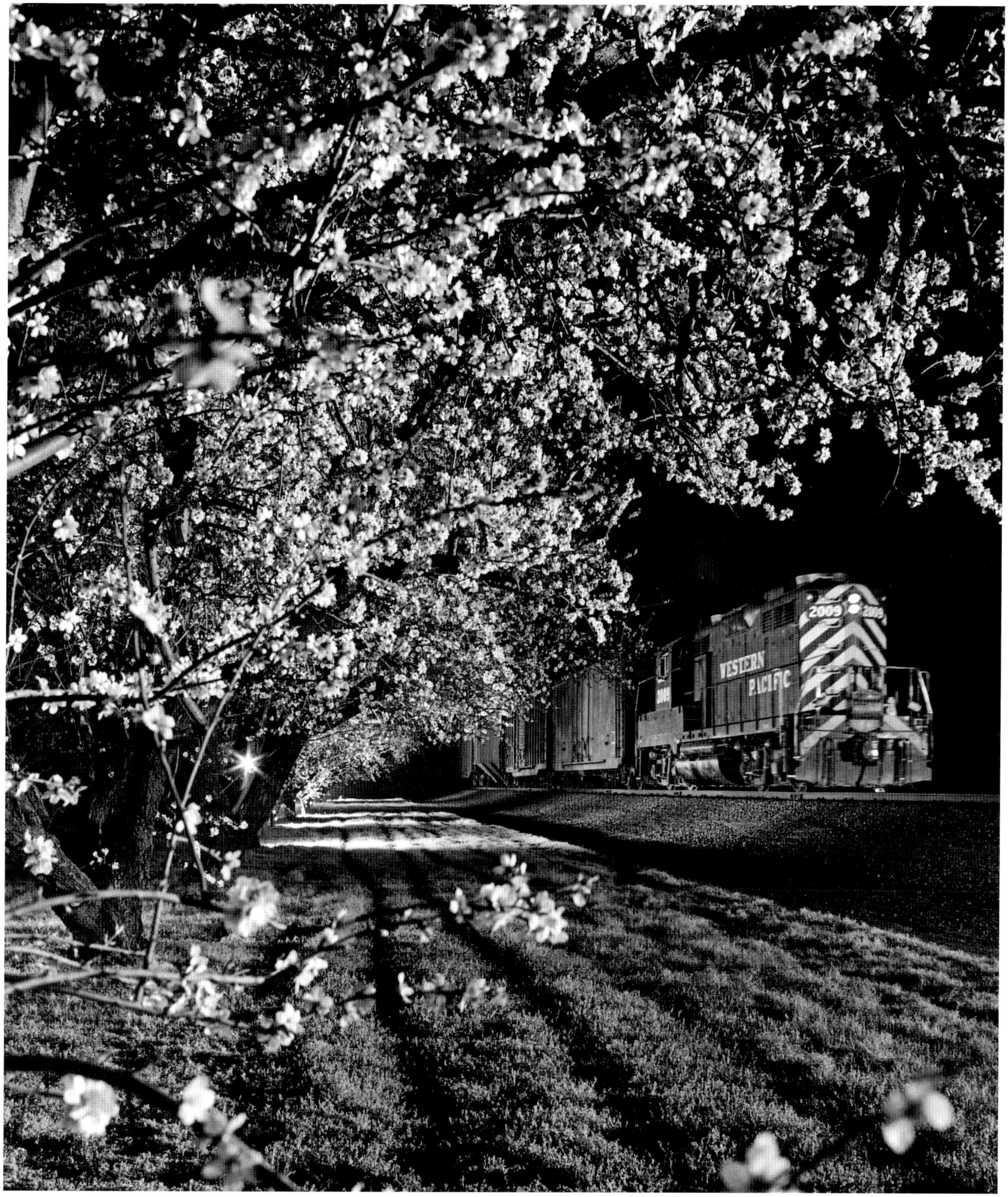

TIDEWATER SOUTHERN'S Stockton Hauler passes an almond orchard in full bloom in February 1982. GP7 #2009 is in charge of this late-night Stockton–Modesto turn during the last year of independence for the Western Pacific and its subsidiary lines, among them the TS. Soon the Union Pacific's yellow curtain of color will descend and envelop the first of what eventually will be many parts of the western railroad scene.
Ted Benson

far left:

TRAIN #17, The Spirit of California, stops beneath the landmark 123-year-old Moreton Bay fig tree in Santa Barbara on a wet winter night in the early 1980s. Running as a short-lived State of California/Amtrak effort begun in October 1982, the Spirit was an overnight train operating between Los Angeles and Sacramento that failed to capture public attention or extended support. Ridership was poor and service was discontinued a year later.
Jeff Brouws

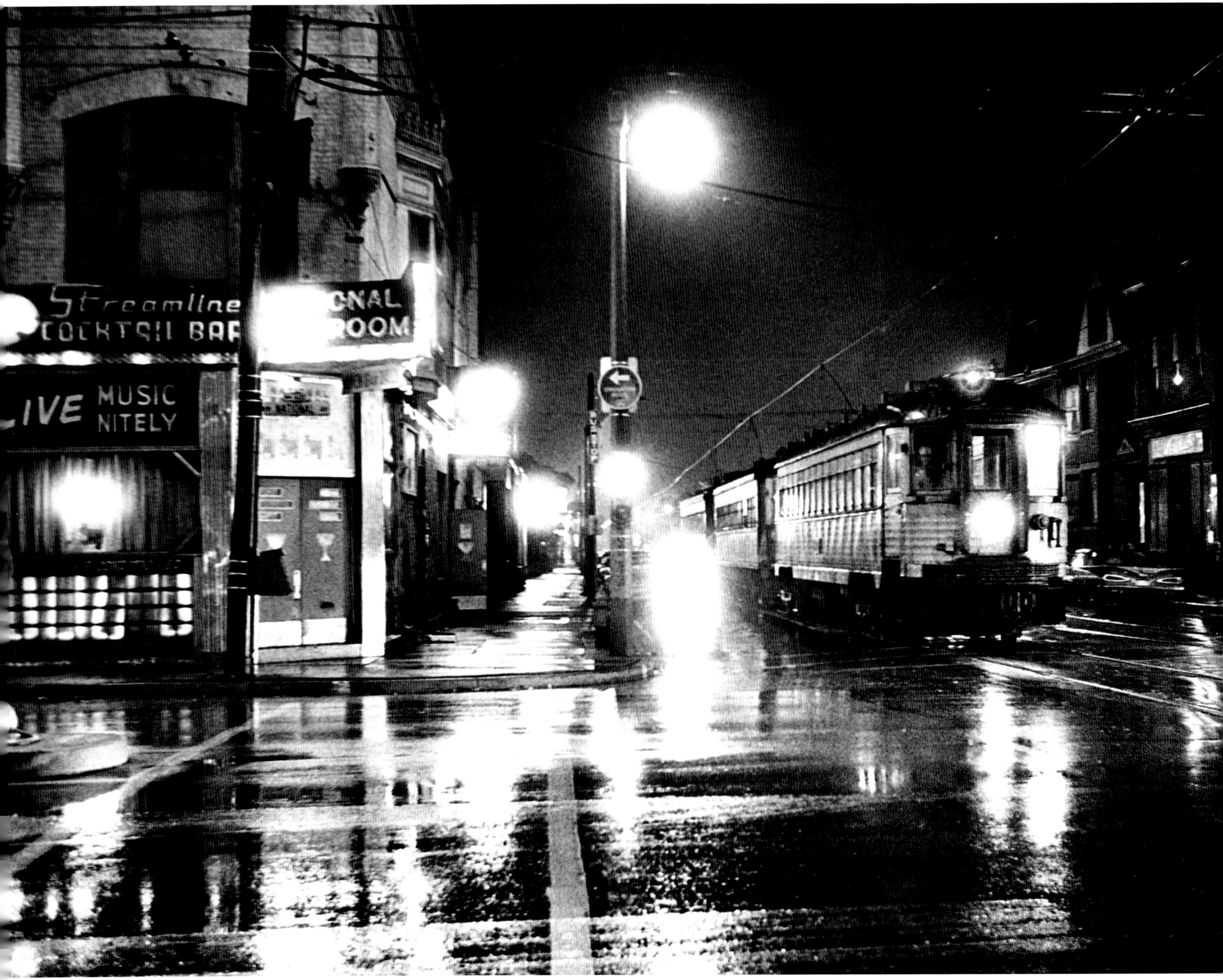
Streamline
LIVE MUSIC NITELY

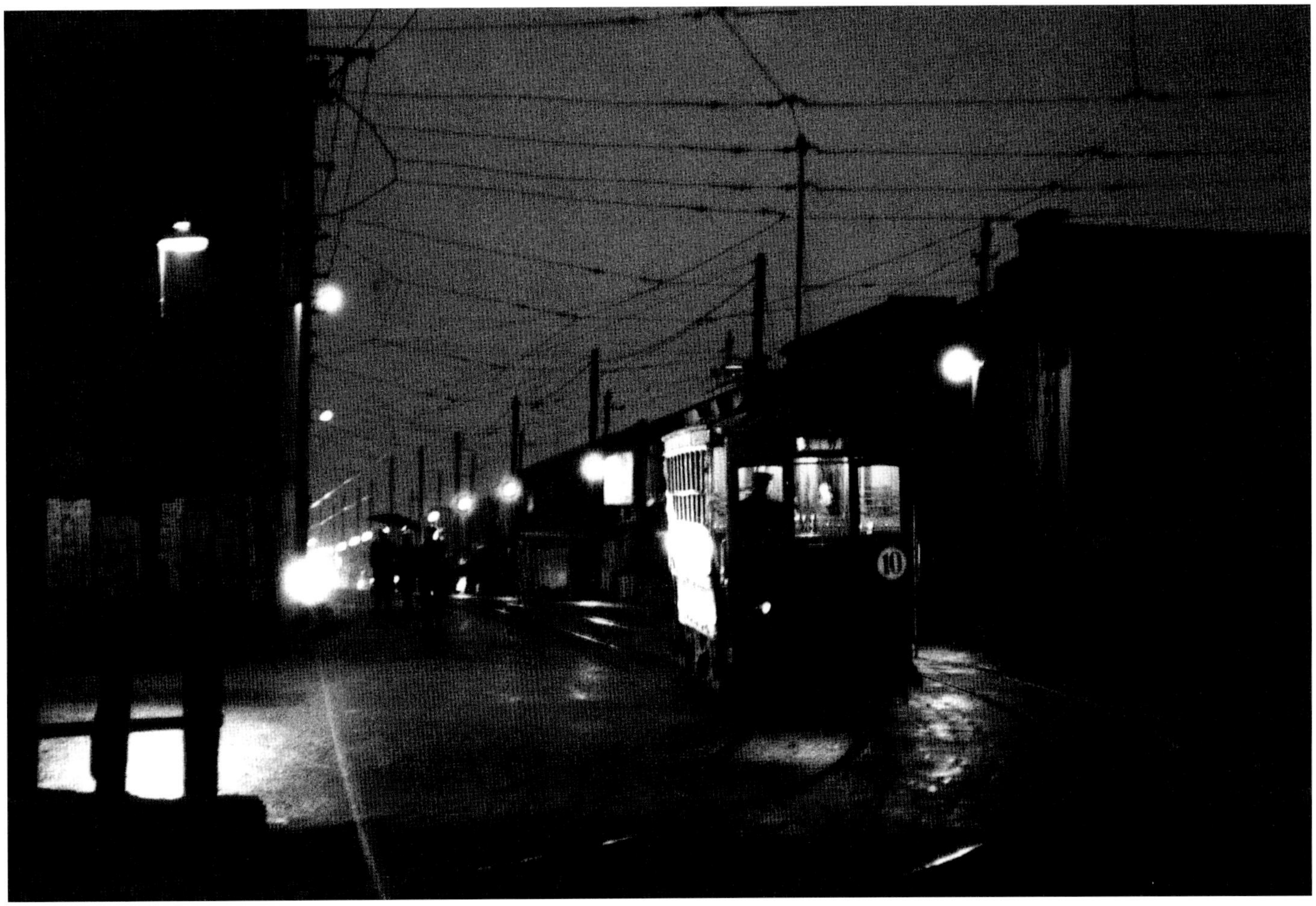

A TRIO OF STREAMLINERS linger at the intersection of 6th and National, in Milwaukee, Wisconsin, 1961. The Chicago, North Shore & Milwaukee Railroad, under the tutelage of utility tycoon Samuel Insull, was at one time the preeminent interurban line in America. Trolley service, begun in the early 1890s, lasted more than seventy years, ending in 1963.
John Gruber

right:
A RAINY NIGHT ON the Horikawa Nakadachiuri line in Kyoto finds a vintage Brill-like streetcar rounding a tight curve after a station stop. Passengers with umbrellas huddle against the windy dampness in this December 1957 view.
Naotaka Hirota

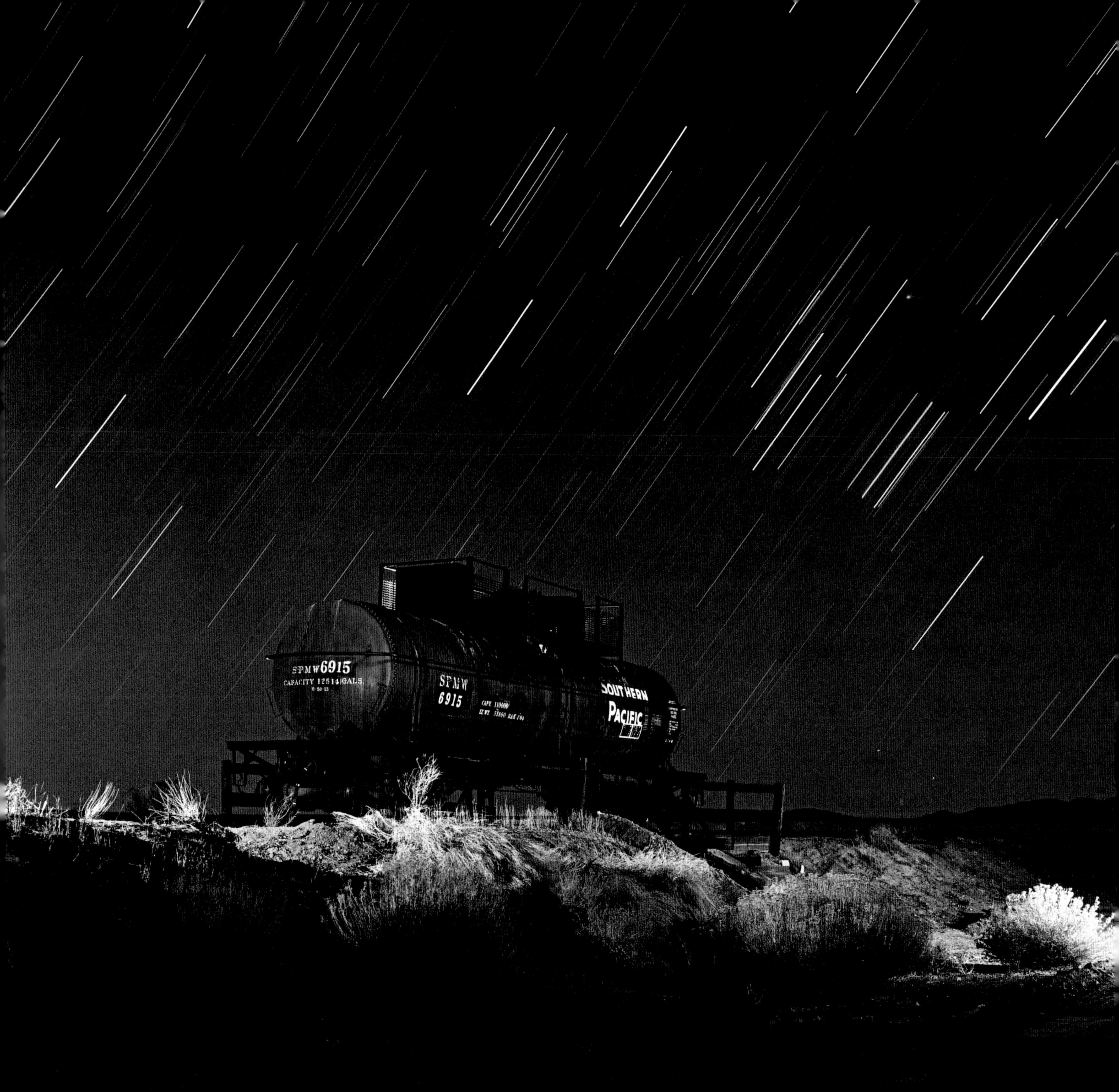
SPMW6915
CAPACITY 12514 GALS.
SPMW
6915
SOUTHERN
PACIFIC

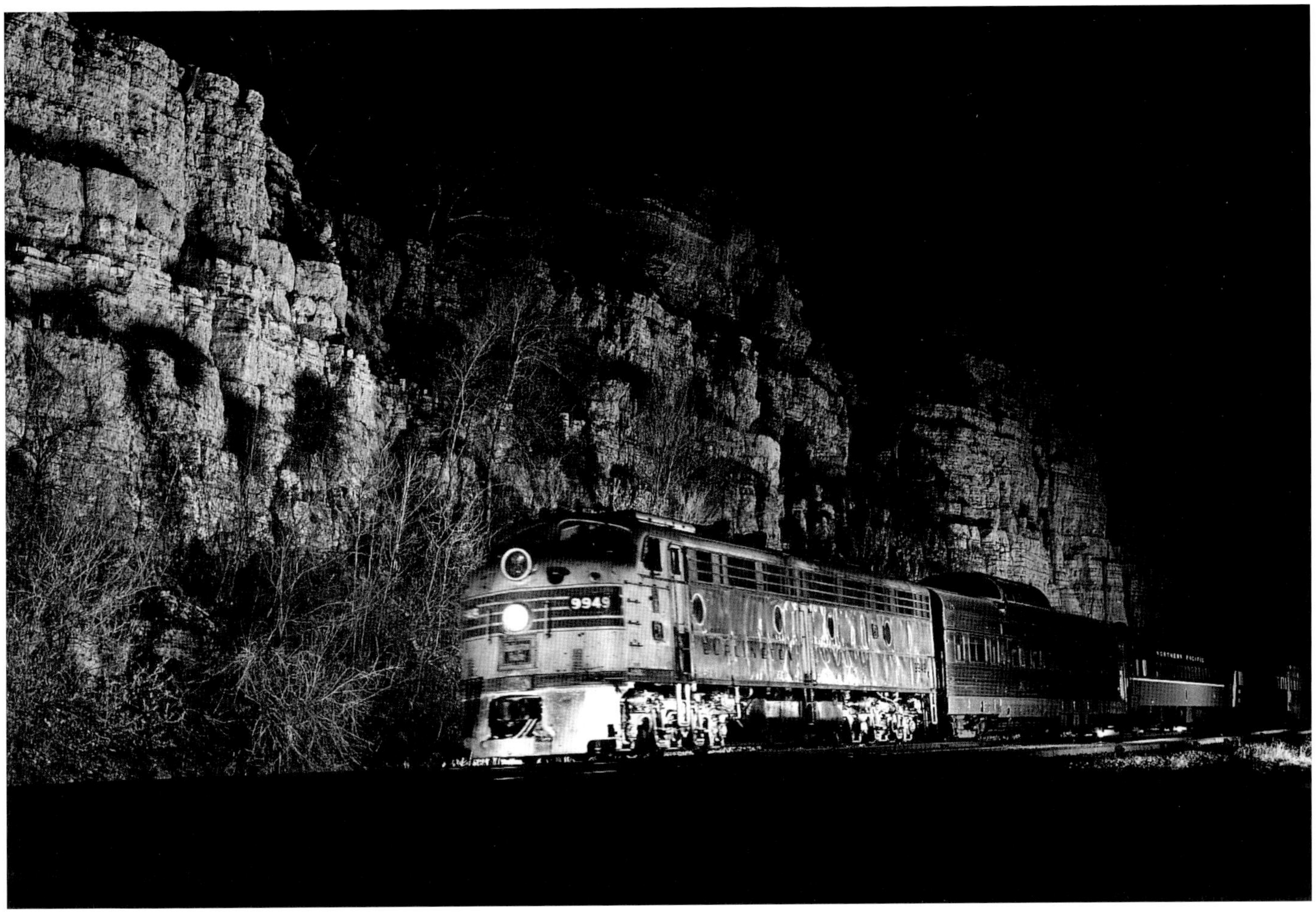

far left:

THE CONSTELLATION Orion arcs above a tank car filled with water—a precaution against brush fires started by stray locomotive sparks in arid regions—at Searles, California, 1982.
Ed Delvers

left:

A BURLINGTON E9 with an abbreviated Twin Cities Zephyr in tow skirts the banks of the Mississippi River near East Dubuque, Illinois, April 1971.
Mel Patrick

overleaf:

IN THE "BE SPECIFIC, ship Union Pacific" world of UP's East Los Angeles yards, a switchman helps shuttle boxcars around in the predawn hours, 1950s.
Donald Duke Collection

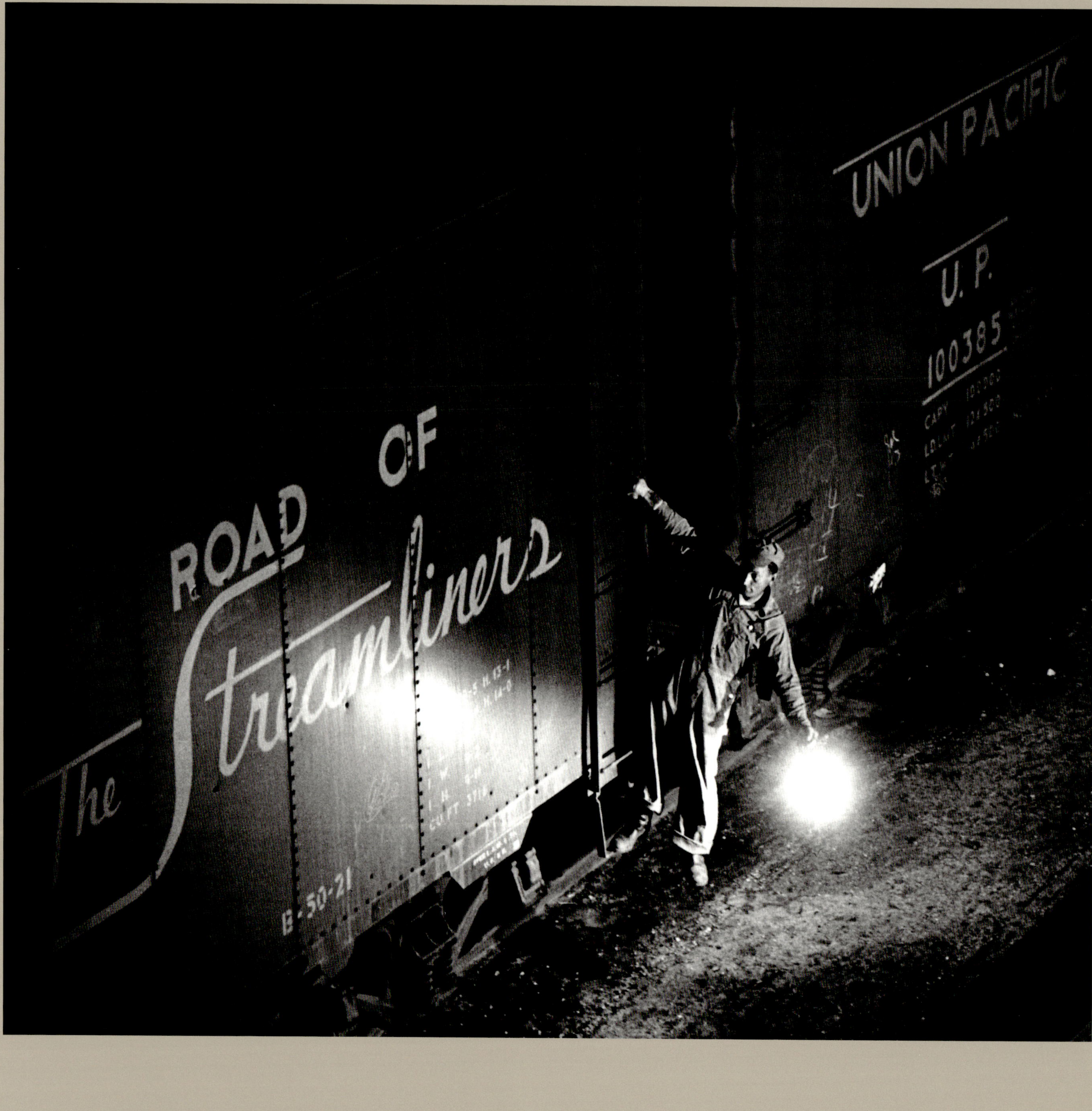
ROAD OF
The Streamliners
B-50-21
UNION PACIFIC
U. P.
100385

Chapter Four NIGHT MOVES

Down in the Yards

Clanking into the yards at Watsonville, we sit at the edge of the boxcar's door, peering out into the fog-shrouded darkness of this isolated rail junction. Having departed from San Luis eight hours earlier, we are bone-tired—a weariness attainable only after a prolonged ride in an empty fifty-footer at sixty miles per hour. With the train now stopped, we eagerly jump to terra firma and revel in its solidity—the same way a sailor on a freighter must feel when alighting on dry land after a storm at sea. As we gather our belongings, the sounds of the train yard surround us: the abrupt collision of boxcars being made into new trains; the stop-and-go cadence of diesel exhaust; the eerie high-pitched whine of steel wheels on rail. It is a varied, busy commotion, wrestled and brought under control.

Up ahead switchmen are signaling with lucid, arcing sweeps of their lanterns: a mystifying light show. An engine trundles down the lead from the north, headlamp illuminating tracks that stretch past infinity, like the arteries of some giant circulatory system. Behind, the yard tower hovers in the sky, a frail sentinel watching over an ocean of boxcars. The third-trick man, wrapped around a smoke and a cup of coffee, relays messages below. To the left stands empties waiting to reenter the cross-country flow.

THE HUMPMASTER WATCHES the nightly parade of freight cars cascading over the retarders at the Southern Pacific's sprawling Taylor Yard in the summer of 1953. Originally completed in 1925 and modified twenty-four years later, this facility at one time oversaw the classification of 2,900 freight cars daily. In 1996, with the completion of the UP/SP merger, the site was deemed redundant and now serves as a MetroLink engine terminal for the Los Angeles commute pool.
Richard Steinheimer

Beyond the yard proper lie the Pajaro and upper Salinas valleys, thousands of acres planted in celery, beets, and lettuce. Woody Guthrie riding the top of a fruit block comes to mind, as does Cesar Chávez and the plight of the farmworkers. The shadowy forms of dilapidated packing sheds crouch nearby, and the air is filled with the rich aromas of this busy nexus of agricultural production.

As ballast crunches beneath our boots, I reflect on the places these freight cars might go and the routes they would take—not unlike our own human wanderings: an endless circular pattern of recurring destinations and departures.

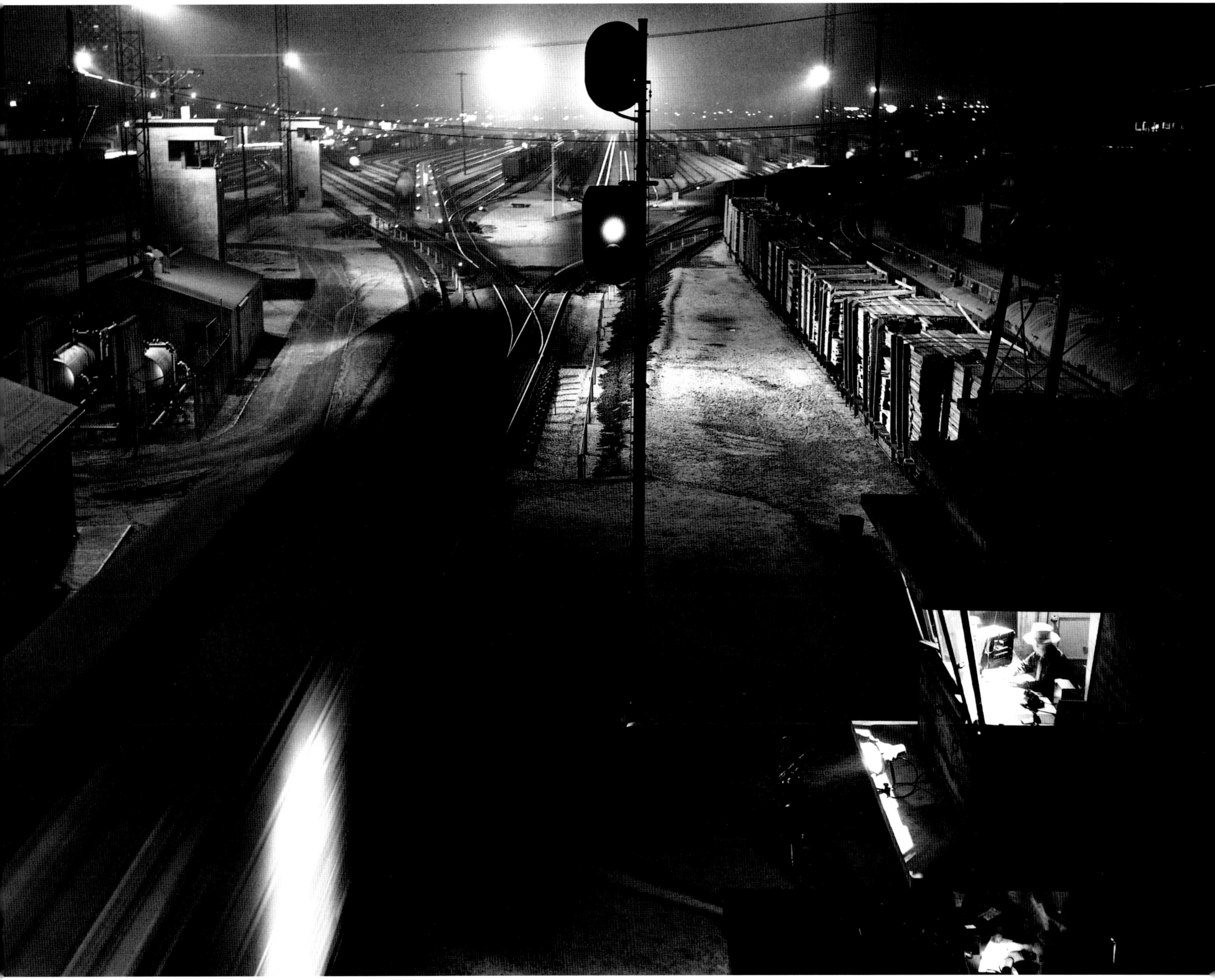

THE COMMERCIAL studio of Hedrich-Blessing, based in Chicago, made dramatic industrial photographs of the rail environment while employed by the Illinois Central Railroad between 1945 and 1970.

Working in conjunction with the IC's in-house PR firm, the Caples Company, Robert Herr and Ken Hedrich did carefully orchestrated publicity photos, relying mainly on a large format 8 x 10" Deardorf camera for all location photography.

The Illinois Central, more so than most of its competitors, took an active interest in visually documenting its many construction projects, types of motive power, architecture, trackage, and workers. A cache of the H-B photographic archive was recently rediscovered in the attic of IC's Champaign, Illinois, depot. It, along with other corporate records, was rescued from the refuse pile by the Illinois Central Historical Society.

In a fine example of H-B's industrial imagery, a Trailer-Train autorack loaded with Dodge Monacos and Buick Le Sabres is shuttled around Markham Yard in Chicago, 1964.
Hedrich-Blessing: R. Herr
ICHS collection

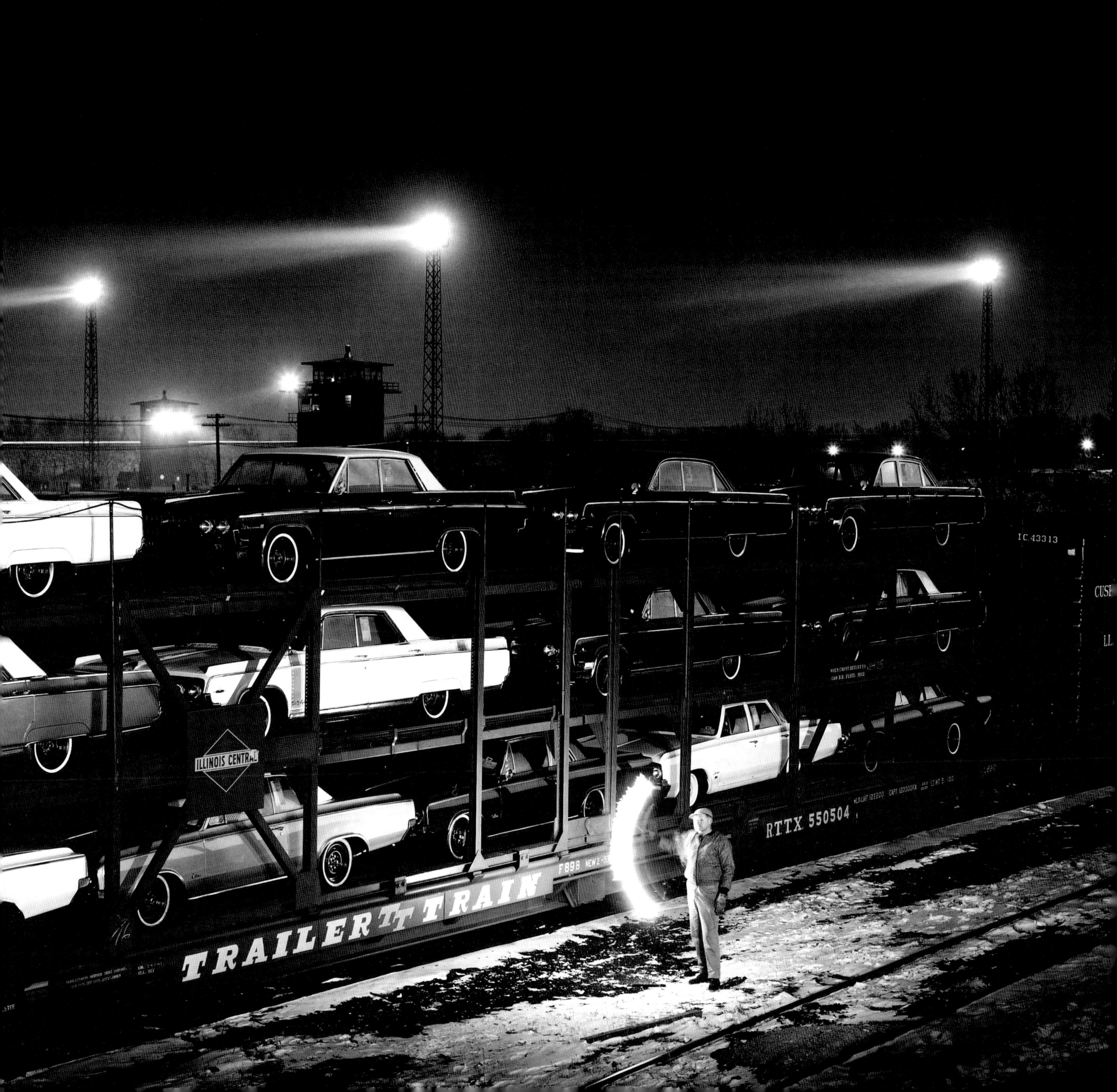

IC 43313
ILLINOIS CENTRAL
TRAILER TT TRAIN
RTTX 550504

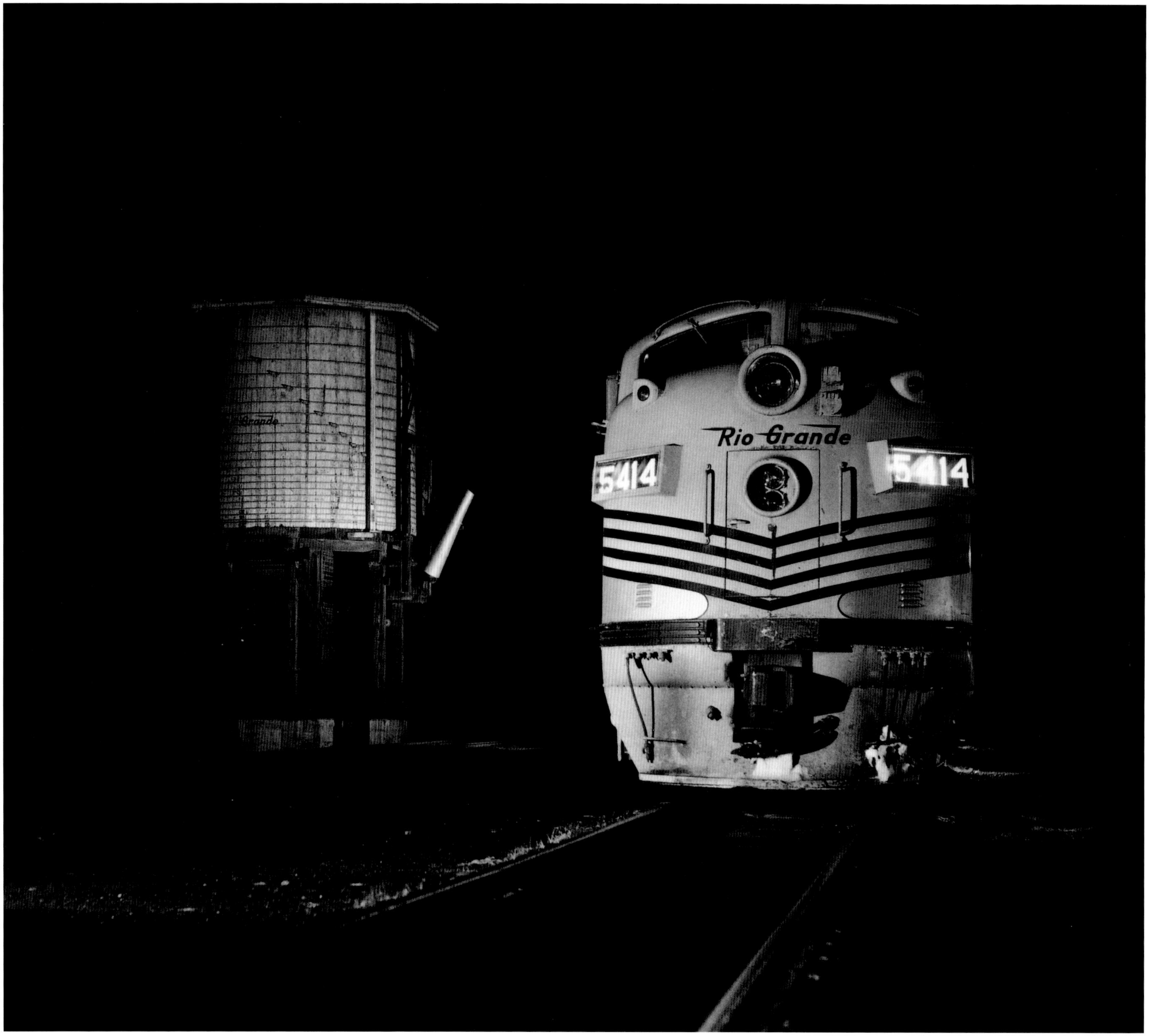
Rio Grande
5414
5414

IN A SCENE DEPICTING an encroaching diesel presence beside an architectural remnant of the steam era, D&RGW FT (for "freight") #5414 sits idling near the aging water tank at Alamosa, New Mexico, in 1959. Jim Shaughnessy, once described by Lucius Beebe as "a photographer skilled in the technique of night lighting and the massive effects of black and white," captures the realities of inevitable change with his Rollei flash gun, 4 x 5" Speed Graphic, and assorted flashbulbs.

Alamosa, once considered the geographic heart of the Rio Grande narrow-gauge, was platted in 1878 and evolved from early Hispanic agricultural communities. Deemed a logical terminus point for rails that would eventually extend to Creede, Santa Fe, Durango, and Farmington, it handled trains hauling silver ore, timber, and petroleum: the riches of the Rocky Mountain Empire. From its earliest days, Alamosa also served as an important staging area for mining camp supplies, as well as boasting a roundhouse, locomotive shop, and car repair facility. Later it became one of the few places where vestiges of D&RGW founder General Palmer's dual gauge vision could still be seen intact, the slim rails lasting well into the late 1960s.

Tomorrow, at the other end of the yard, in seeming defiance of age and history, 2-8-2 K-37 class Mikados will whistle off into the twilight of their lives on a westbound run to Durango, battling the stratospheric elevations of Cumbres Pass. The F and its standard gauge brethren—in a far more modern, albeit somber, display of tractive effort and aesthetics—will muscle their time freight to Denver and points north.
Jim Shaughnessy

following pages:

CONDUCTOR S. M. SURRATT picks up waybills and running orders for time freight #209, due out of Winston Yard at 12:01 A.M. on the Winston-Salem Southbound Railway, Winston-Salem, North Carolina, 1955.
Philip Hastings / CSRM

BOSTON & MAINE GP9s prepare to pick up train MB-6 at the throat of Mechanicville Yards, 1950s.
Jim Shaughnessy

LOMPOC LOCAL switches cars at Surf, California, 1983.
John Roskoski

SPENCER YARD looking down into the classification bowl from the tower, Linwood, North Carolina, 1982.
William D. Middleton

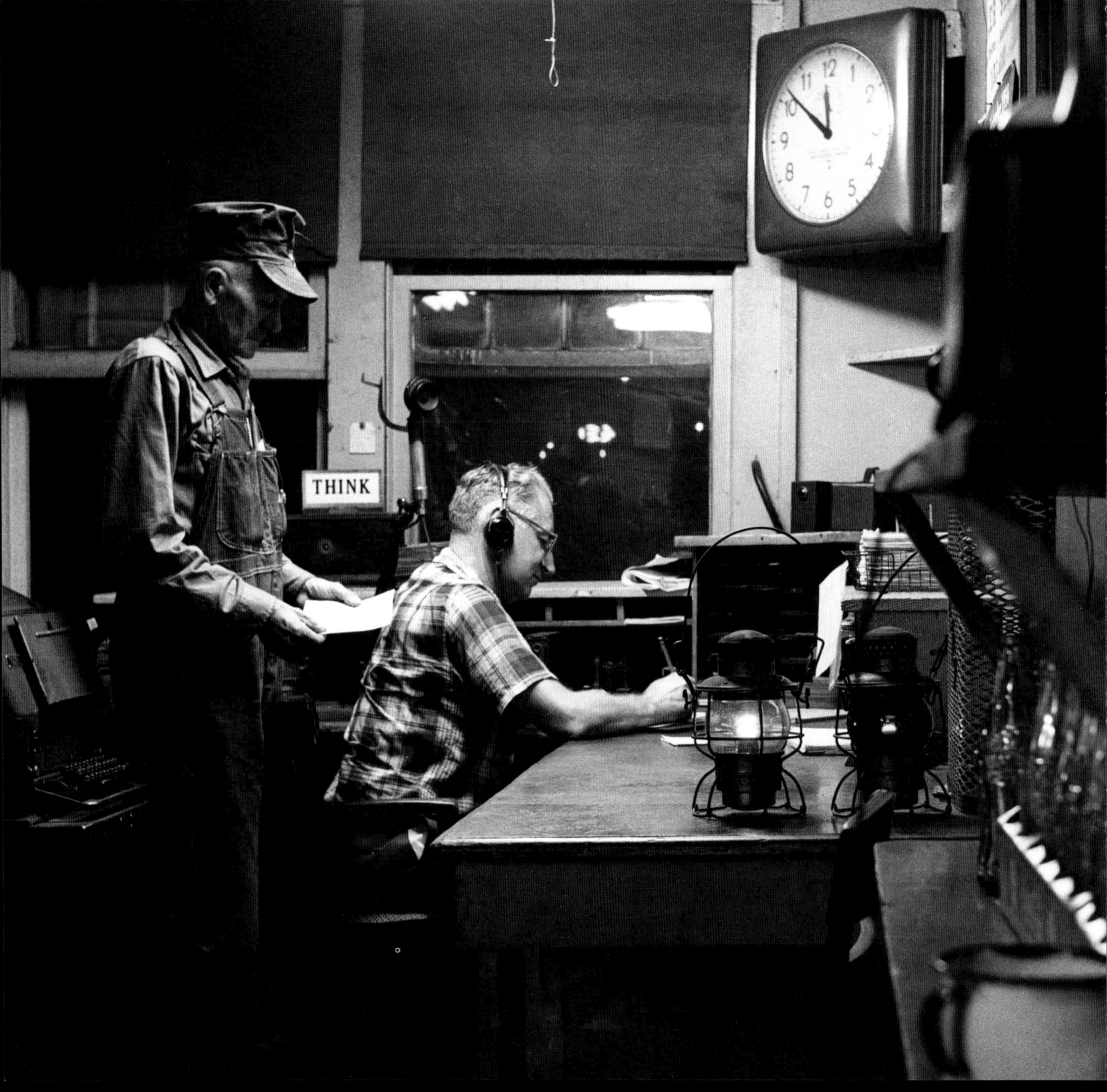
THINK

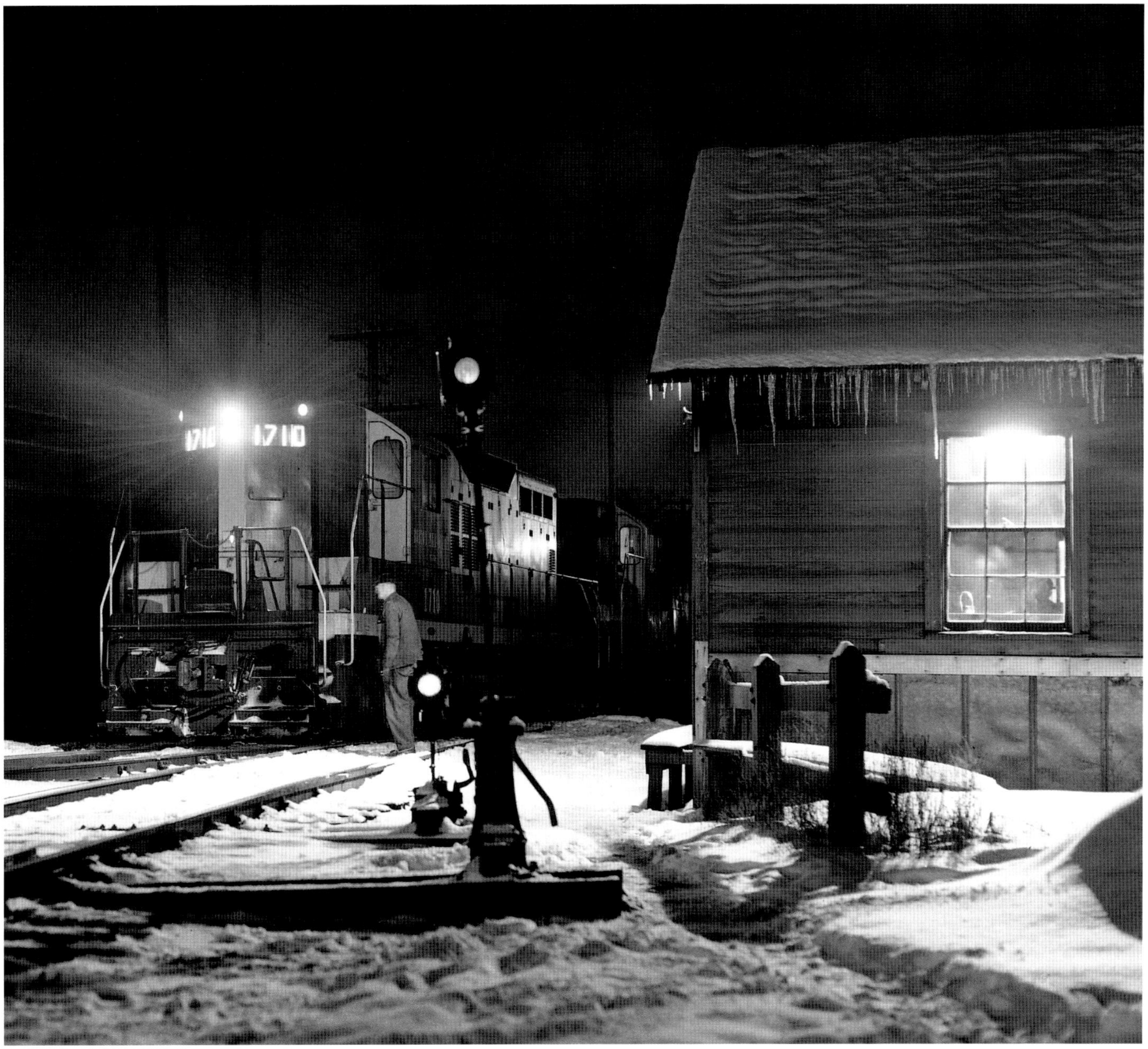
1710
1710

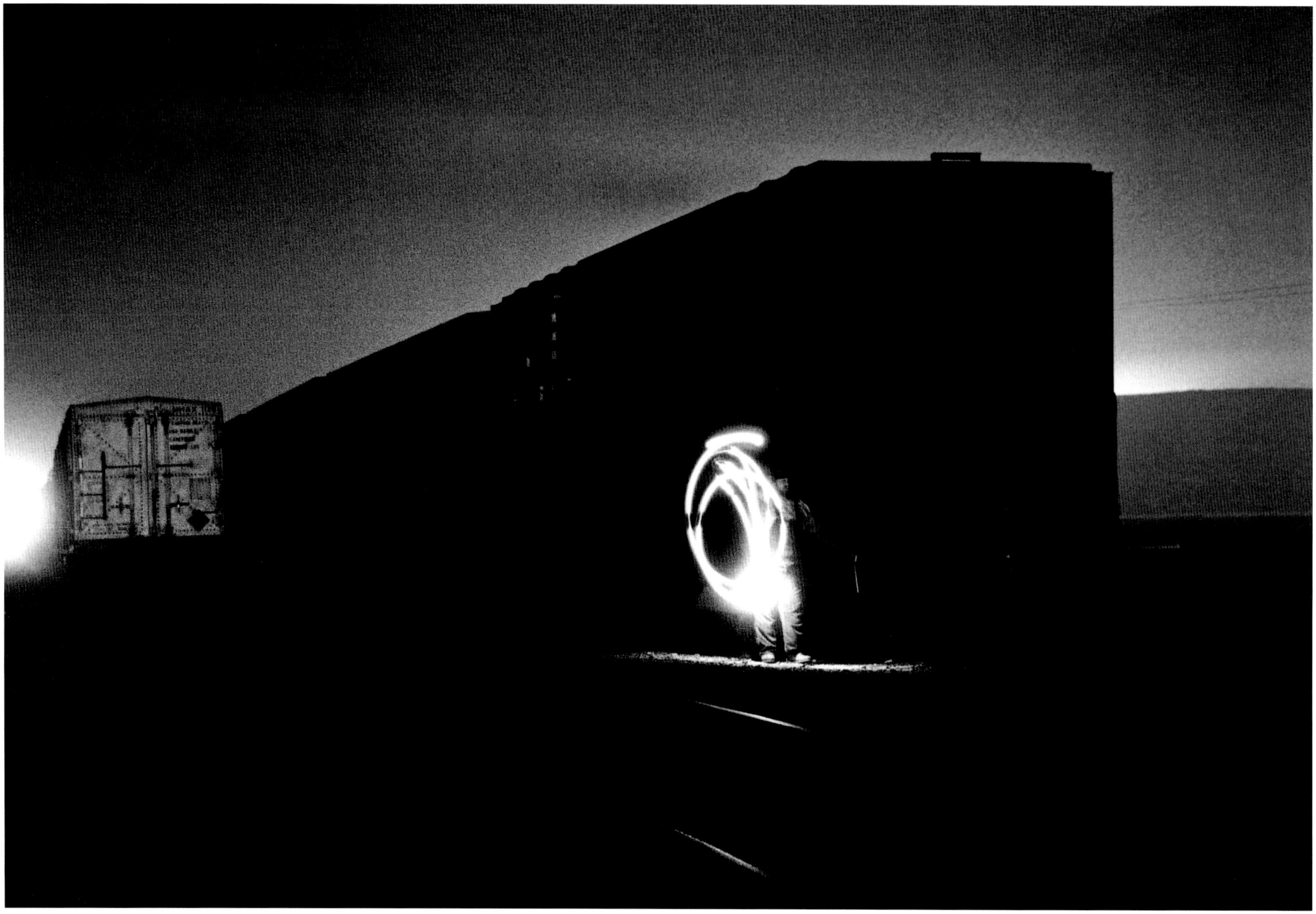

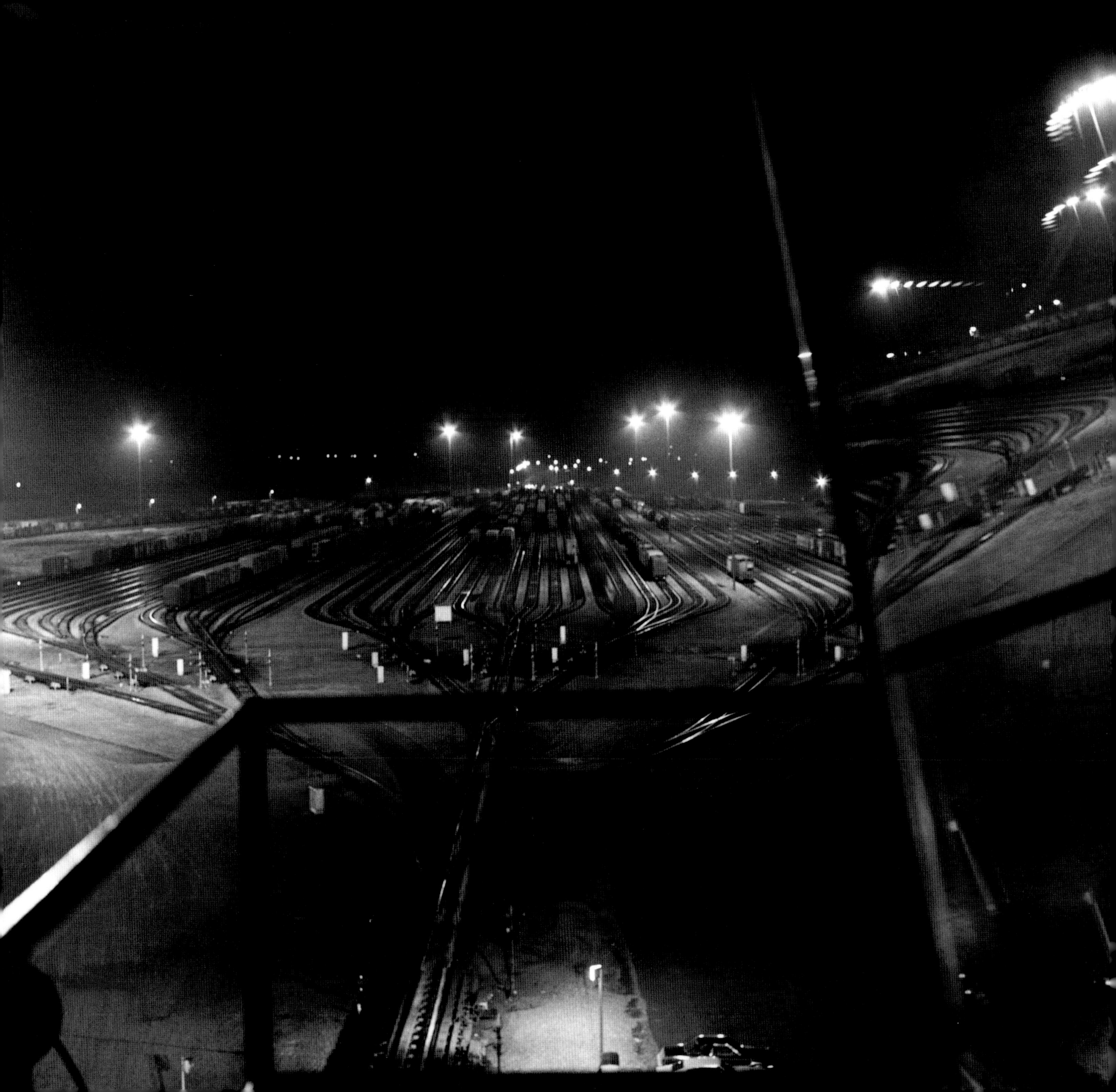

IN THE LAND OF Saroyan and Steinbeck, a chilled switchman on the Tidewater Southern gathers a cut of cars amid the gloom of an all-encompassing Central Valley tule fog. As a former interurban line running between Stockton and Turlock, California, the TS once sported Jewett parlor cars and steeple-cabs. Now, under the control of the Union Pacific and powered by diesel instead of electric traction, it continues as an important feeder line for canning and packing plants adjacent to its high iron.
Richard Steinheimer

far right:

A REEFER-LADEN Santa Fe hotshot highballs out of Fresno's vast Calwa Yard, creating an ethereal time-exposure in 1972. Produce grown in this fertile area accounts for a staggering 25 percent of America's table food. The loop at Tehachapi and the vacant distances of the Mojave desert beyond Barstow await this night train.
Thomas L. Taylor

overleaf:

HOSTLERS HAVE just finished lubricating CNR U-2g 4-8-4 #6234 at the roundhouse in Hamilton, Ontario, 1958.
Philip Hastings / CSRM

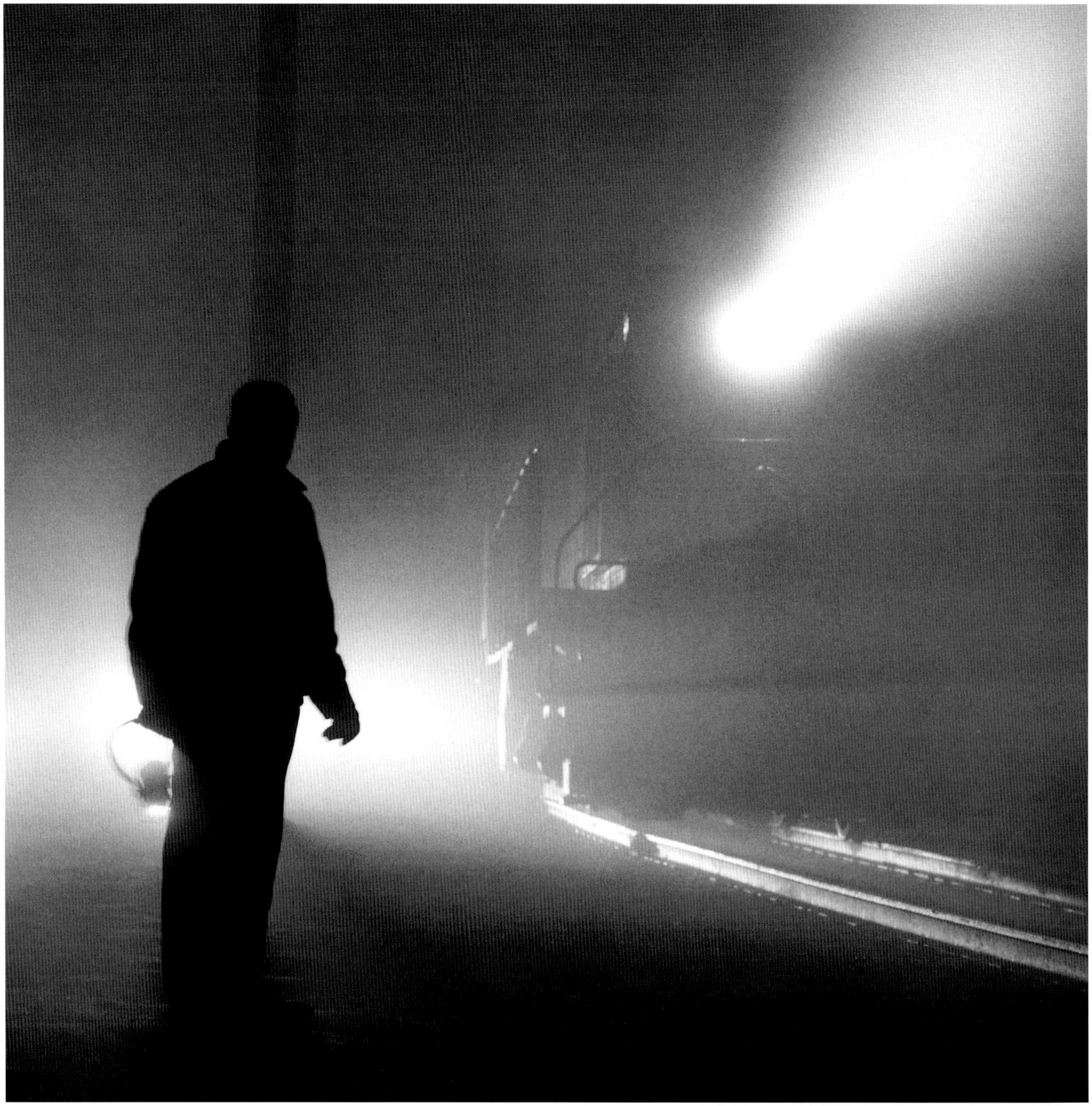

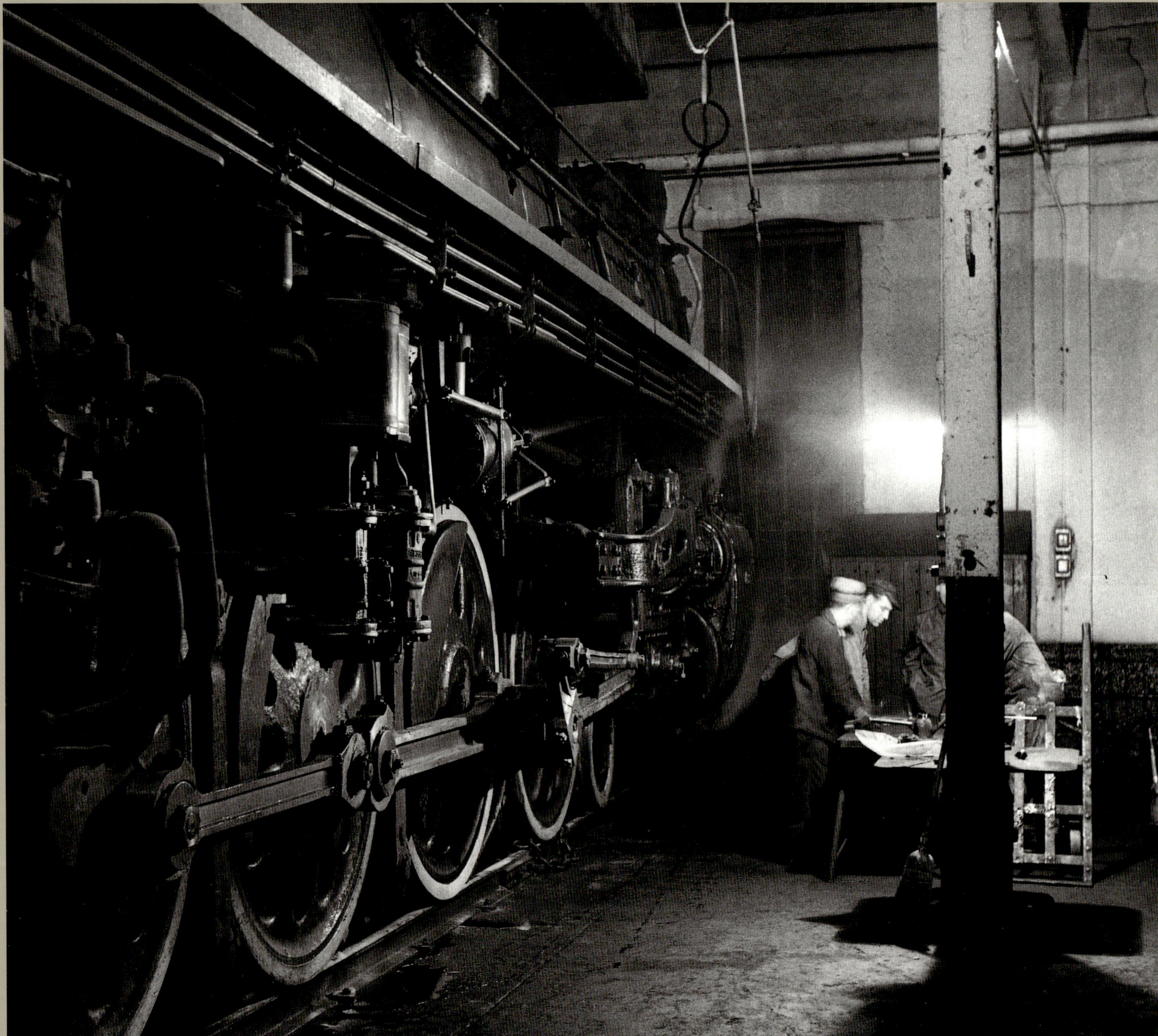

Chapter Five 'ROUND MIDNIGHT

'ROUND MIDNIGHT

The Roundhouse Experience

Soft yellow light pours out of the rear windows of the roundhouse at Bayshore. With expectation and excitement, we creep toward the opening, pressing our faces against the glass. We peer into this microcosm of sight and sound and smell, eavesdropping on engines slumbering away the night, watching a railroad caught between acts, in a state of repose.

Imagine it's 1952. Inside, stout men wearing grease-encrusted overalls, handling machinery and tools made for giants, are lilliputians among the massive locomotives on the house tracks. A lone engine tender keeps watch over the fireboxes of the Consolidations and cab-forwards. As the hours elapse on the Standard clock, he'll periodically check his charges. The butterfly doors yawn open, and, seeing all is well, he continues his rounds.

Against the wall a chalkboard hangs askew, displaying the night's assignments in a scribbled shorthand, the foreman's yellow scrawl discernible to those who already know. Smoke curls above the roofline, ventilators sucking it up into the evening air forming gray exhaust trails that climb toward the starlight. A switch engine pops off a trio of notes, their echoes floating operatically across the adjacent yard. Drivers slip on wet rail. A quiet stillness returns for just a moment, covering the landscape.

A TRIO OF FERROCARRILES NACIONALES de Mexico 2-8-0 steam locomotives stand beneath the "semi open air" enginehouse in Tierra Blanca, Veracruz, in 1962. Consolidation 1563 will soon head up a *directo* fast freight south to Jesus Carranza on the line across the Isthmus of Tehuantepec. The N de M 1500s were ex-Chicago & North Western Z-class power. Mainline steam lasted south of the border until 1966. *Victor Hand*

Out front locomotives wait at the opening of their bays like eager children anxious to embark on another trip. Dark and hulking against the wood and brick doorways, they recall an Otto Kuhler etching filled with dramatic life force. The acrid smell of alamite and lubricants floods the senses. On the turntable, an invading member of a new motive power tribe—the diesel—takes a ride to one of the garden tracks. A fast freight on the cutoff zips by in the distance: #394, the nightly Coast Merchandise.

In the background, hissing injectors and clanging bells, signifying a hostler's move, complete this roundhouse rondo.

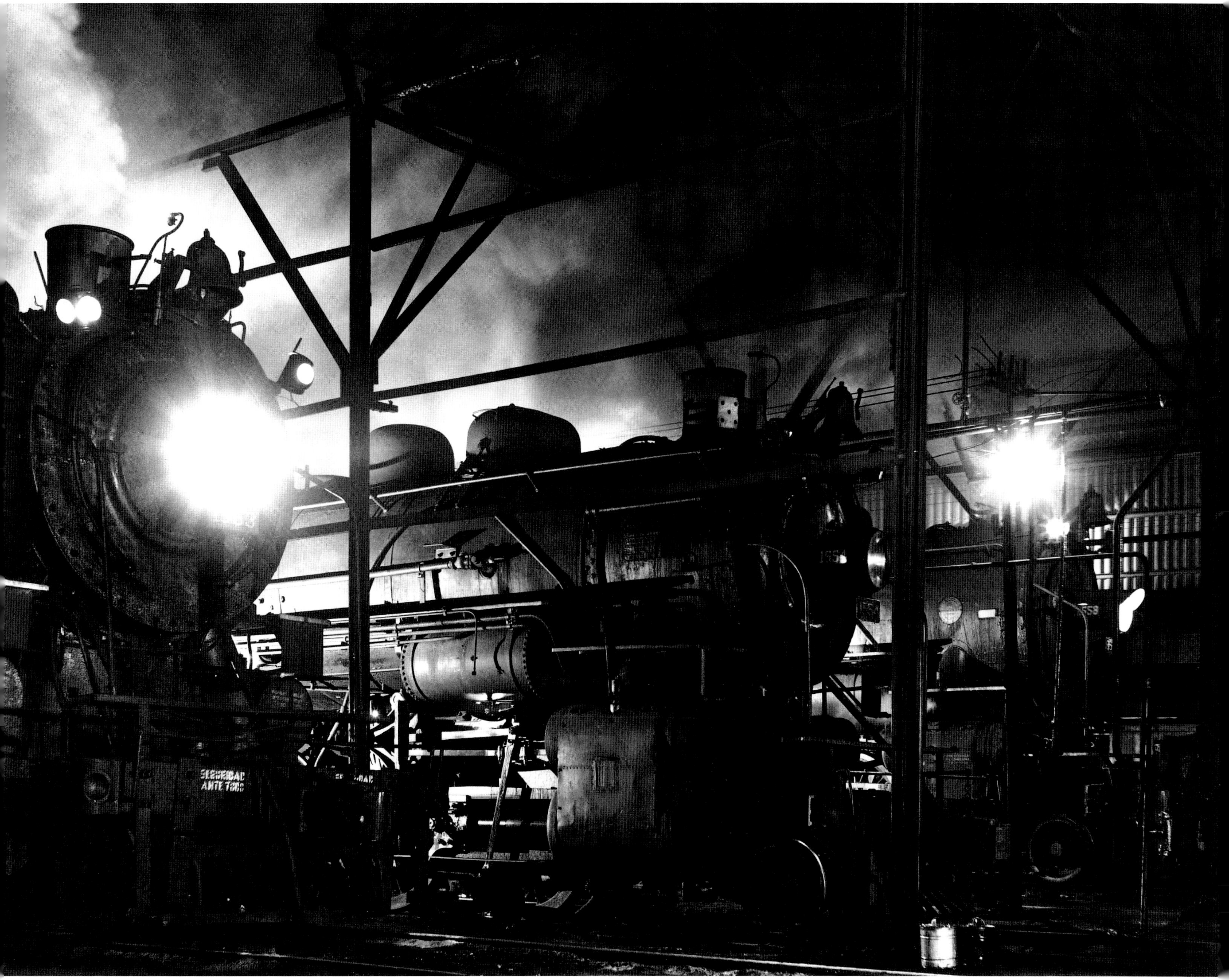

right:

THIS PHOTOGRAPH was taken in 1949 at the zenith of Japan's steam era, when thousands of locomotives of mixed ancestry and lineage—including Porters, Vulcans, Alcos, and Baldwins—plied the rails in the Land of the Rising Sun. A JNR C11-class 2-6-4T is viewed through the panes of the engineer's warming shed at the Okagi roundhouse located on the Tokaido line, the major rail artery for the nation.
Katsusaburo Nishio

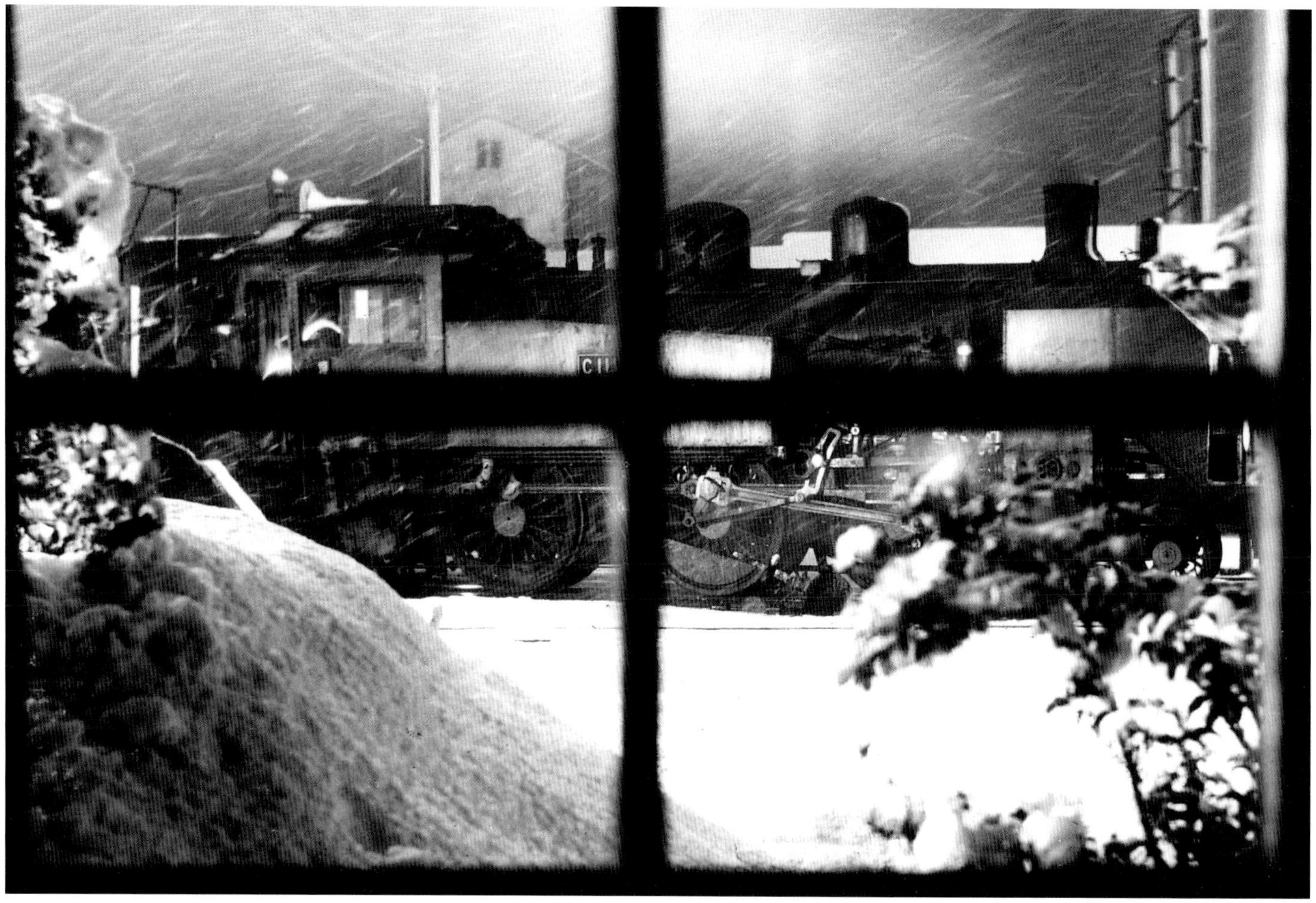

below:

FRENCH ACCENTS blend with the language of steam as workers ready CNR #6179 for a run on the Maritime Express, Rivière du Loup, Quebec, 1953.
Philip Hastings / CSRM

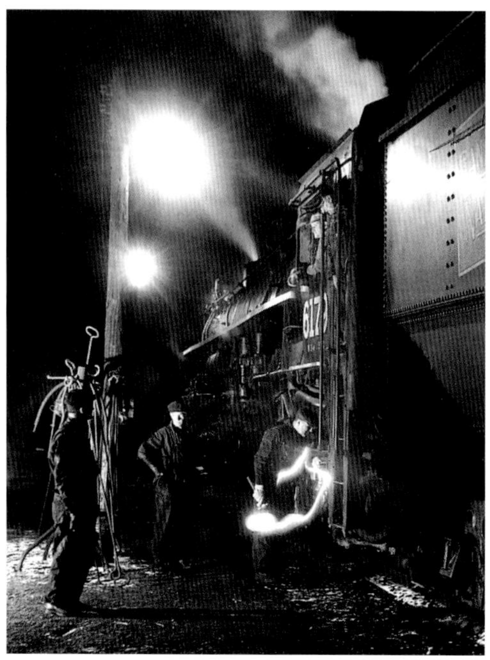

opposite:

FAMILY TIES: a Seaboard Coast Line Geep and Louisville & Nashville FP7 idle away the night at the Tilford Yard roundhouse—a facility used jointly by the two roads—in Atlanta, Georgia, 1969.
Jim Boyd

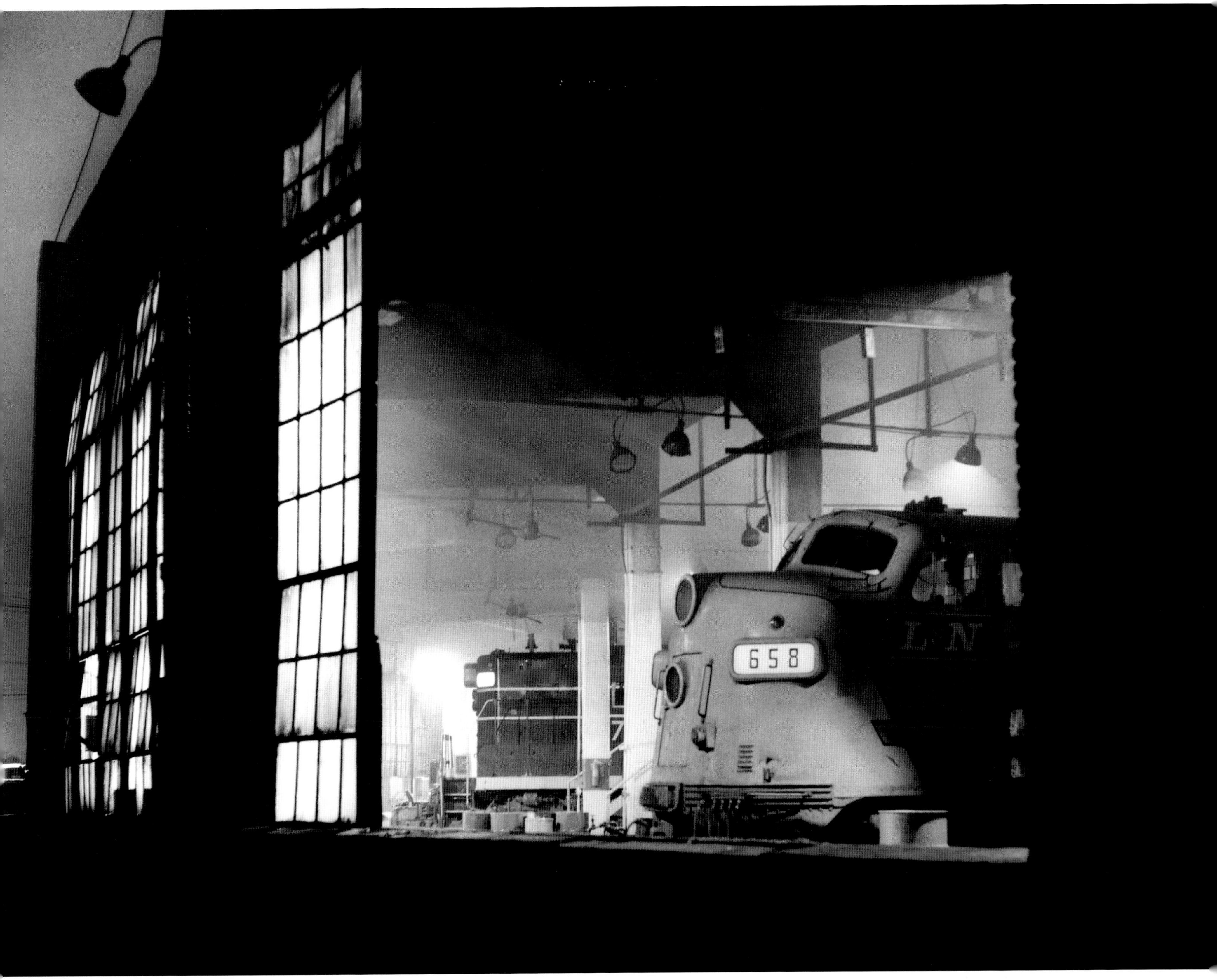
658

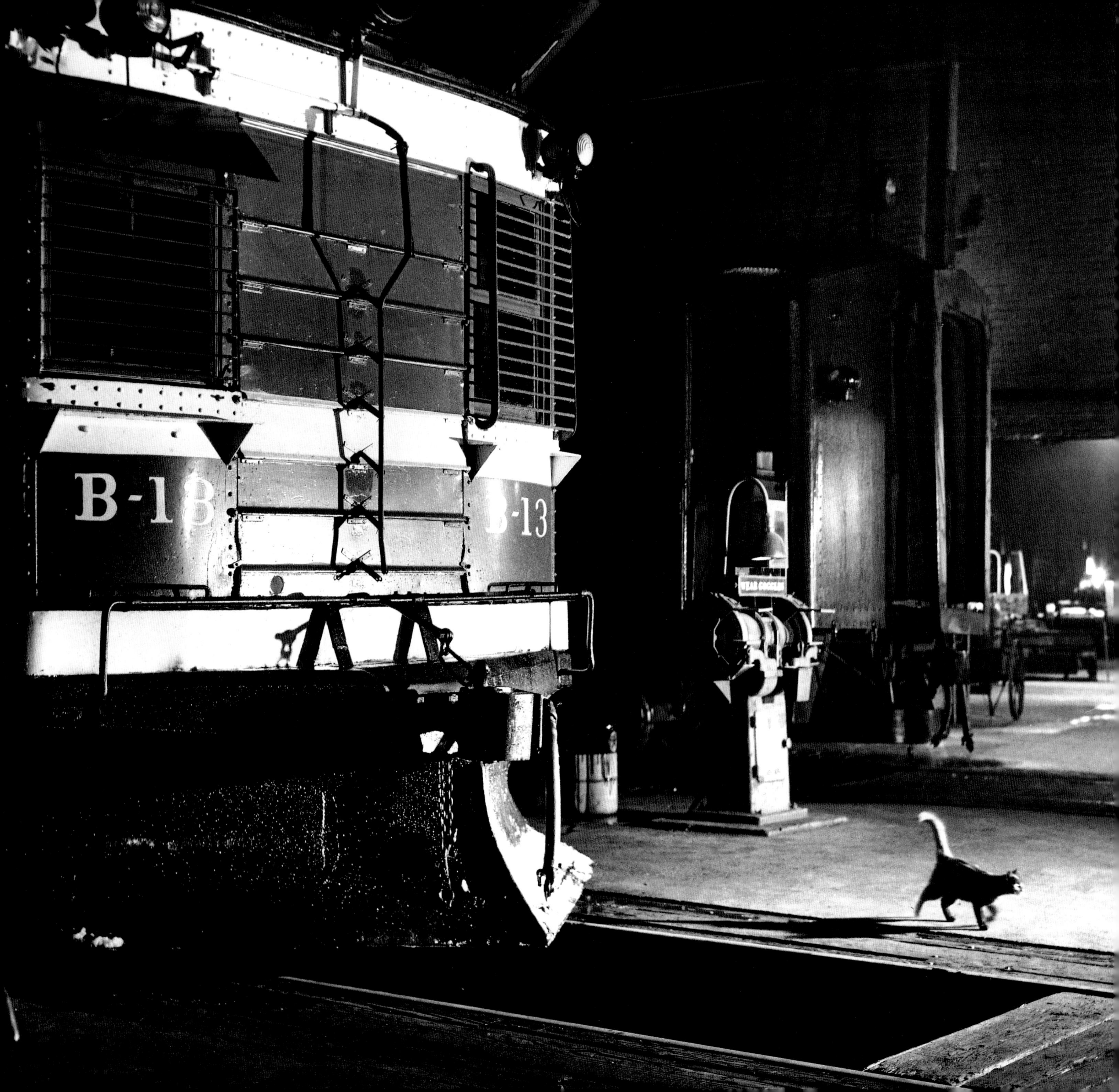
B-13
B-13

EVEN A LARGE roundhouse belonging to a major transcontinental railroad can be a quiet place at midnight, virtually devoid of human activity save for a hostler or watchman. This was especially true on smaller branchlines in rural America where heavy engine repair and servicing, normally requiring a phalanx of engine wipers, machinists, and other roundhouse laborers, wasn't necessarily a 24 7 affair. The house at Jamestown, North Dakota, is just such a place. The only "worker" on duty tonight prowls for four-legged interlopers as it strolls past Northern Pacific B-13, a 1920s-vintage Doodlebug, tucked away from a brisk November snowstorm raging outside. On the Dakota plains, circa 1957, the state regulatory requirements of the "Century Code" mandated that public conveyance be provided on all rail lines throughout the state—oftentimes a money-losing proposition for the common carriers.

In a typical scenario employed by many granger lines, the railroad pressed the cost-effective gas-electrics, with their three-man crews, into operation. It was one way to meet transportation needs in small communities where the ridership was sparse but passenger, mail, and express service essential. The last "puddle-jumper" ran to Wilton, North Dakota, on a summer's eve in 1961. *Richard Steinheimer*

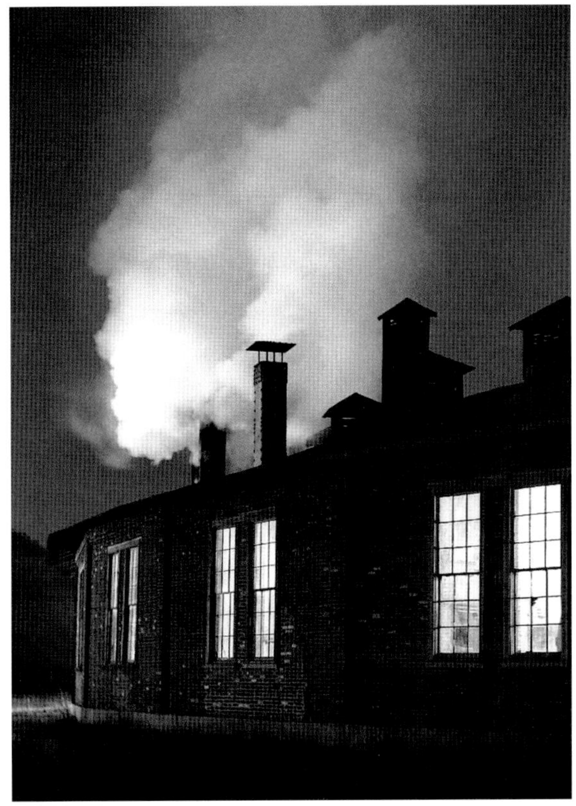

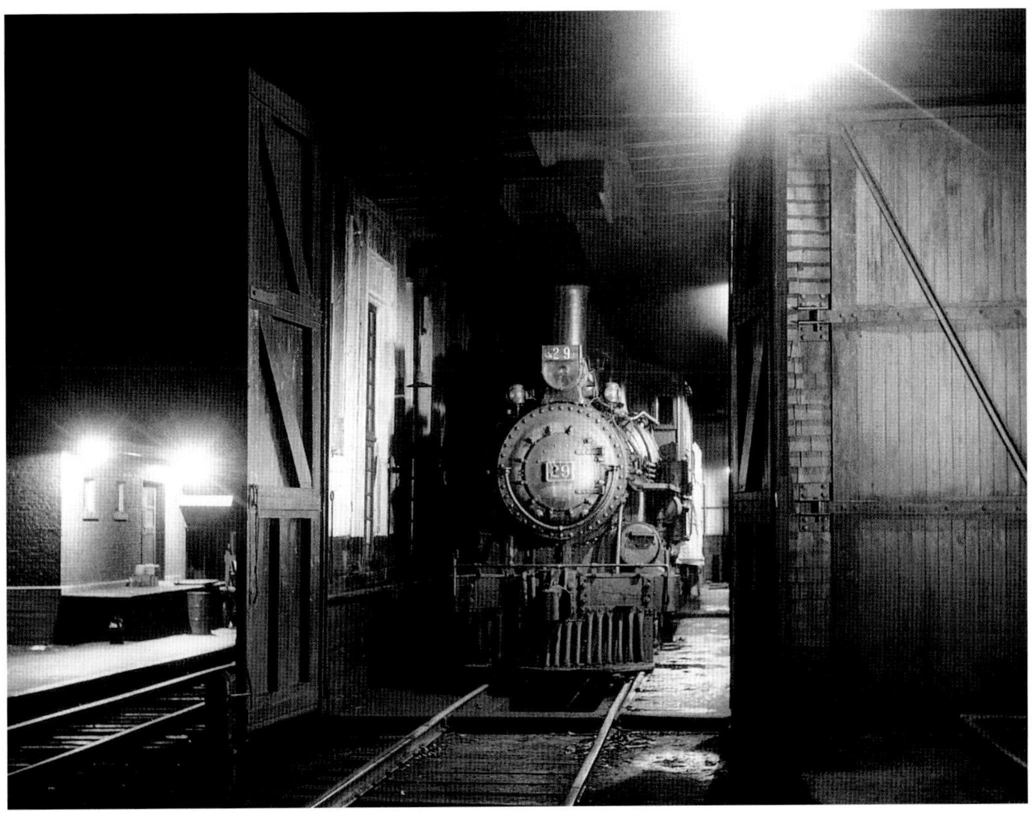

EAST BROAD TOP Roundhouse, Orbisonia, Pennsylvania, 1955. *Philip Hastings / CSRM*

left:

CANADIAN PACIFIC 4-4-0 #29 sits in her stall at Chipman, New Brunswick, 1953. *Philip Hastings / CSRM*

following pages:

480-CLASS MIKADOS, Chama, New Mexico, 1965. *Victor Hand*

ENGINE TENDER Ed Kettle watches over his narrow-gauge charges in Durango, Colorado, 1961. *Richard Steinheimer*

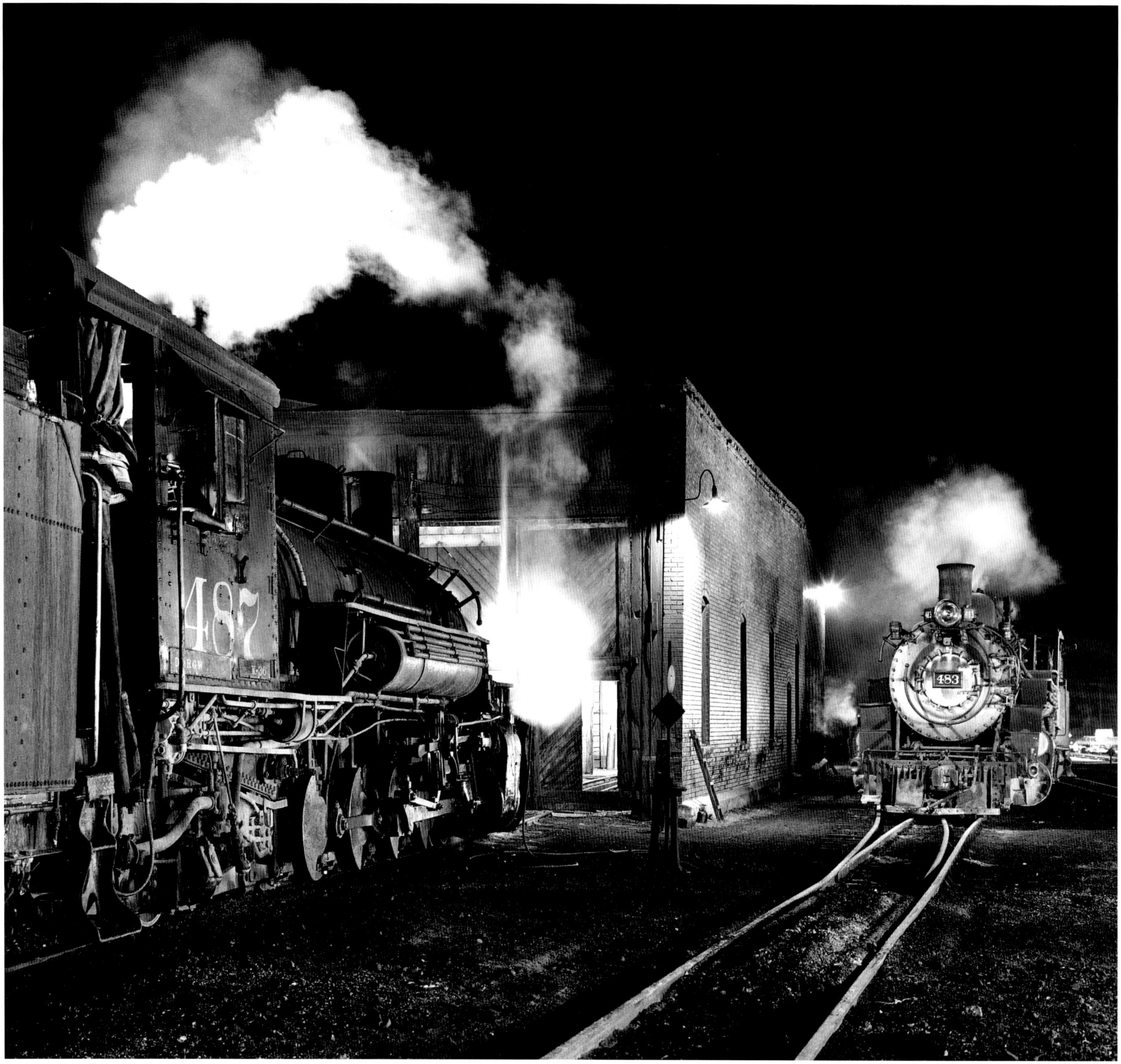
487
483

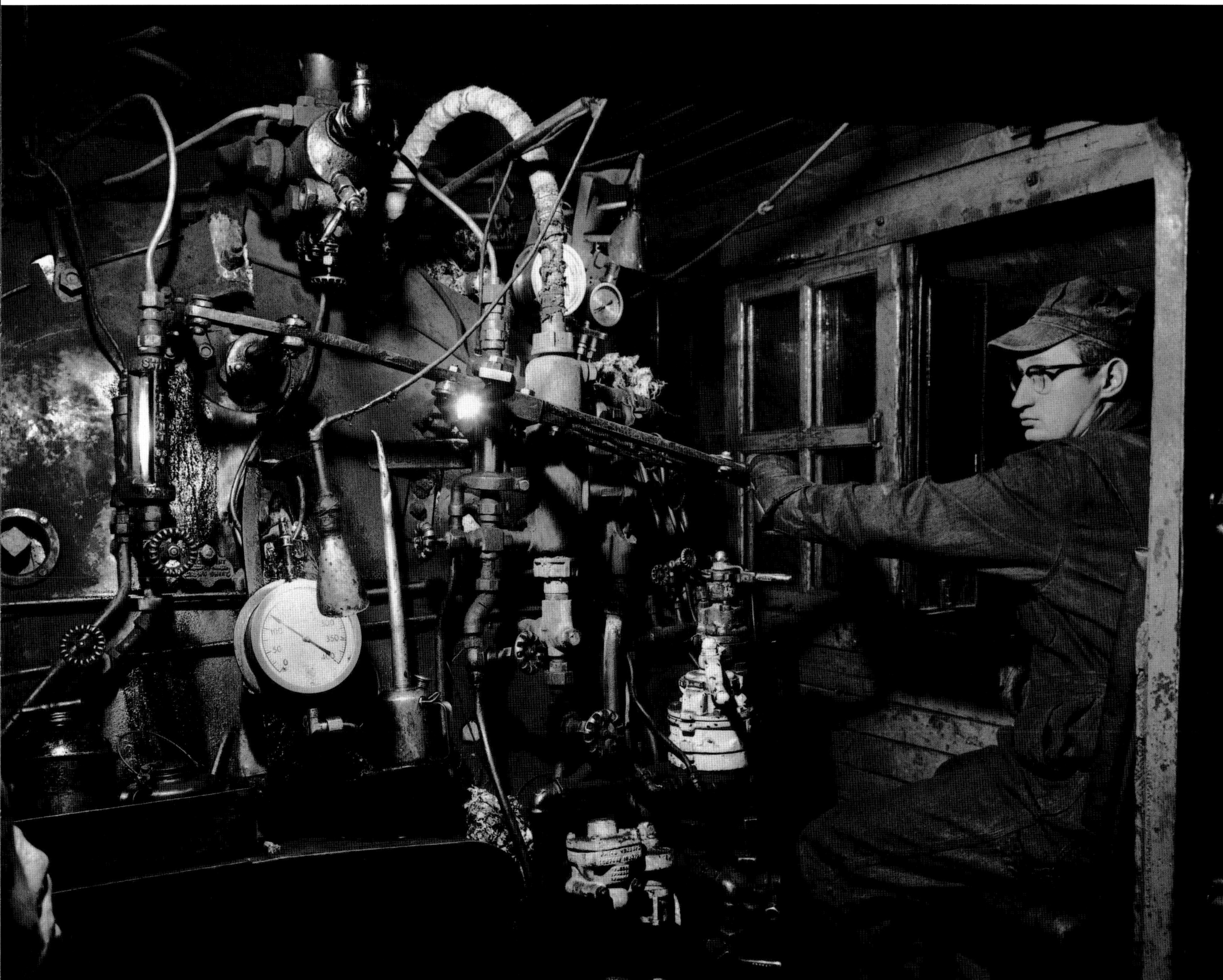

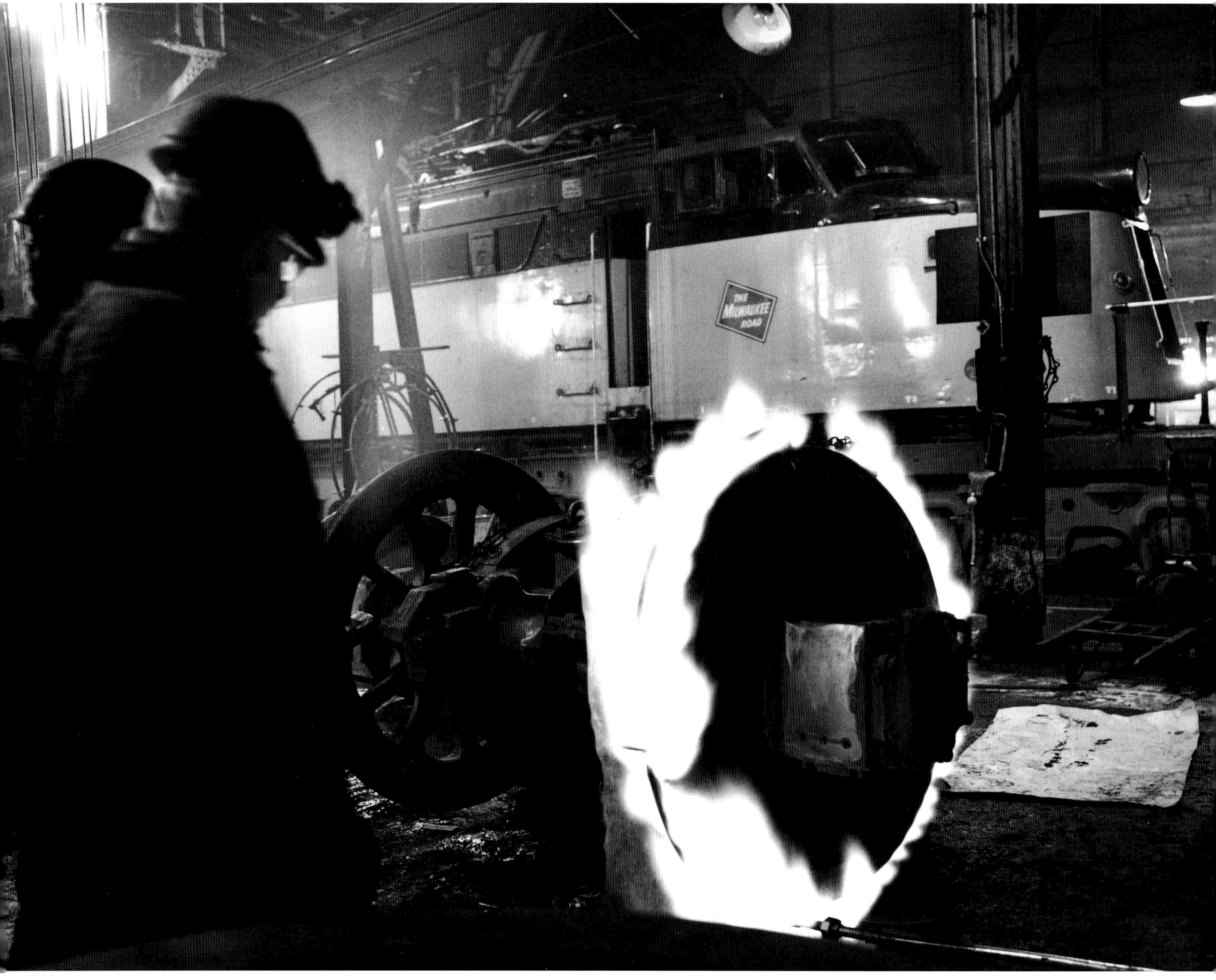
THE
MILWAUKEE
ROAD

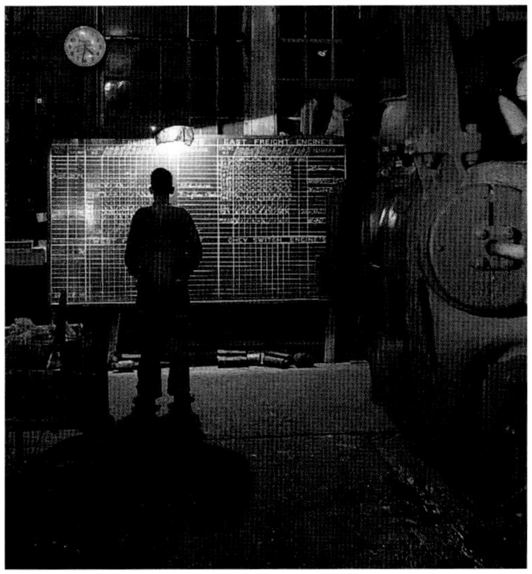

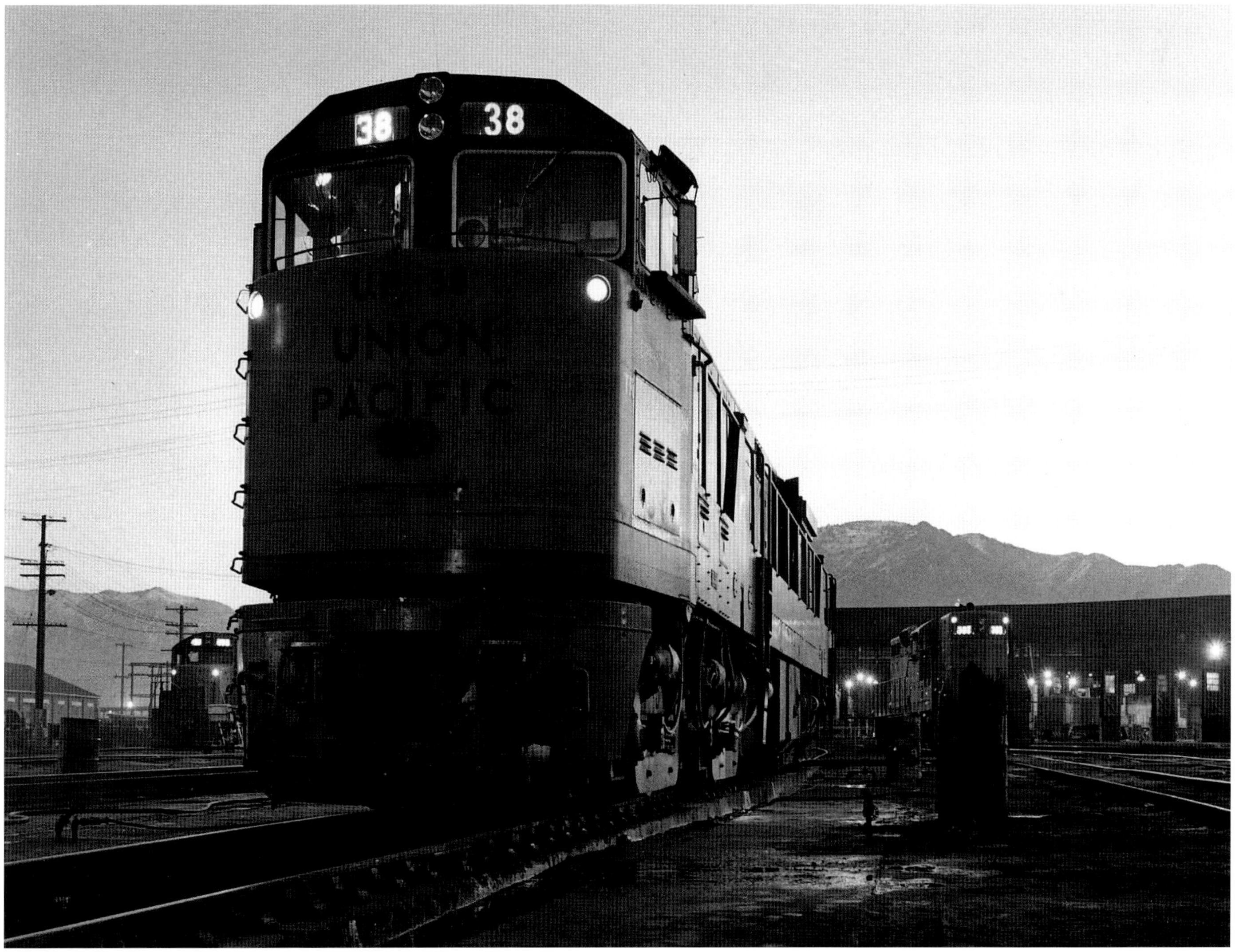

ALL TYPES OF motive power can be found in the roundhouse. At 8 P.M. on a brisk January night in Deer Lodge, Montana, two Milwaukee Road workers sweat a new tire into place on a Little Joe wheel set. It's 1974, and in five months salvage operations will begin as the electrification ends. Most of the Joes will go west to Seattle or Chehalis, Washington, to meet their maker—their demise under the scrapper's torch, a sad certainty of fortune.
Richard Steinheimer

above:

A MECHANIC CHECKS the engine availability board, Cheyenne, Wyoming, 1957.
Philip Hastings / CSRM

right:

UNION PACIFIC U50, Ogden, Utah, 1972.
Richard Steinheimer

overleaf:

UNION PACIFIC Park City Local, Morgan, Utah, 1958.
Richard Steinheimer

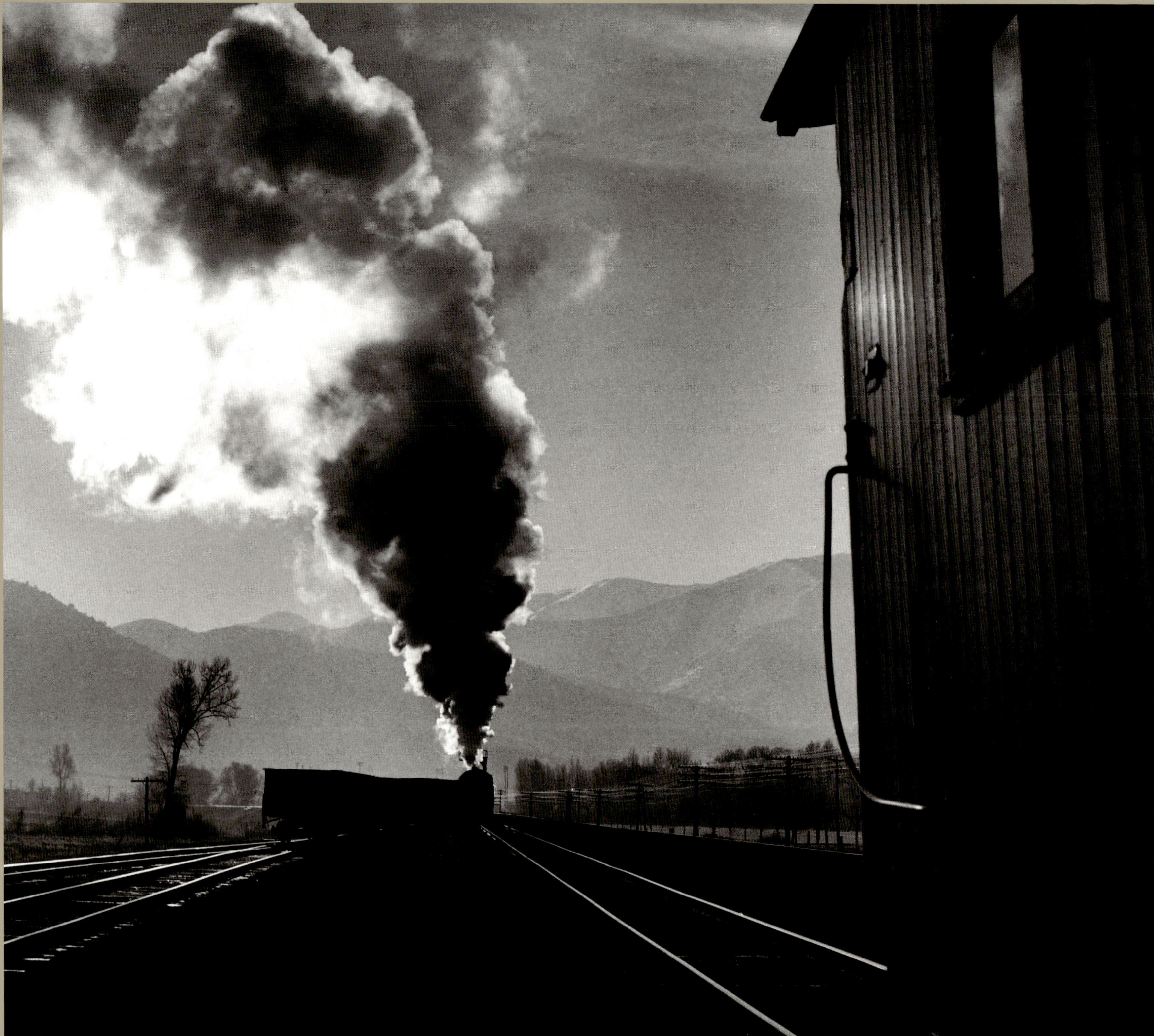

Chapter Six SOFTLY AS A MORNIN' SUNRISE

Daybreak on the Railroad

It's November, and dawn arrives as a pinkish tint. Ed and I scramble from our sleeping bags, shaking the cold stiffness from our bodies, and watch the first sunlight fire the snow-capped tops of the eastern Sierra. Mt. Whitney towers above Lone Pine Station, a majestic granite sculpture carved by tectonics and erosion. To the east, the Panamint and Inyo mountains lie shrouded in cool blue shadows. The temperature is touching the teens. The smell of creosote and sage permeates the air. We think of hot coffee and the solace of open spaces; we think to ourselves there is no finer place to witness the daybreak on this railroad earth.

Sharp chiaroscuros of bright winter light delineate and outline the yard and the eight boxcars scattered in front of the Southern Pacific depot. A solitary GP9 idles on the ready track, with four big hopper cars and a caboose tied to its back. Soon the crew for the Lone Pine Local pulls up in a battered Plymouth and begins to assemble the train, the switching moves taking on a balletic quality. By year's end no train will travel to this part of the line; twelve months later the tracks will be torn from the land, another favorite outpost in the annals of western railroading doomed to oblivion. Trains will still deliver loads of potash out of Searles

EARLY MORNING SUNLIGHT, combined with the still coolness of a Cheyenne, Wyoming, dawn creates a montage of steam, man, and machine. The Union Pacific's two venerable steam locomotives—the 4-8-4 #8444 and the Challenger #3985—are being readied for a trip to Railfair '81 and the opening festivities of the California State Railroad Museum. *Pat Barry*

from the Trona Railway to Mojave. But the north end of the Jawbone and its historic ties to the Carson and Colorado narrow gauge, which last saw trains ply its slim rails in 1960, will further recede from our memories with these latest rounds of abandonment. Time and the elements will eventually erase what we can remember.

But for now, the sun continues its ascent as we drain our cups. Gloves come off as we fumble with cameras and lenses. The sunrise plays itself out as we take our last photographs. The salty conductor highballs the Local out of town, his caboose now a retreating dot on the thin line of desert horizon.

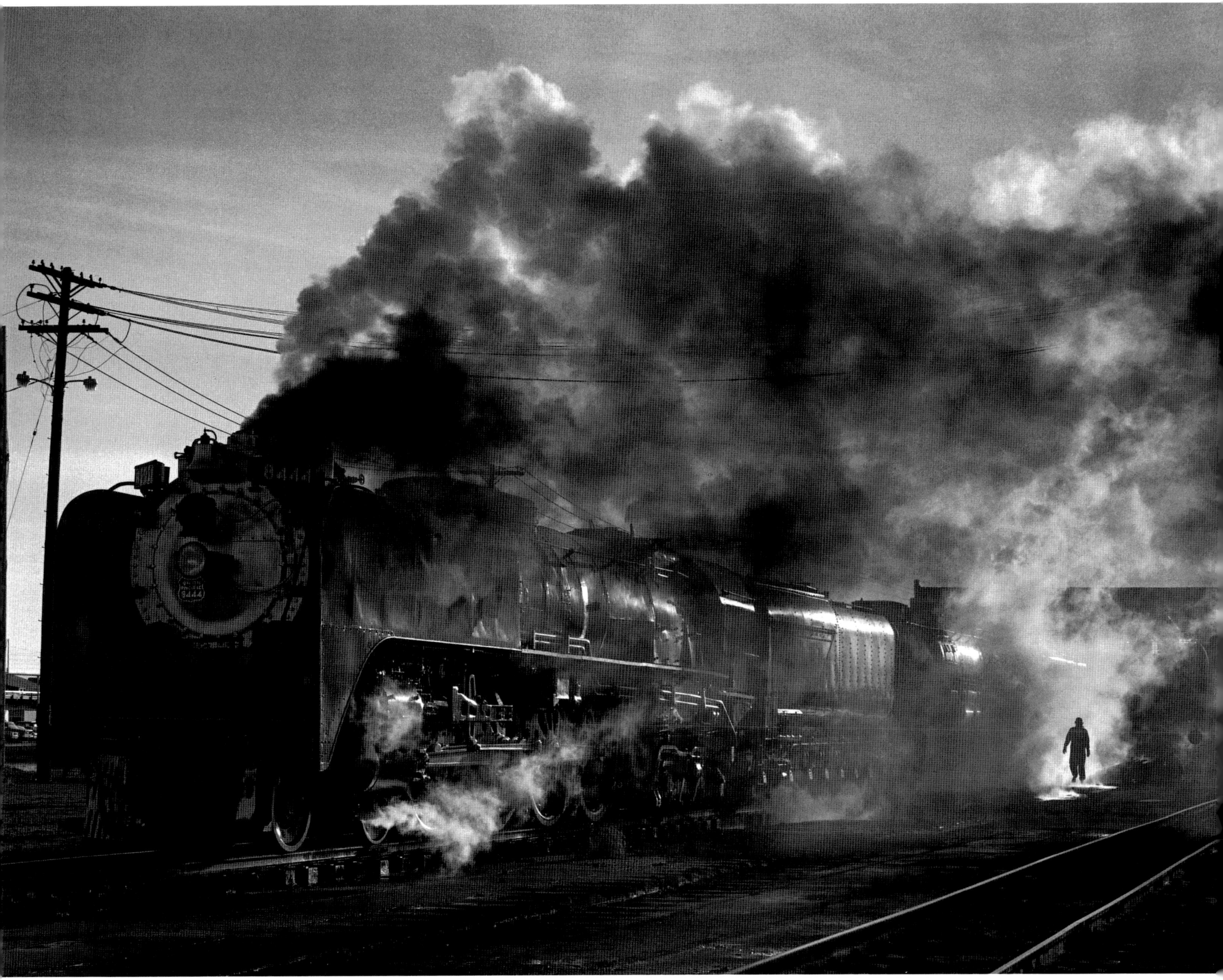

FIELD NOTES, 1984: Late last winter, while driving by Santa Clara on my way to Northern California, I took a detour to investigate an old haunt—the Espee's Newhall yards. Once there, I climbed out of my car to watch from an access road as a switching crew went about its morning chores. The car spotter conducted the show with switchlist in hand. The yard engine, an aging Alco diesel, prowled the throat, its sputtering stop-start exhaust a noisy punctuation against the dawn. The sun began its ascent along the horizon. I raised the camera to my eye ready to make a few exposures. As I released the shutter, something clicked elsewhere in my mind.

A memory, tucked away like a discarded boxcar on an overlooked siding, suddenly appeared. I was eighteen and wanted to become a railroader—a switchman, in fact. I was fascinated with yards and the people who worked there. The job had a taut muscular nature that seemed very appealing: how often do you command objects the size of small suburban houses?

Learning of my interest, an older friend more wise than I (an ex-railroader with switching experience) decided that a weekend trip to Roseville, site of the Espee's large marshaling yards, was essential to my railroading "education." There, he'd arranged a meeting with an aged acquaintance of his who'd had a long career as a cinder cruncher. At the outset, I suspected underlying motives for this visit. My suspicions proved warranted. Roger greeted us at the door of his home in a wheelchair—both legs severed below the knee, the result of a fall beneath a rolling boxcar.

As the night wore on and the talk grew intimate, I learned of Roger's life, railroad career, and tragic accident. The purpose of bringing me here was now clear and to the point: a switchman's job had its dangers. While Roger's calamity did not rob me of the romance, it certainly reinforced the hazardous realities of working on the high iron. I got religion that night.

For whatever reason, I moved on to other things, never to become a railroader. Perhaps thoughts of Roger lingered. Regardless, I still remained enamored of those men who plied the myriad tracks, beckoning boxcars here and there. And now, on this winter's day, as I watched the crew work the ladder tracks, I felt as though I were seeing what I might have become but for a different chain of circumstances. Like all of us at certain stages in life, I had discarded one dream for another. And like this switchman sorting out his lists, determining the speed, velocity, and direction of his charges, I changed the rail's alignment and sent my life toward other destinations.

right:

AN SW1500 cow-and-calf start the day's switching duties at Clearing Yard on the Belt Railway of Chicago, 1965.
John Gruber

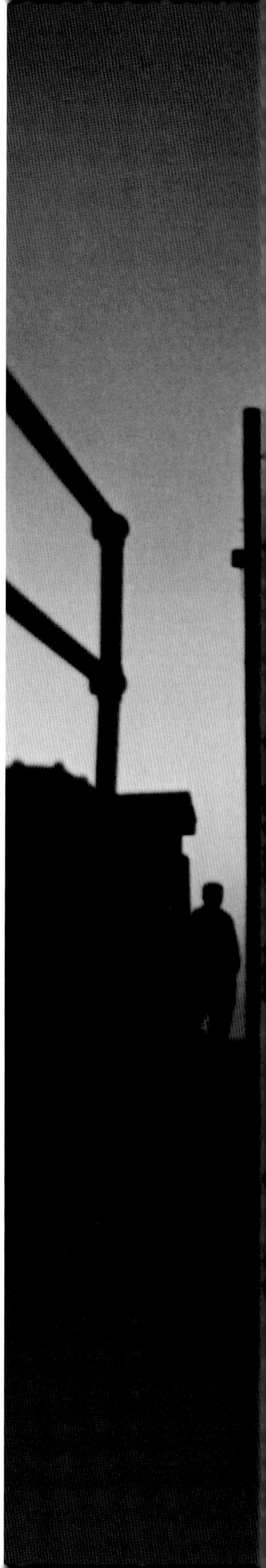

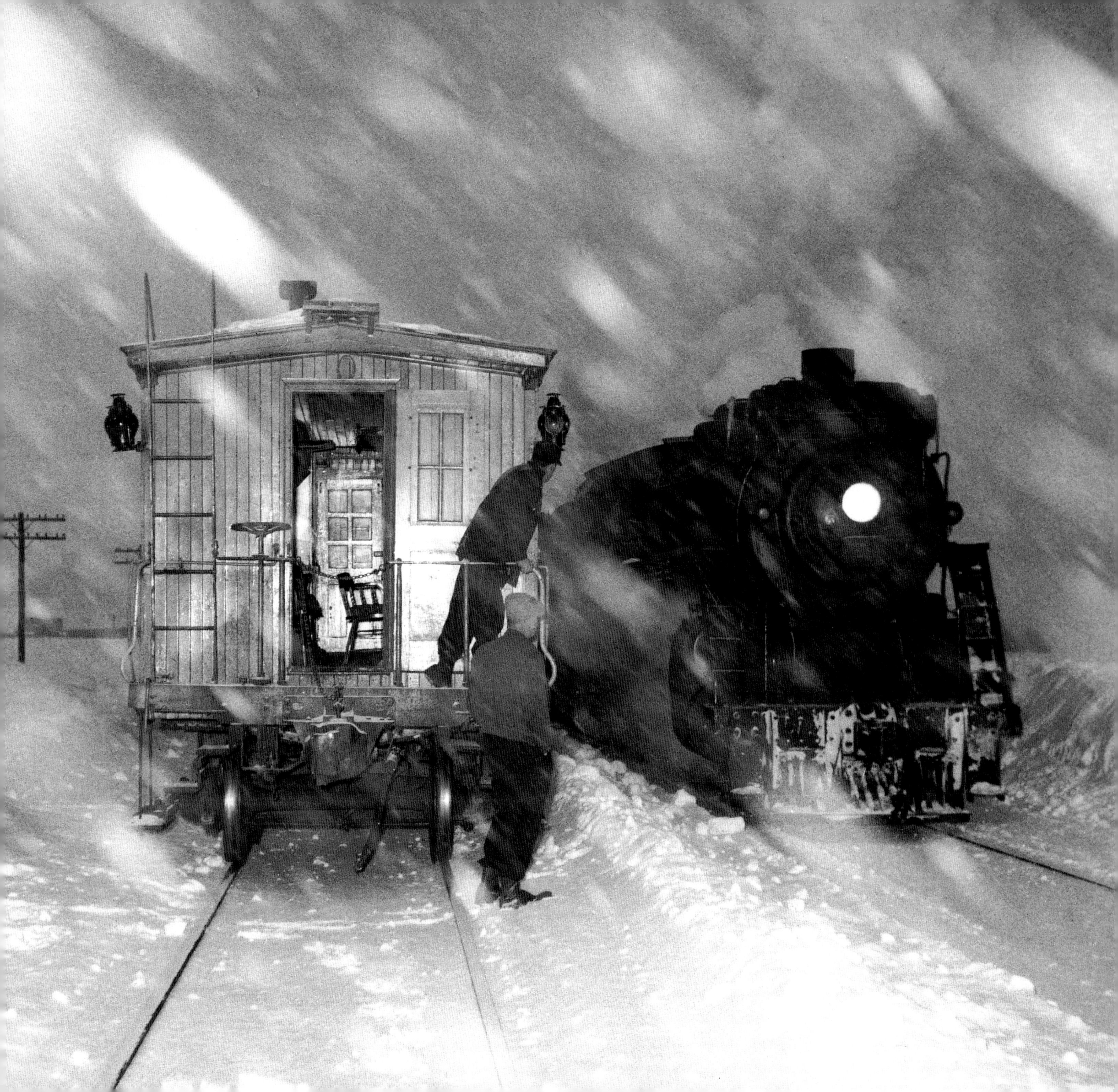

DAWN AND THE SEVERE winter realities of blizzard conditions greet the arrival of two opposing Canadian National freight trains at Green River, New Brunswick, in 1955. On the ground, taking brief leave of their caboose, conductor and rear brakeman survey a westbound extra headed by 4-6-2 #5258 and Mikado #3313. With the mercury hovering below zero, the combination of fill-flash and snowflakes creates a virtual whiteout in the Canadian wilderness.
Philip Hastings / CSRM

right:
MINUTES BEFORE SUNRISE a CNR brakeman returns from flagging protection. The stray light from his lantern bobs and weaves in an interesting combination of time-exposure and flash photography. When a train was stopped on the tracks, item 99 in the book of rules required the rear "brakie"—with flags, torpedoes, and fusees in hand—to walk back at least a quarter mile along the mainline to alert approaching traffic.
Philip Hastings / CSRM

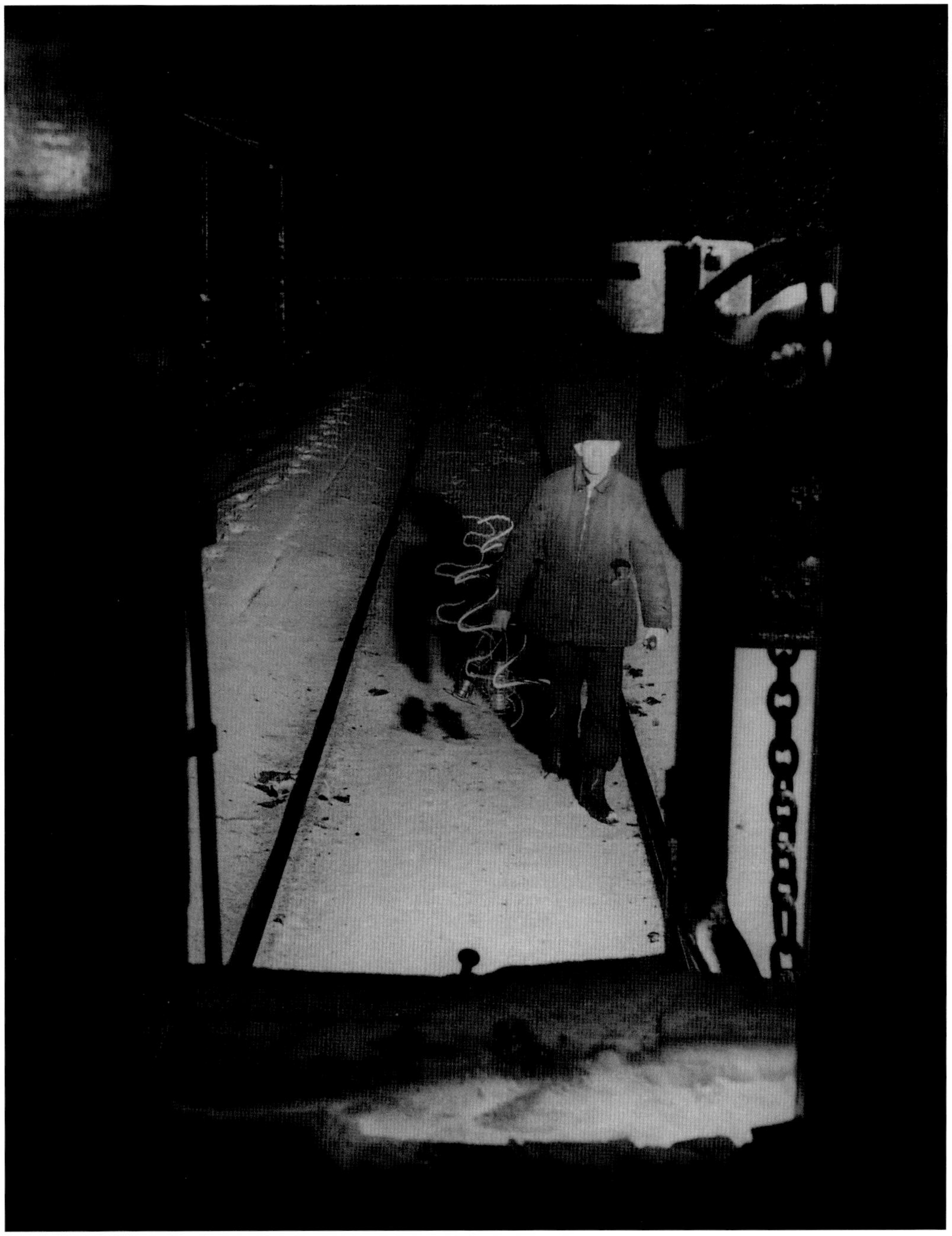

TWO SANTA FE freight trains hurriedly pass one another outside the railroad town of Mojave, California, in 1981. The conductors leave their cupolas momentarily, stand on rear platforms, and perform a traditional "roll-by," mandated by the rule book.

The caboose cupola, long a mainstay on the AT&SF, was invented in 1863 by T. B. Watson, a Chicago & North Western conductor. With his own waycar temporarily unavailable on a worktrain, Watson took a boxcar with a hole in its roof, improvised a perch atop stacked boxes, and was able to survey his entire train from this "crow's nest." Realizing this overview would change the nature of railroad operations, he relayed this discovery to the master mechanic at Clinton, Iowa. Two waycars then under construction were outfitted accordingly, making the C&NW the first railroad to employ this new breakthrough in caboose architecture.
Jeff Brouws

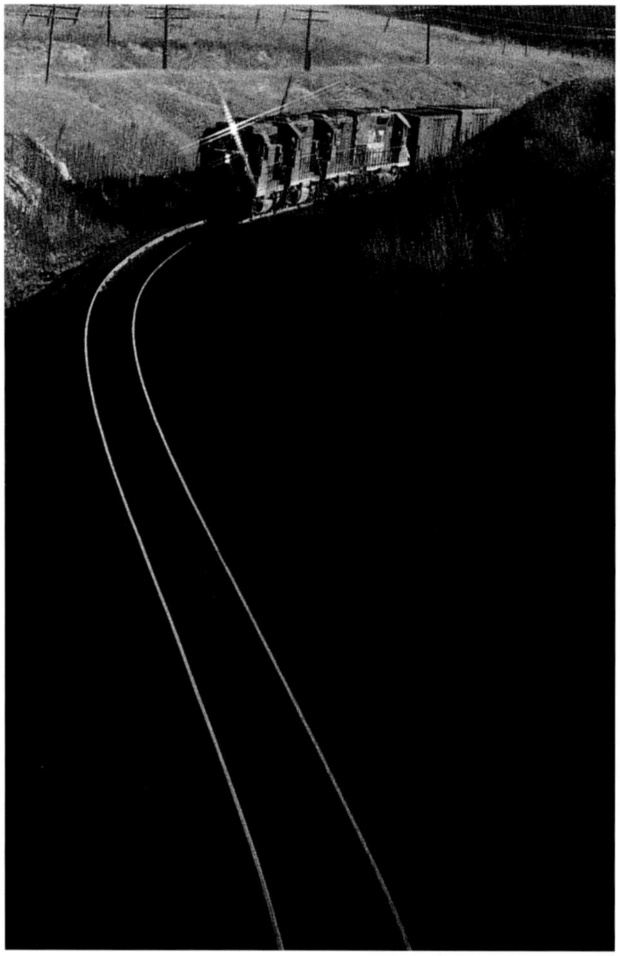

FOUR D&RGW DIESELS lead a freight east of Arvada, Colorado, in 1975. Moffat Tunnel and the precipitous assault of the Rockies is straight ahead.
Jeff Brouws

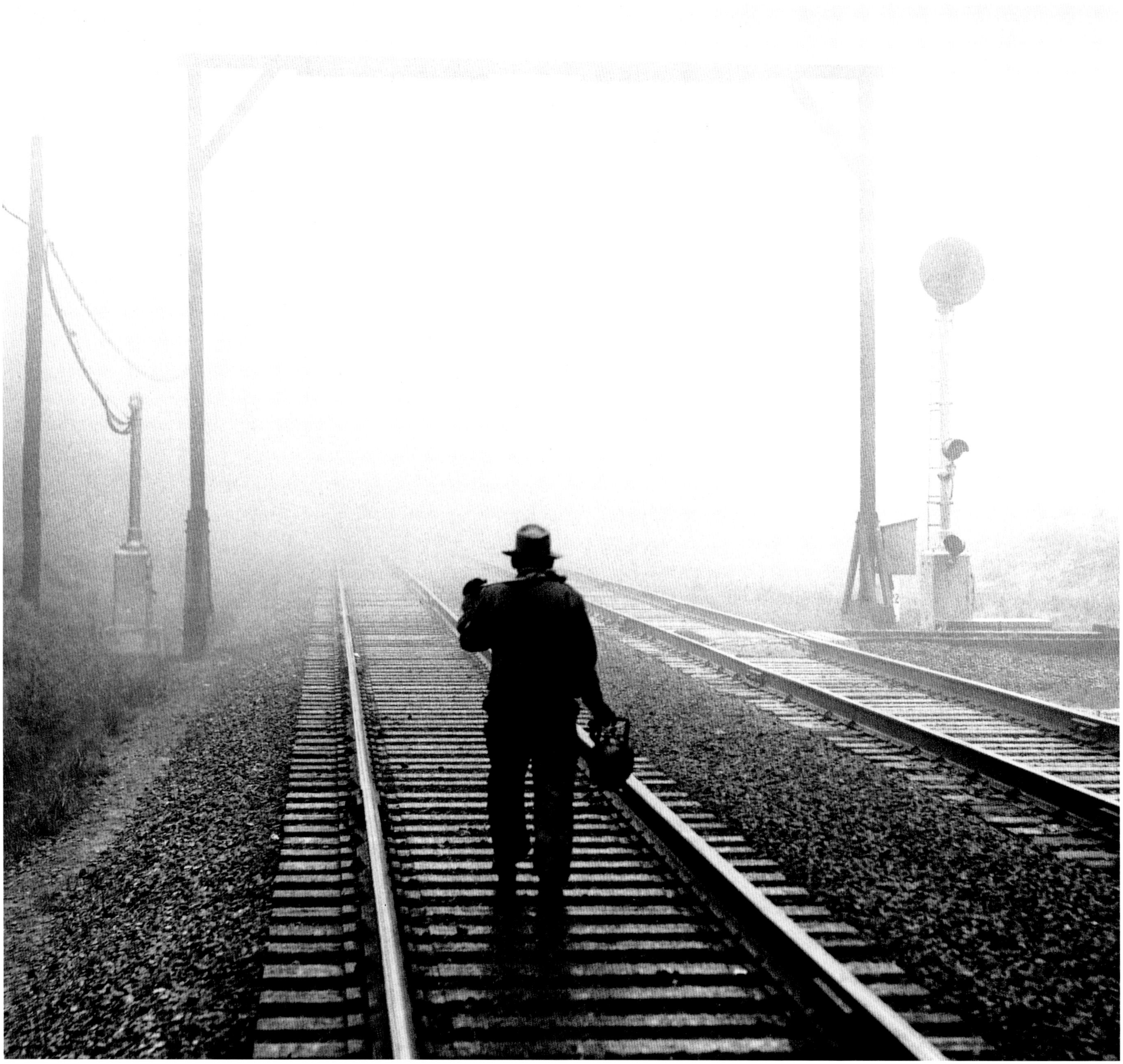

A BLEAK SAN FRANCISCO fog rolls off the Coastal Range and engulfs a solitary track-walker as he starts his morning rounds. With spike maul and lantern in hand, he'll walk fifteen to twenty miles today over the Espee's Bayshore Cutoff near the town of Brisbane, California.

As a member of the section gang—and usually the lowest man on the rail-road totem pole—the track-walker ironically had the most important job: to insure the safe passage of trains over his territory.

Weather could often play havoc with track. The heat of summer dried out ties and expanded rail joints; the cold temperatures of winter fouled switch points and cracked fish plates; rain-soaked ballast weakened the roadbed.

But now, while studying the rail, the laborer also becomes vigilant to other sounds ahead. The daily parade of commuter trains will soon arrive. GS4 4-8-4 locomotives, pulling strings of Harriman coaches, will rocket past on their sprint toward San Jose. The flat-lands of Visitacion Valley will echo again with the sounds of steam—breaking the silence that is the track-walker's sole companion on this murky day in 1949.

Richard Steinheimer

ACKNOWLEDGMENTS

Jeff Brouws

THINKING BACK ON MY CHILDHOOD, I find it very easy to trace where and when my interest in trains at night began. One Saturday evening when I was twelve, as we were returning from a family outing to Paso Robles, I caught a glimpse of a fast-moving freight from the backseat of my parents' car. I was enthralled by the train's wide-sweeping Mars light. It engulfed the landscape, illuminating the rich farmland of the Salinas Valley. The neon main streets of Coyote and Gilroy were highlighted by it, as were the slung-together wooden fruitstands by the side of the two-lane Highway 101. As we played tag with the train for the next five miles, I sensed the beginning of a fascination with railroading that has yet to abate.

Later that year as I heard the passing parade of late-night commuter trains whistling for the downtown crossings into San Mateo, I felt a certain comfort in this nocturnal continuity, as if train sounds in the night—a blues tune to the blackness—could bring solace. Around this time I also discovered my first train books at the local library: very browsed-over copies of *The Railroad Men* by Simpson Kalisher and *Night Train* by Donald Duke, as well as a complement of Lucius Beebe and Charles Clegg manifestos like *Highball* and *The Trains We Rode*. In my freshman year, a buddy of mine, Norm Landes, sold me his used 35mm Exacta for twenty-five dollars. Immediately I went out to try and imitate some of the fine photography I had just been exposed to via the pages of these wonderful pictorials. The steam engine no longer plied the rails but, even at that early age, I was attracted to the gritty aesthetics of the railroad environment. The love of the printed page and photography later merged, becoming a life-long passion, prompting the creation of this book.

The publication of *Starlight on the Rails* has been an eighteen-year journey. Ed Delvers and I met in the summer of 1981. After initial outings to shoot trains in the Mojave Desert of California, we realized we were taking mostly night photos. What was mundane, ordinary, and uniform during the day seemed to take on a new life, depth, and dimension at night—even a dash of mystery. And from a technical standpoint, photographing trains after dark was like playing poker with a couple of wild cards in the deck.

Fond memories abound of our chasing the Lone Pine Local out of Mojave, California, watching it switch cars at Searles, and then following it farther up the line, through the Owens Valley, to its terminus. It was mesmerizing to watch that white string of light wind its way through the barren but beautiful open spaces of that landscape. That same night, while we were shooting at the station in Lone Pine well past 1 A.M., the mercury reached 15 degrees. We wrestled with tripods and time-exposures, trying to capture the essence of that special place. A lifelong friendship was forged between us as we endured the cold ordeal that can be the eastern Sierra in November. Ed simply was (and is) the best of traveling companions: patient, easy-going, and tolerant of other stubborn photographers who want to keep on driving, whether it's in search of propane for morning coffee or new locations to see. Our companionship clicked effortlessly.

Several months later, on our return from another trip, an idea came to mind. A book was a way to put our interest between covers. We did some initial research, sent letters off to other photographers, and received a tremendous outpouring of images to cull through. From this correspondence several friendships developed and some were deepened. Of special note is our friend Richard Steinheimer, who, in his unwavering belief in the project and profound generosity, is the pictorial and spiritual foundation for this book. As a devout fan of Dick's, ever since I met him in Palo Alto when I was fifteen, I want to acknowledge two things: at this writing, after just completing the final photo edit, I had the pleasure of going back through our files and was once again astounded by "Stein's" seemingly inexhaustible creativity. Second, I want to thank him for his humanity. There isn't a nicer guy on the planet. It has been an honor to have him as a friend and guiding presence for *Starlight on the Rails*. Thanks too, Dick, for the fine introduction.

Other friends have played an equal role in their enthusiasm, use of photographs, and support for this project: Mel Patrick (who came forward early with a magic box of 8 x 10s); the late Philip Hastings (for his exquisite studies of the human side of railroading); Wayne Depperman, whose willingness to talk, analyze, and philosophize about railroad photography added immeasurably in shaping *Starlight*; and S. R. Bush, whose graphic sensibilities and suggestions are evident on every page.

I'd also like to thank our very patient contributors and a couple of other friends: Ted Benson, Shirley Burman, Jim Boyd, Dick Dorn, Donald Duke, Chris Goepel, John Gruber, and Ellen Halteman and the California State Railroad Museum for generously allowing us to use photographs from the Philip Hastings, M.D., Collection, (which now resides at the California State Railroad Museum), Victor Hand, Robert Hart Jr., Kentaro Hirai, Naotaka Hirota, Joel Jensen, Stan Kistler, Paul Lukens, William D. Middleton, Dianne Miller (our retouching goddess and genius), Katsusaburo Nishio, Al Papp, Howard Pincus, John Roskoski, Jim Shaughnessy, David Styffe, and Thomas L. Taylor.

Equally important are some of the players in the "backshops," behind the scenes. An incalculable debt of gratitude is owed my wife and best friend, Wendy Burton Brouws. She not only helped with production, enduring late-night printing campaigns, but also successfully got the manuscript and rough layouts into the very able hands of our talented and kind editor at Abrams, Eric Himmel. Without them, this book might have remained in the flat files for yet another twenty years—a dream unrealized. Ed and I are extremely grateful for your support and belief in the validity of our project. Many thanks.

Jeff Brouws
Red Hook, New York

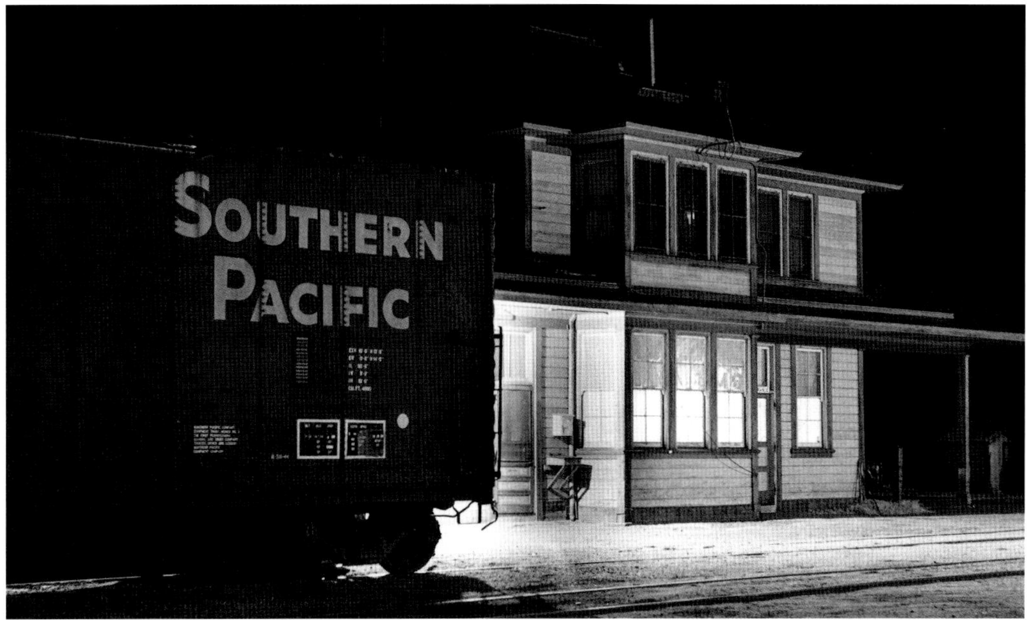

IT'S A FEW HOURS before dawn in California's Owens Valley and the station agent at Lone Pine is already busy at work. A Hopperesque feeling pervades the nighttime atmosphere at the loneliest railroad outpost in America. It's 1982 and the northern end of the Jawbone Branch will soon fade into history.
Jeff Brouws

ACKNOWLEDGMENTS *Ed Delvers*

HEAR THAT LONESOME WHISTLE BLOW. A universal incantation. When people learn of my interest in trains they often share their recollections with me. It is remarkable how often their memories include that whistle in the night—far away, haunting, lonesome, unforgettable. And not just in the United States.

The sensual experience of trains is the same the world over—that sound, that whistle in the distance, slipping drivers on a starting train, staccato messages in switching moves; crossing gates and rushing express trains bound for glory; the smells (bordering on taste) of coal smoke and lubricants, electric sparks, idling diesels; the feel of wet rails and greasy metal, the radiant heat of fireboxes; and the sights of trains at speed, at rest, at dusk and dawn, in rain, in snow, in farmland and industry.

This experience is heightened at night. As extraneous details blend into the background, our senses shift to some kind of survival mode, a world of contrast and shadow in which we need to see the unseen, for somewhere danger lurks. How to capture that emotion in a photograph—on a mere piece of paper.

Night photography evolved to have a special place in my heart. At fifteen I was fascinated to discover that a camera with the shutter held open on a tripod would gather enough light (with time) to produce a picture even by moonlight. Stationary subjects worked best, but a whole new world opened up when I found that motion in the scene caused unique effects. For additional lighting, early attempts with consumer-type electronic flash units resulted in underexposed pictures, but the discovery of a more ancient technology, namely the flashbulb, was a major breakthrough. (To this day, I marvel at the amount of light an egg-sized bulb can generate—equivalent to electronic flash units costing thousands of dollars.) Then, as if to complete the circle, it became a challenge to record the night as seen by the naked eye—no flash, no tripod, just shooting as if by day.

I was fortunate to have spent my youth in Japan, the land of the bullet train. The old and new coexisted there, and the era of steam railroading in regular service lasted into the 1970s, allowing a relative youngster like me to experience a time of trains that I believed should never end. When I moved to America, as if from past to future in one move, steam was supplanted by the allure of modern railroading: trains heavier, faster, longer, louder, and larger, and still all running through the night.

Later, upon arriving in California, I was introduced to Jeff Brouws. Catering truck driver, freelance publisher, book collector, blues fan, railfan, ardent student of classical photography, a good guy all around, and now an acclaimed contemporary photographer, he introduced me to such California icons as the Tehachapi Loop, Winterail gatherings, and Richard Steinheimer. We had fun as we discovered each other's fascination with things that go bump in the night, especially trains.

We went out every so often to record the railroad scene. There was never any lack of subject matter. The mainlines had their draw, but the train-a-day branch-line and lone cars on desert sidings were also part of the picture. And it did not end at sundown: with time-exposures and flashbulbs we were able to have fun with cameras late into the night. The thrill lasted all the way into the darkroom, when the results of gambled exposure settings and setups were revealed.

In addition to night photography, I discovered that nocturnal audio recordings had their own flavor. What differences are there between the sounds of night and day? Perhaps that abatement of daytime noise, the highways not so rushing, the creatures asleep, the accentuated way that sounds come out of darkness unexpectedly. The way the night air carries sound differently. Jeff will attest that during that phase of my explorations he would be trackside with tripod while I would be standing somewhere in the dark, microphone in hand, having admonished him not to call out to me until I re-emerged. Thus one of my favorite recordings was of the Tehachapi Loop on the Southern Pacific, where above the silence of the highway a train can be heard for twenty minutes as it makes its way up the valley to the loop, first dim in the distance, crickets chirping, drawing near with locomotives thundering, wheels screeching, circling round and above unseen in the dark before passing into the night with the light of the caboose disappearing into Tunnel 10 as crickets chirp again. It's just not the same during daylight hours... I know, having recently moved to Tehachapi.

It was natural that with many interests in common we would eventually embark upon a night train book project. The experience and success of Jeff's publication of *The Railroad Photographer's Calendar* series emboldened us to solicit the works edited for this presentation. To these individuals we owe the success of this project. Their patience has been remarkable. What started in 1982 has taken almost twenty years to come to fruition. Fortunate we are that the subject matter is timeless, and as well that what we envisioned at the outset was allowed to age and sufficiently mature to take the form of this book you now hold in your hands. Now listen, and you too can hear that lonesome whistle blow. . . .

Ed Delvers
Tehachapi, California

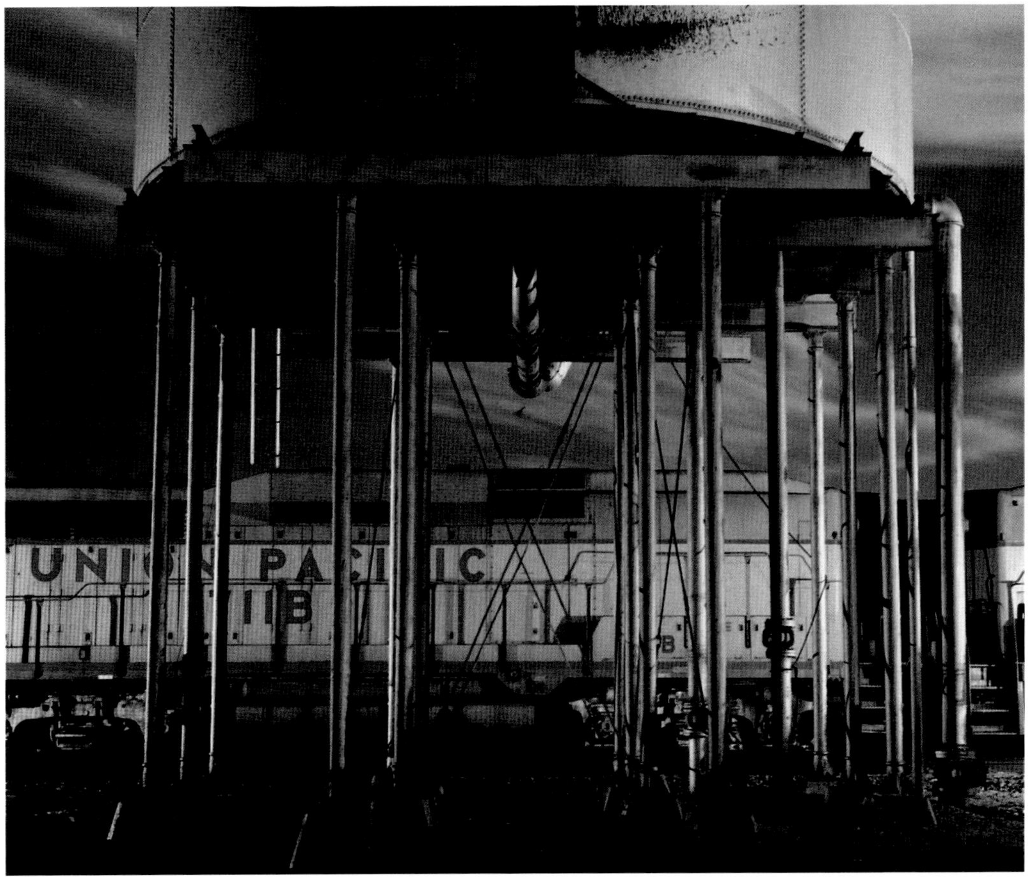

IN A SURREAL INTERPLAY of tone, light, and time-exposure, the pipes and supports of an ancient Union Pacific water tank frame the more modern contours of GP30B engines. It's 100 degrees at 2 A.M. in Yermo—a desolate rail yard in the Mojave Desert of California.
Ed Delvers

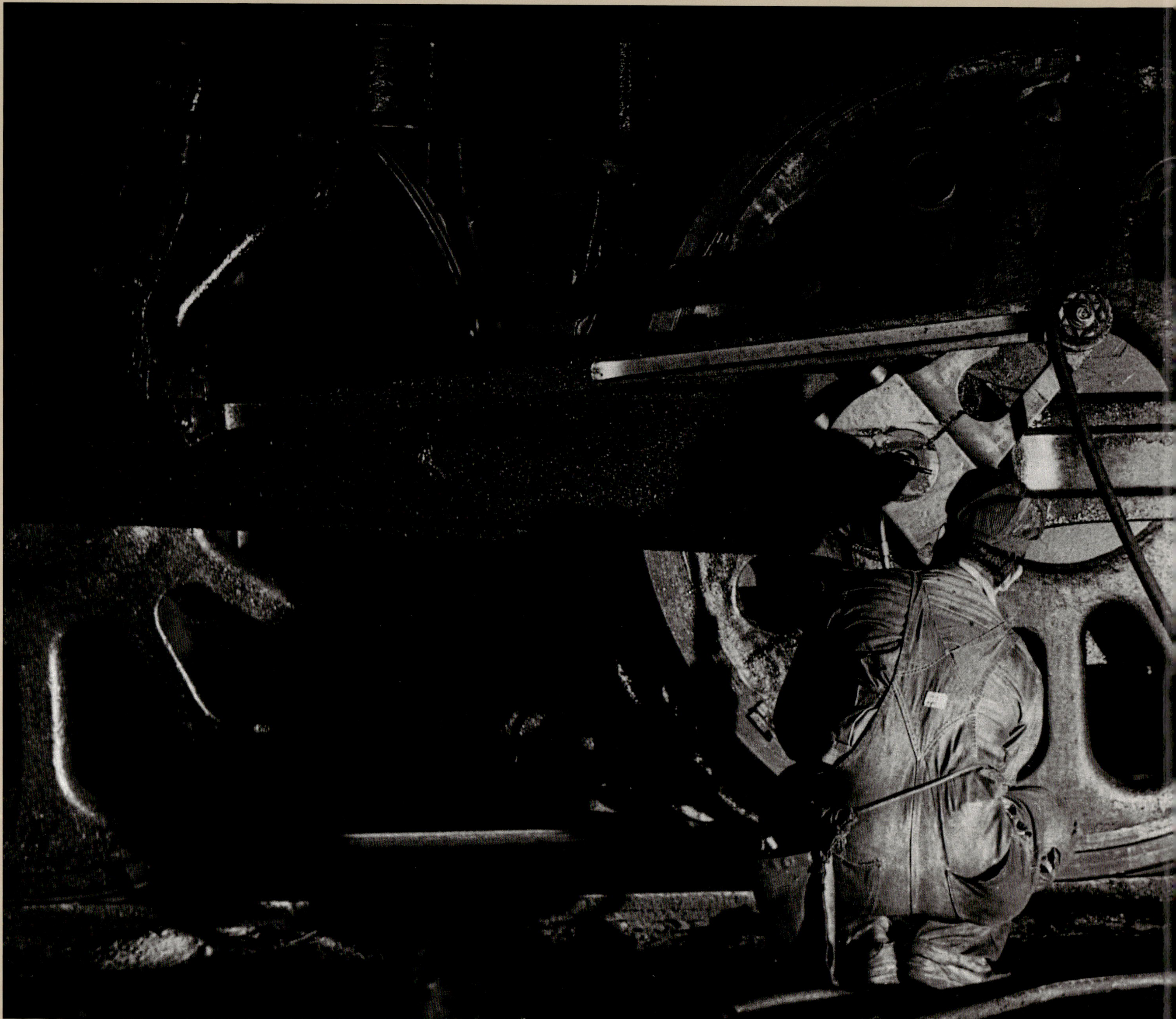